Lady Maclean's
Book of

SAUCES
AND SURPRISES

Lady Maclean's
BOOK OF

SAUCES
AND SURPRISES

Collins
Glasgow and London

By the same author
Lady Maclean's Cook Book
Lady Maclean's Diplomatic Dishes

First published 1978
by William Collins Sons and Company Limited
Glasgow and London
© Veronica Maclean 1978

Printed in Great Britain

ISBN   0 00 435126 6

CONTENTS

FOREWORD

Cooking is rather like conjuring. Sometimes a repertoire of tricks gets too well known, both to the performer and his audience. The surprise element has disappeared and a dreary staleness replaces it. When your cooking becomes dull and repetitive it is time to take up a new challenge. I would suggest to my compatriots that this challenge should be sauces – and the art of making them. For sauces are the branch of cooking most neglected by even the keenest British amateur cook, and to my mind, quite mistakenly so.

Sauces are an intrinsic part of good cooking and great dishes. Far from obscuring, they complement and enhance good materials and a perfect sauce can transform everyday food into a perfect feast.

Sauces can be both the key to new inspiration and the ladder to greater skills.

Sauces are a ladder which will lead the average cook rung by rung into the altogether different world of *la grande cuisine*, and it is surprising once a foot has been set on that ladder, how easy and exciting the ascent can be, and how satisfying to everyone concerned.

The saucemaker's skill is probably the highest form of gastronomic art, for it is the most creative and individualistic. Every year new sauces are invented, while old ones are re-discovered or re-defined, as I hope this book will show; for the same French classic sauce will never be cooked in exactly the same way by two different *maîtres sauciers*, however skilled and punctilious they may be. Each one will put something of himself into his version of a Beurre Blanc or a Bigarade and the result will always be just a little bit different. The techniques of classic cooking may be rigid but the interpretation of those techniques are left in saucemaking entirely to the individual. Readers will notice that in the chapter on French Classic Sauces few exact measurements are given. It is up to the *saucier* to choose, and to taste, the ingredients and their combinations.

What is a classic sauce, the uninitiated may well ask, and why should it be French? Classic sauces are so called because they have been created either by some great chef or gastronome of the past, or by the jealously guarded traditions of a certain town or region, and continue to be used, in more or less that same form, as the acknowledged and perfect accompaniment of a certain dish. Many classical dishes are called after the sauce that accompanies and identifies them –

eg Tournedos Rossini, Sole Meunière, Poulet Chasseur or Boeuf Bourguignonne.

It was the Italians who revived the skills of classical cooking during the Renaissance and transformed them into a new art. It was Catherine de Medici who brought her culinary scientists and artists to France in the sixteenth century, but it was the French who developed these techniques (including the art of sauce-making) throughout the next two centuries into a formal school of cooking – until a gastronomic peak was reached towards the end of the eighteenth century and the first thirty years or so of the nineteenth century, a peak that has probably never been surpassed. The classic school of French cooking crossed over to England from France with the refugees from the French Revolution, their chefs and *maîtres sauciers*.

During the next hundred years – indeed until the social revolution that followed the 1914–18 war – it flourished in Britain under discriminating royalty and gastronomically distinguished private patrons and clubs, whereas in France, strangely enough, it followed an entirely different destiny. There, the Revolution, the wars of the Empire and the troubled peace of their aftermath, created a climate of inflation and profiteering, a climate which rapidly accelerated the establishment of public restaurants and restaurateurs who in their turn kept alive the sacred flame (and incidentally the finances of the country) by depending on the public and foreign tourists for their new patrons.

In Victorian England the plain school of English cooking died hard, and one must acknowledge that in those days of superb materials it had its own merits – but it was only the particularly prejudiced and ignorant who maintained that the French 'merely made good sauces to disguise bad materials'. If this were so there would be something very wrong indeed either with the sauce or the saucemaker, for one of the basic rules of saucemaking is that a sauce 'should always relate to the dish that it accompanies – either by enhancing its taste, or by subtly contrasting with it', and the second and no less cardinal rule is that a good sauce should be based on (a) first-class fresh ingredients, and (b) classical disciplines. Some amateurs may flinch from the implied severity of the last two words – but good cooking is a very technical and slowly acquired skill which can only be called an art after many years of apprenticeship; like all other arts its techniques must be taken seriously or it cannot develop and succeed. Even the naturally-endowed kitchen genius who seems to cook by instinct, cooks all the better for learning a basic technique from which he or she can take flight, and there is no good cook who does not take pains. That is why the first two chapters of this book briefly describe the basic classical techniques of sauce-making and give recipes for the major French classic sauces.

They will probably never be cooked by busy career girls or hostess-housewives whose time in the kitchen is limited, but I think it is important to know at least how these sauces can and should be made and to use the knowledge both as a basis for simpler versions of the classic sauces (which I also attempt to supply) and for sound techniques in non-classical sauce-making, as well as for a yardstick by which one can measure, criticize (and appreciate) the classic sauces that one meets in restaurants or round a rival cook's dining table.

There are over six hundred sauces in this book, collected from generous friends and relations, from professional and amateur cooks, from fellow gourmets and cookery-book writers, from old newspaper cuttings and ancient books and from every country where I have lived or travelled, among which I hope at least some will suit every cooking- and life-style.

Among the many people whose sauce-making skills I admire and without whose inspiration this book would never have been written, I would particularly like to thank:

Mrs Rombauer Becker for *Joy of Cooking*
Mr Cass Canfield and Mr F L Stagg for *A Paris Cookbook*
Mrs Mary Clifford for *Washington Cookbook*
Mrs Caroline Conran and M Michel Guérard for *Cuisine Minceur*
Admiral Ralph Cousins USN for *Golden Trough Cuisine*
Mrs Elizabeth David for *French Country Cookery*, *Italian Food* and *Mediterranean Food*
Mrs Josceline Dimbleby for *A Taste of Dreams*
Lady Dudley for *Cookery Books 1* and *2*
Mrs Theodora Fitzgibbon for *The Art of British Cookery*
Lady Jekyll for *Kitchen Essays*
Mr Ronald Johnson for *Food and Cookery*
Sir Phillip Joubert for *One Man's Meat*
Miss Lily MacLeod for *A Cook's Notebook*
Countess Morphy for *Recipes of All Nations*
Mrs Mary Reynolds for *Italian Cooking for Pleasure*
Mrs Louisa Rochfort for *The St James Cookery Book*
Mr Jack Denton Scott for *The Complete Pasta Book*
Mrs Fortune Stanley for *English Country House Cooking* (Pall Mall/ Phaidon Press)
Vice-Admiral Joe Williams USN for *Dolphin Dishes*
Mrs Windsor for *Secrets of the Great French Restaurants*
The Clarendon College of Further Education, Nottingham, for permission to use the late Mr Alwynne Thompson's excellent handbook *Steps to Saucemaking*
The Junior League of Charleston Ladies for *Charleston Receipts*
The National Cathedral Association, Washington DC for *Herb Cottage Cookbook*
The Tennessee Cookbook

I would also like to thank the following for permission to reproduce individual recipes:

The Right Honourable Julian Amery
Mrs David Bruce

Mrs Stephen Clissold
Mrs Cockerill
Mrs Crickmere
Lady Head
Lady Keswick
Jaimie Maclean
The late Mrs James Young
Mlle de Rothschild
Shura Shivarg
Miss Katie Stewart
Princess Weikersheim
Lady Victoria Wemyss

For their invaluable help and support, I would also like to thank:

Mrs Cockerill
Mrs Diana Cookson
Miss Margaret Hildreth
Mrs Alison Hore
Mrs Rob MacPherson

For permission to reproduce the drawing of the Reform Club kitchen used on the endpapers, I would like to thank Mr Lionel Robinson of Benhams, whose firm was responsible for carrying out Soyer's original designs.

Note on Measures   In certain recipes cup measures are used. They refer to American cups holding $\frac{1}{2}$ US pint or 8 fluid ounces.

We have also not metricated certain personal and traditional recipes.

1

THE
BASICS

THE BASICS

1 THE STOCKS

FIRST, THE CLASSIC, OR SLOW BUT SURE, WAY

GENERAL STOCK OR *FONDS MARMITE*
LIGHT OR WHITE STOCK
    a) Chicken Stock *Fonds de Volaille* also called **(Fonds) Blanc de Volaille**
    b) Veal or White Stock *Fonds de Veau* also called **(Fonds) Blanc Ordinaire**
BROWN STOCK
    a) and b) Brown Bone Stock *Estouffade* **(I and II)**
    c) Golden Veal Stock (*Fonds***) *Blond de Veau***
    d) Game Stock *Fonds de Gibier*
FISH STOCK
    a) Fish Stock
    b) Fish Fumet
    c) Court Bouillon
THE STOCKPOT – a few basic rules
SECOND STOCK

SECOND, THE MODERN AND QUICK WAY

QUICK CHICKEN STOCK
    a) Chicken Stock using Tinned Soups
    b) Simple Brown Poultry Stock
QUICK BROWN STOCK MADE IN THE PRESSURE COOKER
BOUILLON CUBES AND TINNED BOUILLON AND CONSOMME
QUICK FISH STOCKS
    a) Tinned Clam Juice
    b) Quick Clam Fumet

THE STRENGTHENERS

MEAT GLAZE *GLACE DE VIANDE*
JELLIED GRAVY *PETITS FONDS*
BEEF TEA *JUS DE VIANDE*

2 ROUX AND LIAISONS–SAUCE THICKENERS

ROUX
    a) **White Roux** *Roux Blanc*
    b) **Blond Roux** *Roux Blond*
    c) **Brown Roux** *Roux Brun*
LIAISONS
    a) **Egg Yolk Liaisons**
    b) **Farinaceous Liaisons**
    c) *Beurre Manié* **and** *Crème Manié*
    d) **Butter Liaisons or Swirls**

3 SOME INGREDIENTS AND PREPARATIONS (APPAREILS) USED IN SAUCE-MAKING

CLARIFIED BUTTER *BEURRE FONDU*
MARINADE
MIREPOIX
MIREPOIX MAIGRE
DUXELLES
DUXELLES à la *BONNE FEMME*
BOUQUET GARNI FAGGOT
ESSENCES
GLAZE
BROWNING or SUGAR CARAMEL

4 HERBS AND SPICES

5 A FEW COOKING TERMS USED IN SAUCE-MAKING

1 THE STOCKS

FIRST, THE CLASSIC, OR SLOW BUT SURE, WAY

The body of nearly all sauces is made from a stock or liquid base, blended with a roux, or thickening agent; it is given an infinite variety of flavours by their combined essences and by the addition of other ingredients to this base. Sauces and their bases should always relate to the dish they accompany, either by enhancing its taste or by subtly contrasting with it.

Making stock when you want it from a few meaty bones or poultry carcasses is common practice even nowadays in many kitchens, but keeping a stockpot going from day to day is unfortunately not so usual. This is partly because our cookers have changed from solid fuel to gas and electricity, eliminating that convenient *coin du feu* or cool part of the stove that you could stick a broth pan on to look after itself, and partly because of the rising costs of raw materials and of fuel. Yet a stockpot properly used is a very economical factor in the kitchen, and now that a new range of slow-cooking electric casseroles, that run at an extremely low cost, have appeared on the market, a stockpot is once more a practical proposition, and I cannot recommend it too highly, both economically and gastronomically.

A stockpot eliminates waste and is the greatest of all standbys for the careful and dedicated cook: for the sauce-maker it is almost a necessity.

Ordinary or everyday stock has many names; broth; *pot-au-feu*; bouillon etc, but for the purpose of this book it will be called General Stock or *Fonds Marmite*.

As well as General Stock there are several other special stocks which, in French classical cooking, are prepared as the first step in the making of special sauces and dishes. These are the *Fonds de Cuisine* or basic preparations upon which *la grande cuisine* is slowly built.

GENERAL STOCK
FONDS MARMITE

6½ kilo/10 lb beef bones (shin, marrow bones and knuckle)
12 litres/3 gallons cold water
½ kilo/1 lb carrots, peeled
½ kilo/1 lb onions, peeled
cloves
225 g/½ lb leeks, cleaned
100 g/¼ lb celery, cleaned
large bouquet garni

Chop the bones if large and put into a clean stockpot. Cover with the cold water, and allow to come to the boil slowly, thus extracting the flavour from the bones by first dissolving the albumen content. (If boiling water is added to the bones the goodness is sealed in, and cannot escape into the water.) As the stock comes to the boil, skim off the coagulated albumen as it rises to the surface in the form of white scum. When the stock has boiled, add the carrots, whole, the onions, whole, each one stuck with a clove, the leeks and celery and the bouquet garni. Allow the stock to simmer for 6 hours, skimming as necessary to keep it free from scum and fat. Do not let it boil, as this will make the stock cloudy. The stockpot should never be quite covered, allow a gap of about 5 cm/2 inches for steam to escape. The vegetables may be removed when cooked, as their flavour has then been extracted. When the cooking process is finished, strain off through a fine strainer. If not required immediately, the stock should be cooled as quickly as possible to prevent fermentation taking place, and stored, uncovered, in a refrigerator until required.

LIGHT OR WHITE STOCK

a) Chicken Stock
Fonds de Volaille
also called
(Fonds) Blanc de Volaille

a bouquet garni
2 medium onions
3–4 sticks celery, including tops
2–3 leeks or spring onions,
including tops
2–3 kilo/4–5 lb chicken carcass –
necks, backs, wings, giblets and
feet, well scrubbed
5–6 litres/10–12 pints water
1 glass good dry white wine
(optional)
1 tablespoon coarse salt

This is the stock that is used for nearly all the Classic White Sauces. It can be made from poultry or from veal.

Prepare the bouquet garni. Chop the vegetables roughly into 3 cm/ 1-inch pieces.

Put the chicken carcasses into a large heavy soup pot with enough cold water to cover them by 5–8 cm/2–3 inches. You will probably need about 5–6 litres/10–12 pints.

*Bring to the boil and skim away scum carefully for 5 minutes. Add the vegetables and bouquet garni and wine but not the salt. Partially cover the pot, leaving a 3-cm/2-inch gap for the steam to escape and simmer gently, for 2–3 hours, occasionally skimming and never allowing the stock to boil, or it will be cloudy. Boiling water can be added if the liquid evaporates too much and stops covering the ingredients. When the meat is falling off the carcasses, remove them, strain the stock into a clean pan and continue simmering gently for another hour or two until the stock is much reduced. Check the seasoning and add the salt. Put aside to cool, uncovered, and when cold, if you are going to use the stock at once, remove the congealed fat carefully. The stock can be refrigerated for several days, or deep frozen in cubes, for future use. If a larger quantity of Chicken Stock is required proceed as for *Fonds Marmite* (opposite), substituting chicken carcasses and trimmings, or whole boiling fowls, for the beef bones.

b) Veal or White Stock
Fonds de Veau
also called
(Fonds) Blanc Ordinaire

This need only be made if you want a particularly fine Velouté or White Sauce, without any trace of colour and with a great deal of flavour. It is mostly used by chefs or where veal is easily available and cheap.

To the same ingredients as the Chicken Stock Recipe above, add 3 kilo/4 lb shoulder or shank of veal and a 3 kilo/4 lb knuckle of veal. Blanch the veal and veal bones in a separate pan. Skim for 5 minutes. Drain, rinse and cool before adding to chicken carcasses. Cover with cold water and proceed as from * in the Chicken Stock Recipe.

The last two stocks are the ones used in the preparation of classic white sauces. We now come to four more complicated stocks which are mostly used in the making of classic brown sauces. In each case the bones and vegetables of the stocks are coloured by frying or braising before the water is added and despumation begins.

BROWN STOCK

a) Brown Bone Stock Estouffade I

(For a large quantity)
6½ kilo/10 lb beef bones – shin of beef and marrow bones are ideal
225 g/½ lb bacon trimmings, coarsely diced
500 g/1 lb onions, coarsely diced
500 g/1 lb carrots, coarsely diced
100 g/¼ lb celery, coarsely diced
12 litres/3 gallons cold water
bouquet garni
225 g/½ lb leeks, chopped

Chop the bones into pieces 5–8 cm/2–3 inches long, place in a roasting dish and brown evenly in a moderately hot oven, about 350°F 180°C Gas 4 for approximately 45 minutes. Place the bacon trimmings together with a little fat in a frying pan and fry on the stove to extract the fat from the bacon; add the *mirepoix* of vegetables (except leeks) and fry all together to a light brown colour. Then drain off the fat, place the bones in a clean stockpot; add the fried *mirepoix*, cover with cold water, bring to the boil, skim, add the bouquet garni and leeks and allow to simmer for 6 hours as for *Fonds Marmite*. Never let the stock boil again or it will become cloudy. The stockpot should be not quite covered to allow the steam to escape. You can refrigerate this stock in a bowl or stone jar for a week, or deep freeze it in cubes, using ice-trays to set the cubes and plastic bags to store them.

b) Brown Bone Stock Estouffade II

(For a small quantity)
1½ kilo/3 lb beef bones – or mixed beef/veal
1 stick celery
2 onions, quartered
2 carrots, quartered
large bouquet garni
6 peppercorns
3–4 litres/6–8 pints water
salt
6 litres/12 pints capacity saucepan or small fish kettle

Wipe bones but do not wash unless unavoidable. Put into the pan. Set on gentle heat and leave bones to fry gently for 15–20 minutes. Enough fat will come out from the marrow so do not add any to the pan unless the bones are very dry. Slice the celery into 3–4 pieces. After 10 minutes add the vegetables. When the bones and vegetables are just coloured, add the herbs, peppercorns and water, which should come up two thirds above level of ingredients. Bring to the boil slowly, skimming occasionally, then half-cover the pan to allow reduction to take place and simmer 4–5 hours, or until stock tastes strong and good. Strain off and use bones for a second boiling. Although this second stock will not be so strong as the first, it is good for soups and gravies. Use the first stock for brown sauces, sautés, casseroles, or where a jelly stock is required. For a really strong beef broth, add ½ kilo/1 lb or more shin of beef to the pot halfway through the cooking.

c) Golden Veal Stock (Fonds) Blond de Veau

Makes 2 litres/4 pints
3 kilo/4½ lb broken veal bones – shin and knuckle bones
1 kilo/2 lb beef trimmings
100 g/4 oz uncooked ham or bacon
225 g/½ lb carrots, cubed
100 g/¼ lb mushrooms, cubed
100 g/¼ lb onions, cubed
25 g/1 oz celery, cubed
1 teaspoon chervil
1 teaspoon tarragon
2 cloves garlic, crushed
2 shallots, chopped
10 tablespoons dry white wine
4 litres/8 pints cold water
3 fresh tomatoes, de-seeded
2 tablespoons tomato purée
bouquet garni

An excellent new classic light brown stock for most purposes invented by M. Michel Guérard of *Cuisine Minceur*.

Brown the bones in a roasting dish in a very hot oven, 450°F 230°C Gas 8, for 15 minutes, without fat. Turn them several times whilst they are browning with a metal spoon. They must not burn.

Add the trimmings, ham, carrots, mushrooms, onions, celery, herbs, garlic and shallot, return the dish to the oven and allow the vegetables to sweat (cook without browning) for 5 minutes.

Put the bones and vegetables into a saucepan or small deep pot, pour on the white wine and let it boil until it has almost evaporated. Add the cold water, fresh tomatoes and tomato purée, and the bouquet garni. Let it cook slowly, uncovered, for 3 or 4 hours. During this time, take great care to keep the surface perfectly clear of fat and scum by skimming regularly. Then strain the liquid, about 2 litres (4 pints), through a conical strainer into a bowl in which it can be kept until it is needed. To ensure that it is completely free of fat, put the cooled stock in the refrigerator for an hour or more. Any remaining fat will rise and solidify and can easily be removed.

d) Game Stock
Fonds de Gibier

This stock is made exactly the same way as *Estouffade* (see opposite) substituting roasted game – old partridge, grouse or pheasant carcasses, hare, rabbit or venison – for the browned beef bones.

FISH STOCK

Fish Stocks are used in the preparation of nearly all classic fish sauces, and for boiling and poaching fish.

a) Fish Stock

1 kilo/2 lb fish bones and trimmings
1 onion, chopped
a few parsley stalks
mushroom parings
pepper and salt
juice of ½ lemon
10 tablespoons wine

Put the ingredients into a large stewpan with a little butter. Reduce, with the lid on, to about half, shaking the contents occasionally. Now add 2 litres/4 pints cold water, bring to boil and simmer for 20 minutes only, skimming occasionally. Further cooking tends to make the stock bitter.
NOTE: Avoid oily fish for stock.

b) Fish Fumet

The same ingredients and method as above but omitting mushroom parings and lemon juice. Add 8–12 peppercorns and use say 1 litre/2 pints water to 750 ml/1½ pints white wine. Red wine is also used for some fumets (usually for freshwater fish).

c) Court Bouillon

Red or white wine and fish stock with additions of aromatic herbs: chervil, parsley, thyme, sweet basil, bay leaf, fennel, etc.

THE STOCKPOT
– a few basic rules

(i) The stockpot should at all times be kept clean and free from fat. Some foodstuffs, but not others, may be added with advantage, but it must never be regarded as a vessel for garbage disposal.

(ii) Skim and wipe regularly round the inside of the pot with a clean damp cloth.

(iii) Do not add vegetables until the stock has boiled and been skimmed.

(iv) In cooking, the stock must simmer gently and not boil; otherwise chalk from the bones will make it cloudy – and good stock must be clear.

(v) Always cover the stockpot while cooking but never completely or it will go sour. Allow at least a 5-cm/2-inch gap for steam to escape.

(vi) Cook only for the prescribed time.

(vii) Remove the stockpot from the fire when cooking process is finished and cool as RAPIDLY AS POSSIBLE. Leave UNCOVERED in larder or fridge.

(viii) Salt and pepper should not be added, seasonings are used only at a second or further stage.

(ix) Raw vegetable trimmings and some types of meat bones may be added during the cooking process. No pre-cooked or starchy foods should be added. Cabbage, lettuce and some kinds of turnip are to be avoided. Mushroom and tomato debris are excellent and will improve the flavour of *Fonds Marmite* and *Estouffade*.

BOILING water should be added if the liquid evaporates too much and stops covering the ingredients.

(*x*)   Boil up every day for 10 minutes and skim, then simmer for another 10 to keep fresh, even if you do not add to the stockpot – especially when the stock includes chicken carcasses.

(*xi*) Add new materials after the initial boil and skim.

(*xii*) Never leave stockpot in a warm place when it is not actually cooking and never leave it covered.

SECOND STOCK

This is simply the addition of fresh cold water and seasoning to the ingredients of any stock after the first stock has been drained off. It is advisable to boil rather than simmer second stock: this will extract the gelatine from the bones.

SECOND, THE MODERN AND QUICK WAY

The following recipes are for when you have neither the time nor the inclination to make stock properly.

QUICK CHICKEN STOCK

a) *Chicken Stock using Tinned Soups*

375 ml/¾ pint tinned chicken broth or strained clear chicken and vegetable soup
or strained chicken noodle soup
any jellied chicken gravy (*petit fonds*) you have saved from the bottom of the roasting pan
3 tablespoons each onions, carrots and celery, finely sliced
125 ml/¼ pint dry white wine or dry white vermouth
2 sprigs of parsley
⅓ bay leaf
a pinch of thyme or a little fennel

Simmer the chicken broth or soup with the jellied chicken gravy, fresh vegetables, wine and herbs for 30 minutes. Season to taste, but go carefully with the salt. Strain and it is ready. This is a useful stock and you can use it as a base for Velouté Sauce.

b) *Simple Brown Poultry Stock*

the chicken neck, gizzard, heart and scraps
1 onion, sliced
1 carrot, sliced
1 tablespoon rendered fresh pork fat or cooking oil
375 ml/¾ pint white or brown stock or broth
2 parsley sprigs
⅓ bay leaf
a pinch of thyme

Chop the chicken into pieces 4 cm/1½ inches or less. Brown them with the vegetables in hot fat or oil. Pour off the browning fat and add the stock or broth, parsley sprigs, bay leaf and thyme. The chicken should be covered by 1 cm/½ inch. Simmer, partially covered, for 1½ hours or more, skimming as necessary. Strain, de-grease and the stock is ready for use.

QUICK BROWN STOCK MADE IN THE PRESSURE COOKER

1 kilo/2 lb lean beef or soup meat
2 tablespoons melted fat
2 onions, roughly sliced
2 carrots, roughly sliced
4 sticks young celery with the tops, diced
1 wineglass dry white wine or a good red wine
a cracked soup bone, with knuckle if possible
bouquet garni
3 peppercorns
½ teaspoon salt

Wash and cut the meat into 3-cm/1-inch cubes and brown it slowly in the melted fat in the pressure cooker. Push to one side and brown the vegetables. Drain off the fat. De-glaze with a wineglass of wine. Scrape juices together. Add the bone, well cracked, and bouquet garni and seasonings. Pour on 1 litre/2 pints boiling water from a kettle. Do not have the pressure cooker more than half full. Adjust cover and cook at H/15 lb pressure for 30 minutes. Reduce pressure instantly and strain. Cool uncovered.

BOUILLON CUBES AND TINNED BOUILLON AND CONSOMME

a) Bouillon Cubes

These are a bit salty and easily recognized, but don't hesitate to use them in an emergency. They can be strengthened with any jellied gravy (*petit fonds*) you have in the larder or by the method used for Quick Chicken Stock on p. 18. Fortnum and Mason's Beef Extract is an excellent and very strong meat concentrate from the Argentine. It is expensive, but you need to use very little at a time for strengthening weak stocks or gravies.

b) Tinned Soups

Tinned beef consommé is rather sweet. Tinned bouillon is more satisfactory and makes a better stock for sauces. It can be strengthened and improved in the same way as the bouillon cubes.

QUICK FISH STOCKS

a) Tinned Clam Juice

This can be used straight but it is very salty and should therefore be well diluted.

The following recipe although not much quicker than a real fumet is quite useful when fish trimmings are not available.

b) Quick Clam Fumet

225 ml/8 fl oz water
225 ml/8 fl oz dry vermouth
225 ml/8 fl oz tinned clam juice
3 peppercorns
1 small onion, diced or 2 shallots
2 celery ribs, diced
3 sprigs parsley, chopped
some mushroom stalks or peelings (optional)
NO SALT

Boil all the ingredients together, uncovered, for 15 minutes or until liquid is reduced to about 500 ml/1 pint. Strain before using and correct seasoning.

THE STRENGTHENERS

The following recipes may seem contradictory but they both work, incidentally demonstrating the individuality of sauce-making – every good cook has his own method. They are the stand-bys of any good cook.

MEAT GLAZE or GLACE DE VIANDE

All-important and never used enough by amateur cooks. This is simply any everyday stock, white or brown – but with as much bone knuckle and meat as possible boiled down slowly until it has reduced to a syrupy consistency and will coat the back of a spoon. It will become a hard jelly when cold and it refrigerates perfectly; 2½ litres/5 pints stock will make about 375 ml/¾ pint glaze and will last for ages, as you only use a teaspoonful or so at a time. Be careful during the near-syrupy last stage of reduction. Lower heat and stir constantly as it must not catch and burn. The process can be stopped and begun again at your convenience, i.e., start one day, leave overnight to cool, remove all fat, and finish next morning.

Cataldi's Glaze

Glaze must be second stock drawn as for soups, reduced to glaze AS QUICKLY AS POSSIBLE (in other words boiled at a gallop), for if done slowly it will look dark and taste nasty. Never make it from bones.

3 quarts of second stock (no cooked bones in it please) reduced uncovered by quick boiling will make eventually a teacupful of solid glaze. Skim well all the time.

Mrs Thomas's Birk Hall Glaze No. 2
Economical

Twice a week collect all bones, cooked or not, of venison, game, beef or mutton and put in a large pot with any trimmings of vegetables you can muster – carrot, turnip, onion, celery and herbs – boil gently till all the good is drawn out and the bones look dry. Then strain into a large basin and let it get cold. (Any pieces of meat strained out will do for dogs' dinners.) Next day skim off fat (this will do for adding to the chickens' food) and boil the stock at the gallop to reduce the glaze, every now and then adding a small teacupful of cold water to make the scum rise; skim whenever it does; when much reduced finish cooking the glaze in a small saucepan, being careful not to let it catch. At the end when it gets syrupy you must stir it all the time. (Second stock will make nice glaze when it can be spared.)

The last two recipes come from Lady Clark of Tilliepronie's kitchen. She was an Edwardian hostess famous for her good food.

JELLIED GRAVY or PETIT FONDS

This is the jelly which lies under the fat of your cold roast. It must always be saved and used. It contains the very essence of the roast and it is the simplest way of all to give an extra flavour and strength to stocks and sauces.

BEEF TEA or JUS DE VIANDE

Mince 500 g/1 lb lean steak twice and place in a stoneware jar; add 250 ml/½ pint cold water and ½ teaspoon salt. Cover the jar lightly.

Place it on a cloth in a pan containing as much cold water as is possible without upsetting the jar. Bring the water slowly to a gentle boil and continue boiling for 1 hour. Remove the jar. Place on a cake rack to cool as quickly as possible. Strain the juice. Store it in a covered container in the refrigerator until ready to heat and use.

2 ROUX AND LIAISONS-SAUCE THICKENERS

A roux blended with a stock constitutes a sauce.

ROUX

A roux can be white, *blond* or golden, or brown, according to how long you cook it. A white roux is used for Béchamel and Béchamel-based sauces, a blond roux for Velouté and Velouté-based sauces. A brown roux is used for Espagnole and all brown sauces. Sometimes pre-browned flour is used for a brown roux; this is easily made by heating the flour in a very slow oven (300°F 150°C Gas 2) in a very heavy pan, shaking the pan periodically so that the flour browns evenly. Great care must be taken in cooking a roux. It must not become too hot, or the flour will lose its thickening properties; and it must be cooked long enough after the stock has been added, for the flour to lose its unpleasant raw flavour, or this will dominate any other taste.

a) **White Roux Roux Blanc**
3 level tablespoons clarified or unsalted butter
3 rounded tablespoons sifted flour

Melt butter in a thick saucepan very gently. Mix in flour and blend carefully with a wooden spoon (or whisk together rapidly with a wire whisk). Cook gently over low heat, for 2 to 3 minutes, stirring all the time. Do not let it colour.

When making a sauce 75 g/3 oz roux is enough to thicken ½ litre/1 pint liquid, but if you want a thinner sauce, such as a Velouté, 50 g/2 oz roux to ½ litre/1 pint of liquid is enough. All roux should be cooked a little before adding the liquid.

b) **Blond Roux Roux Blond**

This is made in exactly the same way as a white roux, except that you cook it a little longer, until it turns straw-coloured, before you add the stock.

c) **Brown Roux Roux Brun**

Same ingredients and method, but it is easier to make a brown roux with previously browned flour. This roux must be cooked very slowly, either in a cool oven (300°F 150°C Gas 2) or over gentle heat until it is a rich hazelnut brown and smells pleasantly nutty and baked. Use slightly more flour than for other roux as browned flour loses some of its thickening properties. Some people use well clarified dripping instead of butter for this roux as butter burns easily.

For a smooth flowing sauce the weight of the butter in the roux should be very slightly more than that of the flour, otherwise they should be the same. The thickness of a sauce depends on how much flour you use in the roux per ½ litre/1 pint of liquid. Here are some figures that I find useful:

2 heaped tablespoons flour per ½ litre/1 pint of liquid makes ½ litre/1 pint thin pouring sauce

3 heaped tablespoons flour per ½ litre/1 pint liquid makes ½ litre/1 pint medium thick sauce, suitable for coating

4 heaped tablespoons flour per ½ litre/1 pint liquid makes ½ litre/1 pint thick sauce, suitable for a Panada

NOTE: (i) Hot liquid must be added to cool roux, or cold liquid must be added to hot roux in order to produce a smooth texture easily. If the milk/stock and the roux have been mixed at the right temperature, i.e. the one hot and the other cold, stirring all the time, a long period of cooking afterwards is unnecessary.

(ii) Lumps formed in combining roux and stocks beat out very easily when sauce comes to the boil. Merely remove pan from the heat and beat hard with a wooden spoon till smooth.

LIAISONS
These are used to complete an unfinished sauce like Velouté, or to thicken and enrich a too thin or un-homogenous sauce, making it smooth and creamy.

a) Egg Yolk Liaisons
Yolks of eggs mixed with milk or cream should only be added just before serving. The sauce should not be boiling, only hot enough to coagulate the albumen and form a liaison. Nor should it be allowed to boil afterwards or it will curdle and the cream lose its flavour. Beat yolks and cream and mix them with some of the liquid to be thickened, return this mixture to the hot liquid and whisk over moderate heat.

b) Farinaceous Liaisons – **arrowroot, cornflour, potato or rice flour**
Always mix these with a small amount of cold stock, water, white wine or milk before adding to the boiling sauce that is to be thickened, stirring or whisking all the time. Then boil for a good 15 minutes. Allow between 2–6 tablespoons to every litre/2 pints liquid.

c) Beurre Manié and Crème Manié
Use ⅓ uncooked flour to ⅔ cold butter or cream and mix these together thoroughly. This is not strictly a liaison, more a corrective for thickening a too thin sauce. Away from heat, beat the paste into the simmering sauce with a wire whisk in little bits. Then boil for 1 minute, stirring and whisking continuously. It will thicken the sauce almost immediately.

d) Butter Liaisons or Swirls
Add small dabs of butter and mix into sauce by swirling the whole saucepan in a rapid, circular, clock-wise motion away from heat, or over very gentle heat. This will thicken as well as enrich a sauce. Do not stir.

3 SOME INGREDIENTS AND PREPARATIONS (APPAREILS) USED IN SAUCE-MAKING

CLARIFIED BUTTER
BEURRE FONDU

Simply melt butter slowly in a small pan; let it stand and cool; use only the yellow part, throwing away the milky acids at the bottom of the pan.

For regular stock-in-hand: heat 3 kilo/4½ lb salted butter in a double boiler. When melted pour into a larger bowl than it needs. When cool cover with foil and refrigerate. Next day run a knife round the bowl, lift up butter and throw away the milky liquid at the bottom, scraping the bottom of the solidified butter until it is quite clean. Press into four smaller containers. Freeze two. Use others from fridge. Repeat indefinitely.

MARINADE

225 g/½ lb carrot and onion, minced
10 tablespoons olive or salad oil
1 shallot, minced
1 clove of garlic, crushed
bouquet of parsley stalks
pinch of thyme
1 bay leaf
5 tablespoons vinegar
½ bottle Bordeaux white wine
¾ litre/1½ pints water, or less as desired
1 teaspoon salt
6 peppercorns
25 g/1 oz brown sugar

A marinade is a strongly flavoured liquid that you steep meat or fish in to improve flavour and tenderness; the residue is often reduced and used in sauces. There are many marinades. This is a useful all-round one:

Fry the carrot and onion in the oil until golden brown. Add the shallot and clove of garlic, parsley, thyme and bay leaf. Moisten with the vinegar, wine and water. Cook for 30 minutes. Add salt and peppercorns and brown sugar. Cook for a further 15 minutes and strain. Allow to get cold before steeping meat in the liquor.

A more simple marinade can be made from 4 tablespoons olive oil, 1 tablespoon lemon juice with some lemon zest, a bay leaf, sliced garlic clove or shallots, parsley or fresh basil and thyme.

MIREPOIX

Dice an onion, carrot, a little celery and a little ham or lean bacon, a pinch of thyme and a small bay leaf. Stew in a walnut of butter for about 10 minutes. Remove and swill the pan out with a little Madeira wine, then add these juices to the preparation.

MIREPOIX MAIGRE

Exactly as for Mirepoix, but omitting the ham or bacon.

DUXELLES

Lightly sauté a small, finely chopped onion in a pan with a little butter and oil. Add 75 g/3 oz mushroom parings and/or stalks, chopped finely and pressed in a cloth to squeeze out all moisture. Stir over a hot stove until all the moisture evaporates. Season with salt and pepper, and a little grated nutmeg. Add ½ teaspoon of finely chopped parsley. Put into a basin and cover with greased paper until required for use.

DUXELLES à la BONNE FEMME Dry duxelles mixed with the same quantity of pâté forcemeat.

BOUQUET GARNI – FAGGOT Pot herbs; usually bay leaf, thyme, sage, parsley, peppercorn, marjoram and any other flavourings suitable for the dish you are making, tied up firmly in a scrap of muslin.

ESSENCES Concentrated cooking juices sieved and reduced if necessary. Jellied gravy of any sort is the perfect essence.

GLAZE Glaze is a much reduced Brown Sauce such as Espagnole used for coating vegetables or meat to give them a rich brown shiny appearance. Recipes are given for Demi Glace on page 47.

The term is also used for coating cold buffet food with Chaudfroid Sauce and derivations of Sauce Mornay.

BROWNING or SUGAR CARAMEL Browning is used for colouring gravies, glazes, stew, etc. It can be used to replace the more highly seasoned commercial gravy colourings. The intense heat under which it is processed destroys all sweetening power.

Melt 1 cup sugar in a very heavy, old, enamelled pan over low heat. Stir it constantly with a metal spoon until it is burned smoke-coloured to black. Remove from the heat and be sure to let it cool – quick addition of water to intensely hot sugar which is over 300°F 150°C can be explosive and very dangerous. Then add, almost drop by drop, 1 cup hot water. After the water is added, stir over low heat until the burnt sugar becomes a thin dark liquid. Then take off the stove, let it get cold, and bottle.

4 HERBS AND SPICES

All herbs are better fresh from the garden or window-box than dried, and most of them are quite easily grown, so do make the effort.

Herb	Uses
Basil, Sweet Green (annual)	All Mediterranean and tomato sauces; suitable for sauces accompanying eggs, liver, lamb and lobster.
Chives (perennial)	Suitable for all sauces that need the tang and zip of an onion taste, especially all kinds of vinaigrette.
Chervil (annual)	For nearly all sauces where herbs are used – the French use it almost as much as parsley.
Dill (annual)	Suitable for many Scandinavian, Russian and German sauces; use with vegetable, mutton, fish, egg and cheese dishes.
Fennel (annual)	Suitable for fish or chicken sauces.
Shallots (annual)	A more delicate flavour than onion and less strong; much used in sauces.

Garlic (perennial)	Suitable for a great many sauces (if you like it) and essential for some, but it must be used with discretion.
Horseradish	A root, not a herb, but a flavour much used in sauces – especially Scandinavian ones.
Marjoram, Sweet (perennial)	Suitable for sauces that accompany pork, mutton, liver, veal and vegetables.
Mint (perennial)	For mint sauce and all sauces that accompany mutton.
Parsley (annual)	For sharpening flavours in all sauces.
Sage (perennial)	For sauces that accompany pork, white-fleshed meats and eggs.
Savory (perennial)	Used in *Fines Herbes* and for pork; it resembles sage.
Sorrel (perennial)	For sharp acid sauces that accompany fish and eggs.
Tarragon (perennial)	Used in many sauces for eggs, poultry, game, kidneys and fish. Essential for some sauces such as Béarnaise.
Thyme (perennial)	Much used in sauces and an essential part of a bouquet garni; suitable for eggs, cheese, lamb and shellfish.
Bay leaf (a shrub)	Much used in sauces and an essential part of marinades and bouquet garni.
Juniper (a shrub)	The berries are used in sauces for game.
Rosemary (a shrub)	Much used for sauces accompanying lamb, pork, and veal.

Composite Herbs or Herbal Packets

Fines Herbes	Usually a combination of fresh herbs: chervil, parsley, chives, tarragon and thyme.
Bouquet Garni or Faggot	A bunch of herbs including parsley stalks, a sprig of thyme, a bay leaf, all tied up neatly in a muslin bag.
Turtle Herbs	English version of a Bouquet, originally used in the making of Turtle Soup. A combination of sweet basil, sweet marjoram, sage, rosemary, savory and thyme, giving a quite different flavour to that of a bouquet.

Spices and Flavourings

Lemon zest, mace, nutmeg, allspice, black, white (Mignonette) and cayenne peppers, paprika, all curry powders, turmeric, coriander and mustard, saffron, cinnamon and cloves are all used in sauce making.

5 A FEW COOKING TERMS USED IN SAUCE-MAKING

To bind, or cohere	see p. 26 under Liaison.
To braise, *braiser* **or** *étuver*	to cook very slowly and steadily until tender and brown in a covered heavy pan in the oven. Meat is usually braised on top of a mirepoix, see p. 23. Bones are braised in an uncovered pan.
To brown, *rissoler* **or** *sauter*	to colour brown by frying in butter or fat.

To clarify	to clarify butter, see p. 23.
	to clarify stock. This may be done either by adding egg white and crushed shells or raw lean minced beef and fresh tomato skins. Bring the cool stock slowly through to fast simmering but do not let it boil. The impurities will be collected on egg or meat and can be removed with it. Raw meat is preferable as egg shells may affect the flavour of a delicate stock.
To de-glaze, *deglacer*	actually to degrease by swilling the frying or sauté pan (in which you have cooked something) round with an acid liquid such as wine or vinegar, at the same time scraping all the pan juices together. Do this over a gentle heat.
To degrease by skimming, *dépouiller*	to remove impurities and fat which rise as a scum to the top of a pan either by spoon, skimmer, bulb-baster or absorbent paper. The most satisfactory way of removing all the fat from a stock or stew is to let it get cold overnight and then simply lift off the congealed fat, which will have risen to the top, next morning.
To despumate, *raffiner*	to throw up impurities by boiling and slow simmering. Adding a little cold liquid to boiling liquid helps this process. The frothy spume rises to the top of the pan and is removed by spoon or skimmer.
To finish with butter, *finir au beurre*	to give sauce extra thickness and gloss by adding butter at the last minute in the form of butter swirls. These are scraps of butter which you feed into the sauce, twisting the pan so as to swirl its contents round. They must never be stirred with a spoon.
To gloss or make a sauce glossy	boil up a small piece of butter with the sauce for a minute or two over sharp heat. (This is only possible with sauces that cannot 'turn' or separate.)
Liaison	there is no English term for this. To make a *liaison* is literally to bind, to cohere or to make homogenous. A thin, uncohered sauce is made thicker and more homogenous by a liaison. Liaisons are added just before serving and can be any of the following:
	– an egg yolk either by itself or beaten up in cream
	– cream or butter
	– cream mixed with a little cornflour
	– *jus lié*, gravy to which a little cornflour or potato flour has been added.
	Liaisons are added off the heat to a slightly cooled down sauce and when an egg is used the sauce must never boil again, but it can be carefully reheated.
To moisten, *mouiller*	to pour on liquid.
To reduce, *reduire*	to lessen liquid by fast boiling, i.e. to reduce by half, means to boil or simmer until liquid measures only half its original quantity.
To refine, *raffiner*	see Despumate.
To sieve	to pass through a sieve, see Tammy.
To skim, *dépouiller*	see Degrease by skimming.
To tammy, *tamiser*	to squeeze through a tammy cloth, by two people twisting it in opposite directions. This is now obsolete. Instead whirl in a liquidizer for a few seconds or strain through a conical sieve with or without a piece of muslin.
To add wine	when it is used to give richness or flavour to a sauce, wine should generally be added a few minutes before serving and should either be

boiled quickly (burnt off) before it is put in the sauce (if the sauce cannot safely be boiled) or boiled up with the sauce. This gets rid of the alcohol in the wine which tastes acid.

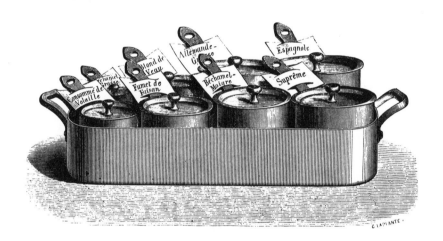

2

THE
CLASSIC FRENCH
SAUCES

THE CLASSIC FRENCH SAUCES
1 THE SLOW BUT SURE WAY

French Classic Sauces are so called because they have been created by some great chef or epicure in the past and have been used in more or less the same form ever since, as the internationally acknowledged and perfect accompaniment or ingredient of certain dishes; they are intrinsically part of *Haute Cuisine* which literally translated means High Class Cooking.

They are easily classified into four groups, according to their basic ingredients:

1 **The White Sauces** ⎫ **flour and butter based**
2 **The Brown Sauces** ⎬
3 **The Butter based and the Butter and Egg based Sauces**
4 **The Oil based and the Oil and Egg based Sauces**
  and finally for lack of a better place to put them
5 **The Compound Butters**

A Note on the Classic Sauces, and a word of Encouragement for the Amateur Cook

The Classic White and the Classic Brown Sauces, by far the largest and most varied group in the business, stem from just three starting or foundation sauces: Velouté, Béchamel and Espagnole. Without these bases, strictly speaking most *Haute Cuisine* sauces cannot be properly made, and certainly cannot be brought to the standard of perfection demanded by a *maître saucier*. This may sound a little daunting to the amateur cook, but please do not be discouraged, or give up before you have begun. It is not as difficult as it sounds.

Of the three foundation sauces, only Espagnole Sauce takes a very long time to prepare, but it is so enormously useful, even in the smallest kitchen – transforming the dullest dish into *haute cuisine* as if by magic – that an occasional Espagnole Day is really worth the effort. It is a perfectly easy sauce, requiring no knack or special skill, only time, trouble and patience, and these can be cut down a lot by good organization. It also has the advantage of storing and freezing remarkably well. Velouté and Béchamel Sauce are more familiar to every cook, and to make them properly is again simply a question of taking trouble, and of how much trouble you are prepared to take. My advice is to master the three foundation sauces the correct and classical way first, and then to experiment with shortcuts or expediencies; in other words to get to know them, and then to come to terms with them: your own terms.

It is at least comforting to know that the second stage, or the additions made to these foundations to give the finished sauces their identity, are, with a very few exceptions, surprisingly easily and quickly made.

In general the word sauce has been omitted in the list of sauces given. For the correct naming of these the simple rule to be followed is: in the case of sauces with French names, the word sauce should precede the name whereas for English (and translated) sauces the word sauce comes after. Thus Sauce Bercy and Cambridge Sauce. The ingredients of all sauces and variations are estimated for approximately $\frac{1}{2}$ litre/1 pint of sauce, except where otherwise stated.

1 CLASSIC WHITE SAUCES

There are two white Foundation Sauces. They are the bases or mothers of a great many classic sauces, some of which also have their own derivatives, grandchildren, as it were, of *Mesdames Velouté* and *Béchamel*.

a) THE FIRST WHITE FOUNDATION SAUCE AND RECIPE: VELOUTE SAUCE

THE DERIVATIVES OF *VELOUTE SAUCE*

ALLEMANDE (PARISIENNE) or SAUCE BLONDE, from which are derived:

Albert	*Russe, à la*	*Villeroy*

AMERICAINE (see also p. 34)
AMIRAL, *à l'*
ARCHIDUC, *à l'*
AROMATES, *aux*
AURORE or ROTHSCHILD
BERCY, from which are derived:

Chicken Bercy	*Marinière*

BORDELAISE BLANCHE, *à la*
BRETONNE
CHAMPAGNE
CHAUD-FROID, for coating, or masking, used cold
CHIVRY
CREVETTES, *aux,* from which are derived:

Duguesclin	*Giselle*	*Lapérouse*

DEMI-DEUIL
ESTRAGON, *à l'*

FLAMANDE
HONGROISE
IMPERATRICE
INDIENNE or CURRY, from which are derived:
   Dino   *Stanley*
JOINVILLE
MAINTENON
MARECHALE
MARGUERY
MATELOTE BLANCHE
MORLEY
NANTUA
NORMANDE, from which are derived:
   Diplomate (or Riche)   *Moules, aux*
   Régence
ORSAY
PAPRIKA
POLONAISE
POMPADOUR
POULETTE
PRINTANIERE
RAVIGOTTE
SUPREME, from which are derived:
   Ambassadrice   *Argenteuil*   *Clamart*
   Doriac   *Ivoire*   *Mathilde*
   Orly   *Souveraine*
VILLAGEOISE I
VIN BLANC, au from which are derived:
   Dugléré   *Fines-Herbes*   *Granville*
   Polignac   *Réjane*   *Saint-Malo*
   Souchet   *Victoria*

b) THE SECOND WHITE FOUNDATION SAUCE AND RECIPE: BECHAMEL SAUCE

THE DERIVATIVES OF *BECHAMEL SAUCE*

ANCHOIS, aux
BOHEMIENNE
CARDINAL
CREME
DUCHESSE
FENOUIL, au
FRANÇAISE, à la
HOLSTEIN
HUITRES, aux

MORNAY, from which are derived:
    Tzarine, and the glazes:
        Bagration   *Infante*   *Montrouge*
        Sullivan   *Walewska* or *Valeska*
    NANTAISE
    SOUBISE, from which are derived:
        Chatham   *Villageoise II*
    VERT-PRE

a) VELOUTE SAUCE

Velouté is a plain white sauce made with a blond roux and stock, carefully refined by despumation. Unlike Béchamel Sauce, but like Espagnole, a Velouté Simple is not considered a complete sauce but is the first stage and foundation of many other sauces, the most important of which are Allemande or Parisienne, Suprême and Vin Blanc. It can be made from different stocks, but the general rule is that it should be made from the stock constituting the dish, i.e. if it is a veal dish the stock should be a veal stock or a mixed stock of veal and chicken bones; if it is a chicken dish, then the stock should be a chicken stock; if it is a fish dish, then it should be a fish stock. The way and time of cooking each stock is identical except that fish stock should be allowed to simmer and despumate for no longer than 20 minutes. *To complete a Velouté Simple and make a sauce a liaison must be added, consisting of yolks of eggs, butter and cream.*

50 g/2 oz lightly cooked roux (25 g/1 oz clarified butter, 25 g/1 oz flour)
500 ml/1 pint cold stock (veal, chicken or fish)
6–8 button mushrooms or parings and stalks
6–8 peppercorns
a few drops lemon juice
a little cream (optional, as more cream will be added with the liaison)

Dissolve the hot roux in the cold stock, put the saucepan on a fierce heat and stir the sauce continuously with a wooden spoon or whisk to prevent lumps and catching while it is coming to the boil. When the sauce begins to bind slightly, add all the other ingredients, and continue to boil for 2–3 minutes. Then remove pan to a moderate heat, wedge the saucepan so that the contents actually boil at one point only (metal wedges can be bought for this purpose, and if you are cooking on gas you can place an asbestos mat over the flame so as to be able to leave the pan wedge-tilted). Now let the sauce despumate and refine, for about 1½ hours, skimming the grease, scum and foam off from time to time and occasionally adding a ladleful of cold stock to allow for evaporation and to assist the refining process. If your aim is perfection, then strain the sauce through a conical strainer into a clean saucepan, add a further 5 tablespoons of cold stock, and despumate again for 30 minutes. Finish by straining through a conical sieve. If the Velouté is to wait, or is to be stored, leave out the lemon juice and cream, pour it into a bowl and cover the surface with either little knobs of butter or greaseproof paper, or paper dipped in cold water, to prevent a skin forming while it cools.

NOTE: A Velouté Simple can be enriched by adding a few drops of lemon juice and a little thin cream, off the heat, just before serving.

THE DERIVATIVES OF *VELOUTE SAUCE*

ALLEMANDE or PARISIENNE or SAUCE BLONDE

1 litre/2 pints veal or chicken stock
1 litre/2 pints veal or chicken Velouté
6 egg yolks
125 ml/¼ pint cream (optional)
125 ml/¼ pint mushroom liquor (made with mushroom stalks and peelings)
juice of ½ lemon
100 g/4 oz unsalted butter

Add the stock to the Velouté and reduce by fast boiling to half. Beat together the egg yolks, cream, mushroom liquor and lemon juice. Pour some of the reduced liquid into this mixture, whisk together, then tip all the ingredients back into the original saucepan. Whisk vigorously until the sauce is thick enough to coat a wooden spoon. Strain through a fine sieve, gently reheat and at the last moment add the unsalted butter in flakes, swirling it into the sauce without stirring. *For sauces derived from Allemande see p. 38.*

AMERICAINE

A basic tomato sauce made with Fish Velouté blended with lobster butter and finished with a little chopped chervil and tarragon. Serve with boiled white fish or lobster.

AMIRAL, à l'

To 500 ml/1 pint fish Velouté add 4 pounded and sieved anchovies (or 1 tablespoon anchovy essence), 1 or 2 parsley stalks, a little lemon zest, 1 tablespoon mixed finely chopped chives and capers. Simmer for 20 minutes. Strain. Add a little lemon juice and seasoning to taste.

ARCHIDUC, à l'

500 ml/1 pint fish Velouté reduced to half, with addition of Madeira wine, whisky and port wine. Garnish with brunoise of vegetables and truffles. Finish with 50 g/2 oz butter and a little cream.

AROMATES, aux

An ordinary Velouté blended with an infusion of aromatic herbs, thyme, basil, marjoram, chives, shallots and peppercorn. Garnish with chopped chervil and blanched tarragon, and finish with a little lemon juice.

AURORE or ROTHSCHILD

To 500 ml/1 pint fish Velouté or Suprême Sauce (see p. 37), add 5 tablespoons thick tomato purée and finish with 50 g/2 oz butter.

BERCY

Lightly sauté 100 g/4 oz chopped shallots in a saucepan with a little butter. Moisten with 250 ml/½ pint white wine and fish fumet and reduce to about one third. Add this to 500 ml/1 pint fish Velouté, simmer for 20 minutes. Finish with 50 g/2 oz butter, a little lemon juice and a teaspoon of chopped parsley.
For derivatives of Bercy see p. 38.
Also Bercy Brun see p. 46.

BORDELAISE BLANCHE, à la

Almost entirely reduce in a saucepan 100 g/4 oz chopped shallots in 500 ml/1 pint Graves, or any white Bordeaux wine. Add 375 ml/¾ pint Velouté (made from the stock constituting the dish); simmer for 20 minutes. Sieve, finish with a little butter and chopped tarragon. Serve with grilled fish or grilled WHITE meat.
See also Bordelaise Rouge, p. 49.

BRETONNE   To a Velouté or Suprême (made from stock constituting the dish) add a garnish of julienne of blanched celery, leek and truffle.

CHAMPAGNE   To 500 ml/1 pint fish Velouté, add 10 tablespoons champagne, and reduce by a quarter; finish with butter. Serve with boiled fish.

CHAUD-FROID   A masking or coating sauce which may be made from a Velouté, Béchamel or Demi Glace Sauce. Boil 500 ml/1 pint Velouté (made from stock constituting the dish), add 375 ml/¾ pint white poultry or fish jelly; reduce the whole by one third, stirring constantly. Take from heat and add 250 ml/½ pint fresh cream; put through a fine sieve or whirl in a liquidizer. Remember to stir the sauce every now and then while it is cooling or a skin will form.

NOTE: This sauce, when cold, should be of such a thickness and consistency that it will readily coat immersed solids such as suprêmes of chicken, poached eggs, etc., at the same time allowing these to be easily dipped into it.

Various game, truffle and Madeira essences may be used to flavour it and colouring matter such as tomato sauce, an infusion of paprika or carmine (cochineal) for pale pink, cochineal for red, spinach purée for green, and caramel for brown. It is used for glazing entrées of fish, meat, poultry, game, ham and tongues, etc., and for making *plats montés* for cold buffets.

CHIVRY   Infuse a large pinch of chervil leaves, tarragon and parsley, a head of young burnet, and a good pinch of chives in 500 ml/½ pint boiling chicken stock for 15 minutes. Strain the liquid through a muslin cloth and add this to 500 ml/1 pint fish or chicken Velouté. Reduce the whole by a quarter and finish with 50 g/2 oz Green Butter (see p. 64). Serve with boiled poultry or fish.

CREVETTES, aux   Boil 225 g/½ lb shrimps together with a few fish bones and trimmings, an onion, a few parsley stalks and a little salt, in 500 ml/1 pint water for 20 minutes. Strain the liquor; shell the shrimps and pass them through a rough sieve; add this to the liquor and proceed as for an ordinary White or Béchamel Sauce with a 50 g/2 oz roux. Finish with a little lemon juice, 50 g/2 oz butter, and garnish with a few small cooked shrimps. Cream can be added just before serving if liked. *For derivatives of Sauce aux Crevettes see p. 38.*

DEMI-DEUIL   A slowly cooked and well refined chicken Velouté, mixed with finely chopped truffle.

ESTRAGON, à l'   A Velouté blended with tarragon purée; finish with chopped tarragon and 15–25 g (½–1 oz) softened butter.

FLAMANDE   A Velouté or Béchamel cohered with the yolks of 2 eggs and a teaspoon of mustard.

HONGROISE   A Velouté or Allemande, in which you combine 2 shallots or 1 medium onion minced and sweated in butter. Carefully mix in $\frac{1}{3}$ sour cream and 2 tablespoons mild Hungarian paprika.

IMPERATRICE   A Velouté, Allemande or Suprême Sauce, blended with chicken and truffle essence. Add cream just before serving.

INDIENNE or CURRY   Sauté about 225 g/$\frac{1}{2}$ lb minced onions, 50 g/2 oz apples in a saucepan until golden-brown. Add 2 tablespoons curry powder, and moisten with a little coconut milk*. Add 500 ml/1 pint Velouté (made from stock constituting the dish) or Espagnole if you want a dark sauce. Simmer for 30 minutes. Strain through a fine sieve. Finish with a little lemon juice. The addition of cream is optional, but an improvement. This sauce is also very good served almost cold, with whipped cream added at the last moment.
For derivatives of Indienne see p. 38.
* See note p. 97.

JOINVILLE   A Velouté, Normandy or white wine sauce, garnished with a cullis of shrimps or prawns and julienne of truffles. Finish with a little cayenne pepper, butter and lemon juice.

MAINTENON   To a Velouté or Suprême Sauce add a purée of onions. Cohere with egg yolks.

MARECHALE   Blend a Velouté, Allemande or Suprême Sauce with a white button mushroom purée.

MARGUERY   Blend together a purée of shrimps and a fish Velouté. Finish with 50 g/2 oz butter and 5 tablespoons cream.

MATELOTE BLANCHE   Combine a strained and well reduced fish Court Bouillon, to which you have added white wine, and 25–50 g/1–2 oz mushroom parings and/or stalks, with a fish Velouté. Sieve and finish with 50 g/2 oz butter and a little cayenne pepper; garnish with white button mushroom heads and small white glazed onions.

MORLEY   A Velouté, blended with mushroom essence. Finish with a little stiff fresh cream.

NANTUA   Sauté a mirepoix of vegetables in 75 g/3 oz crayfish butter. Moisten with a little white wine and cognac, add 3 or 4 sliced tomatoes and 1 tablespoon tomato purée and reduce. Add the whole to a Velouté or Béchamel made from fish stock. Simmer for 20 minutes; sieve; finish with a little cayenne pepper and 10 tablespoons cream.

NORMANDE   A fish Velouté blended with mushroom essence and oyster juice. Cohere with the yolks of 2 eggs. Finish with 50 g/2 oz butter and a little cream.
For derivatives of Normande see p. 39.

ORSAY A veal Velouté garnished with julienne of mushrooms, truffles and tongue. Serve with mutton or lamb cutlets.

PAPRIKA A Velouté or Allemande, highly seasoned with paprika and red Hungarian pepper.

POLONAISE A Velouté with the addition of sour cream, grated horseradish and chopped blanched fennel. Finish with a little lemon juice. Serve with grilled meats.

POMPADOUR Lightly sauté about 100 g/4 oz finely chopped shallots and white button mushrooms in 25 g/1 oz butter; add 250 ml/½ pint thin Velouté made from chicken stock and simmer for 30 minutes. Take off heat, season to taste and cohere with 2 or 3 yolks of egg. Finish with 5 tablespoons cream and 1 teaspoon chopped parsley and a little butter.

POULETTE Flavour 500 ml/1 pint of Velouté with aromatic herbs (sweet basil, dill, tarragon) and 5 tablespoons mushroom liquor; simmer for 20 minutes. Take off heat and cohere with 3 egg yolks. Finish with 50 g/2 oz butter, a little lemon juice and chopped parsley.

PRINTANIERE A Velouté of the stock constituting the dish blended with green vegetable purée. Finish with 50 g/2 oz butter.

RAVIGOTTE (warm) Add 10 tablespoons white wine to 5 tablespoons good malt vinegar. Reduce the whole by half. Add 500 ml/1 pint Velouté and simmer for 10 minutes. Take off the heat and cool. Finish with 50 g/2 oz shallot butter, 1 teaspoon mixed chopped parsley, capers, tarragon, chervil and chives. Serve lukewarm, with boiled tongue, fish or poultry. Do not confuse it with cold Ravigotte Sauce which is a kind of Vinaigrette.

SUPREME Prepare 500 ml/1 pint chicken Velouté. Add to it 500 ml/1 pint more chicken stock, and 4 tablespoons mushroom liquor, made with mushroom stalks and peelings. Boil together over a high heat to reduce by half, stirring carefully all the time. Turn down the heat and cool the sauce a little. Add 125 ml/¼ pint thick fresh cream, gradually, stirring all the time. Take off the stove and swirl in 50 g/2 oz unsalted butter in flakes. If you have some meat glaze or jelly made from veal or chicken stock or pan juices, 2 tablespoons of it will enrich the sauce still further. Add it before you start swirling in the butter.
For derivatives of Suprême see p. 39.

VILLAGEOISE I A Velouté or Allemande enriched with meat glaze or chicken essence.

VIN BLANC, au To 500 g/1 pint fish Velouté add 5 tablespoons fish fumet, preferably that in which the fish has been cooked, and 5 tablespoons white wine. Reduce by one third. Take off heat and cohere with 3 egg yolks. Finish with 50 g/2 oz butter and a little cream.
For derivatives of Vin Blanc see p. 39.

AND NOW THE GRANDCHILDREN

Sauces derived from ALLEMANDE (see p. 34)

Albert Reduce a little tarragon vinegar, 1 finely chopped onion, or 2 shallots, and 1 tablespoon grated horseradish slowly over moderate heat. Blend together with an Allemande, and finish with 10 tablespoons cream, 50 g/2 oz butter and 1 tablespoon chopped parsley.

Russe, à la An Allemande or Béchamel with the addition of grated horseradish, finely chopped ham and shallot, reduced in 8 tablespoons white wine and vinegar mixed. Finish with a little sour cream, sugar, pepper and salt.

Villeroy To an Allemande add 2 tablespoons truffle essence and 2 tablespoons ham essence. Reduce until it is thick enough for coating, for which this sauce is most often used.

Sauces derived from BERCY (see p. 34)

Chicken Bercy Sauté 100 g/4 oz chopped shallots in butter, moisten with white wine and chicken jelly (glaze), then reduce to half. Add this to 500 ml/1 pint Velouté and garnish with poached beef marrow cut into dice and chopped parsley. Serve with chicken sauté.

Marinière To a Bercy add the reduction of the cooking liquor of mussels, and garnish with quarters of poached, bearded mussels.

Sauces derived from CREVETTES (see p. 35)

Duguesclin A Shrimp Sauce garnished with artichoke hearts cooked in butter and chopped, and a few whole shrimps.

Giselle A Shrimp Sauce garnished with shrimps and asparagus heads.

Lapérouse Two thirds Shrimp Sauce, one third Sauce au Vin Blanc, garnished with quartered, poached mussels and shrimps.

Sauces derived from INDIENNE (see p. 36)

Dino A Sauce Indienne, made with either Velouté or Espagnole and garnished with a little julienne of chicken and mushrooms.

Stanley Blend a Sauce Indienne, made with either Velouté or Espagnole, with a Soubise Sauce; finish with a little cream.

Sauces derived from NORMANDE (see p. 36)

Diplomate or Riche   A Normande Sauce with which Lobster Butter is also blended. It is garnished with small diced pieces of lobster and truffle.

Moules, aux   A Normande Sauce with the addition of the cooking liquor of mussels, and garnished with poached, quartered, bearded mussels.

Régence   A Normande Sauce reduced with the addition of a little white wine, and blended with truffle essence.

Sauces derived from SUPREME (see p. 37)

Ambassadrice   To a Suprême Sauce add 3 or 4 roughly chopped lambs' sweetbreads, some asparagus heads and a little chopped truffle.

Argenteuil   Garnish a Suprême Sauce (stock constituting the dish) with asparagus heads.

Clamart   Blend a Suprême Sauce with green pea purée. Garnish with a julienne of truffles.

Doriac   A Suprême Sauce, garnished with julienne of tongue and a little chopped truffle.

Ivoire   A Suprême Sauce finished with white or pale meat glaze, which gives it a shiny white appearance.

Mathilde   Garnish a Suprême Sauce with 75 g/3 oz lightly sautéed chopped onion and diced blanched cucumber. Add 5 tablespoons champagne.

Orly   Blend tomato purée with a Suprême Sauce, adding also a little meat glaze; finish with a little butter.

Souveraine   Blend with a Suprême Sauce a purée of green asparagus, and a julienne of truffles.

Sauces derived from SAUCE AU VIN BLANC (see p. 37)

Dugléré   Blend 250 ml/½ pint Sauce au Vin Blanc and 250 ml/½ pint Tomato Sauce together and add a little fish essence or reduced fish fumet. Finish with chopped parsley. This is the sauce that is so often mis-spelt and mis-cooked in English hotels.

Fines-Herbes   Sauté 1 minced shallot, 2 finely chopped parsley roots and 2 tablespoons chopped chervil in a little butter. De-glaze with 10 tablespoons white wine. Reduce by one third. Add 500 ml/1 pint chicken Velouté and reduce again. Off the heat add 4 tablespoons fresh cream and 2 tablespoons softened butter. At the last moment add 1 tablespoon chopped fresh tarragon. Serve with poached eggs, chicken and sweetbreads.

Granville A Sauce au Vin Blanc garnished with shrimps, mushrooms and truffles.

Polignac A Sauce au Vin Blanc made with chicken Velouté, enriched with cream and garnished with a fine julienne of chicken, truffles and mushrooms.

Réjane A Sauce au Vin Blanc blended with Watercress Butter (p. 64).

Saint-Malo A Sauce au Vin Blanc flavoured with shallots and enriched with Anchovy Butter (or a few drops of anchovy essence), a little French mustard and some more melted butter.

Souchet Slice, and then make a julienne in equal proportions of young carrot, whites of leeks and celery – about 155 g/6 oz in all. Stew in butter. Moisten with a little fish fumet and then reduce drastically. Add 500 ml/ 1 pint Sauce au Vin Blanc and finish with a little butter and cream.

Victoria A Suprême or Sauce au Vin Blanc made with fish Velouté and blended with Lobster Butter (p. 64).

b) BÉCHAMEL SAUCE

This is also called White Sauce and, in America, Cream Sauce. Although the recipe below may seem a more elaborate preparation than the usual plain roux-and-milk mixture, the white sauce that most cooks think of as Béchamel today, it is in fact a simplified modern version: the original recipe, called after the great Béchamel, Marquis de Nointel, Louis XIV's Lord Steward, contained minced veal and many other ingredients. Escoffier refers to it as 'The Queen of Sauces'.

½ an onion, or a small shallot, roughly chopped
a slice of carrot
a little celery (optional)
nutmeg, a blade of mace, ½ bay leaf, a little thyme, parsley and sage
8 peppercorns
salt
1 clove
250 ml/½ pint milk, 250 ml/½ pint veal stock (if veal stock is not available, lightly sauté a little finely chopped ham and add this to 500 ml/1 pint milk)
75 g/3 oz lightly cooked roux (15 g/½ oz butter, 15 g/½ oz flour)
5 tablespoons cream (optional)

Infuse the vegetables, herbs and spices in the stock-and-milk mixture and bring slowly to the boil. Reduce the heat and allow it to simmer slowly for 20 minutes, then take it off the heat and cool and strain it. Meanwhile prepare your roux in another pan. Some people prefer to cook this, once it is amalgamated, in a very slow oven rather than over the heat. Remember a roux should never be overheated, as this destroys the thickening properties of the flour. Leave it in the oven for about 10 minutes while you strain the cooled stock through a conical strainer. Now add the stock to the roux, slowly at first, stirring continuously. Allow the sauce to boil, and beat it vigorously at this point to make it smooth, then lower the heat and let it despumate at the side of the stove for a further 20–30 minutes, skimming it every now and then; when it is really cooked there should be absolutely no taste of raw flour. If cream is used, add it at the last moment before serving and do not reboil. You can now put the sauce into a bain-marie or leave it to wait on top of the stove, but be sure to butter the top, or cover it with greased paper to prevent a skin forming. For simpler versions of Sauce Béchamel see p. 67.

THE DERIVATIVES OF
BECHAMEL SAUCE

ANCHOIS, aux
Here you can use either a Velouté, Béchamel, Normande or even a Sauce au Vin Blanc, providing you use a proportion of fish stock in the preparation. Blend anchovy butter with the sauce, and garnish with diced anchovy fillets. Add lemon juice and seasoning to taste.

BOHEMIENNE (a cold sauce)
Put the yolks of 3 eggs in a basin with a little salt and pepper. Whisk in a few drops of tarragon vinegar. Add 1½ tablespoons cold thick Béchamel. Now add approximately 500 ml/1 pint olive oil, feeding it in slowly at first and then more quickly in the same manner as for Mayonnaise Sauce. Finish with a little chopped tarragon or tarragon vinegar. Serve with cold eggs or sautéed chicken.

CARDINAL
To 500 ml/1 pint Béchamel add about 10 tablespoons fish fumet. Reduce by a quarter, then add 100 g/4 oz Lobster Butter, together with a little truffle essence and tarragon vinegar. Finish with a little cayenne pepper and lemon juice.

CREME
A Béchamel enriched with cream. Reduce by one third and finish with a little lemon juice, 3 tablespoons butter and 4 tablespoons cream. Do not let it boil after you have added the cream.

DUCHESSE
A Béchamel garnished with finely chopped tongue and mushroom. Finish with butter.

FENOUIL, au
To a Béchamel add 10 tablespoons fish stock, and 10 tablespoons white wine, and reduce by one third. Take off heat, allow to cool; then cohere with the yolks of 3 eggs over a moderate heat; finish with a little grated nutmeg and butter.

FRANÇAISE, à la
Reduce 500 ml/1 pint Béchamel with 250 ml/½ pint fish fumet to about 375 ml/¾ pint. Add 1 minced clove garlic, a little nutmeg and 2 tablespoons mushroom essence. Boil together for 5 minutes, pass through a sieve and finish with chopped crayfish tails (or Dublin Bay prawns). Serve with fish mousse or quenelles. The great Carême created this sauce for Prince Paul of Württemberg.

HOLSTEIN
To 500 ml/1 pint Béchamel add 10 tablespoons fish stock and 10 tablespoons white wine and reduce by one third. Take off heat, allow to cool. Then cohere with the yolks of 3 eggs over a moderate heat. Finish with a little grated nutmeg and butter swirls.

HUITRES, aux   A Béchamel or Normande garnished with quartered bearded oysters. Finish with lemon juice.

MORNAY   To 500 ml/1 pint Béchamel add 10 tablespoons stock constituting the dish. Reduce by a quarter. Add 50 g/2 oz grated, Gruyère cheese and the same amount Parmesan cheese and whisk well together. Finish off the heat with 50 g/2 oz butter and a liaison made with the yolks of 2 eggs diluted in a little cream.
For derivatives of Mornay see below.

NANTAISE   To 500 ml/1 pint Béchamel add 4 chopped shallots, 3 chopped gherkins, 1 teaspoon Dijon mustard and a little vinegar. Simmer for 30 minutes. Rub through a fine sieve and finish by binding the sauce with 2 egg yolks and a little butter. Serve with pork.

SOUBISE   Scald and drain about 1 kilo/2 lb finely chopped onions and then stew them in butter. Add 250 ml/$\frac{1}{2}$ pint thick Béchamel Sauce. Season with nutmeg, pepper, salt and 1 teaspoon caster sugar. Cook gently for 20 minutes. Strain. Finish with 50 g/2 oz butter and a little cream. Do not hurry this sauce.
For derivatives of Soubise see p. 43.

VERT-PRE   Scald a handful of parsley and chervil with some spinach and tarragon leaves. Dry them and pound them in a mortar together with 2 or 3 gherkins, 1 tablespoon capers and 25 g/1 oz butter. Sieve and use the butter to blend with a Béchamel.

Sauces derived from MORNAY *(above)*

Tzarine   A Mornay garnished with small diced cucumber; season with paprika pepper.

Bagration   A Mornay garnished with julienne of truffles. Used as a glaze.

Infante   A Mornay garnished with julienne of white button mushrooms. Used as a glaze.

Montrouge   This is the same as Infante except that it is finished with 10 tablespoons cream. Used as a glaze.

Sullivan   A Mornay garnished with asparagus heads, and julienne of truffles. Used as a glaze.

Walewska or Valeska   A Mornay garnished with slices of truffle and lobster collops. Used as a glaze.

Sauces derived from SOUBISE (see p. 42)

Chatham A thin Soubise garnished with sliced tongue and mushrooms. Served with veal.

Villageoise II A Velouté mixed with a Soubise. Dilute with veal gravy and mushroom liquor; reduce, and cohere with the yolks of 3 eggs. Finish with 50 g/2 oz butter and a little cream.

---

2 CLASSIC BROWN SAUCES

There is only one brown Foundation Sauce. It is called Espagnole, Spanish or, by some British chefs, Rich Brown Sauce. It is the base, or father, of a great many classic sauces, which also have their own derivatives, grandchildren, as it were, of The Great Spaniard.

a) THE BROWN FOUNDATION SAUCE AND RECIPE: ESPAGNOLE SAUCE

THE DERIVATIVES OF *ESPAGNOLE SAUCE*

BERCY BRUN
BOURGUIGNONNE
BRESSOISE
BROGLI
CHAMPIGNONS, aux, I and II
CHASSEUR, au
CHATEAUBRIAND
CHEVREUIL, au
DUXELLE
GENOISE
DEMI GLACE, from which are derived:

Tomato Demi Glace		*Algérienne*
Bigarade	*Bordelaise Rouge,* from which is derived:	
	Rouennaise	
Castelaine	*Catalane*	*Czarine, à la*
Doria	*Epigrammes, aux*	*Gratin, au*
Huîtres à Brun, aux		*La Vallière*
Lyonnaise	*Marchand de Vin, au*	*Marigny*
Matelote Brune	*Mironton*	*Moëlle, à la*
Périgourdine	*Piccadilly*	*Piment*
Piquante	*Poivrade,* from which are derived:	
	Cerises, aux or *Badoise*	
	Conti	*Diane*
	Grand Veneur	*Moscovite*
	Nesselrode	*Nora*
	Pignole	*Viennoise*

Porto	*Réforme*	*Salmis*
Tortue, à la	*York, d'* or *Yorkshire*	
Zingara		

HUSSARDE
ITALIENNE
MADEIRA, from which are derived:

Alexandra	*Archiduc*	*Financiere, à la*
Génevoise	*Nancy*	

Périgueux, from which are derived:

	Continental	*Masséna*
Richmont	*Rossini*	

OLIVES, *aux*
PARISIENNE
PAUVRE HOMME
POIVRADE and **GAME POIVRADE**
ROBERT
ROMAINE
SICILIENNE
VERJUS, *au*
ZOUAVE

ESPAGNOLE SAUCE

Though not a complete sauce on its own, Espagnole Sauce is a necessary ingredient of practically all classic brown sauces. It can be made in 2 hours or so, but ideally it should take 6–8 hours. Despumation is a steady, slow business and cannot be hurried. A perfectionist *saucier* of the old school would think nothing of keeping a special Espagnole on the stove for 2–3 days!

Making a good Espagnole is more a question of organization and patience than sustained effort; if you have a stove or cooker that will produce a steady, low heat then the sauce can be left to look after itself most of the time while you get on with other work. Nevertheless, in most small kitchens it is practical to make a larger quantity of the sauce than you need at one time and then refrigerate the excess in 250 ml/½ pint or 500 ml/1 pint jars. It will keep perfectly for two weeks or more in a fridge and it can also be deep-frozen quite successfully.

Here are two traditional methods for making this all-important sauce.

First Recipe

2–3 carrots, chopped
1 large onion, chopped
4 stalks of celery, chopped
2 leeks, chopped
any other braising vegetables
100 g/4 oz butter
tomatoes, fresh or tinned
100 g/4 oz mushroom parings and/or stalks
100 g/4 oz flour, browned (see p. 21)
3 litres/6 pints good brown stock
bouquet garni

Take a 3–4 litre/6–8 pint saucepan and sauté the vegetables in it in the butter for about 10 minutes. Then add the tomatoes and mushrooms. (These should dominate the other vegetables. It is a question of taste exactly how much tomato is used in Sauce Espagnole. There is no doubt that it helps speed up the refining process but some perfectionists are against using too much for fear the tomato should dominate all other flavours.) Sauté for 5 minutes.

Sprinkle in the flour and add 3 litres/6 pints good brown stock (see p. 16). Prepare a bouquet garni and throw it into the stock. Keep stirring until the contents boil, then lower heat, and wedge the saucepan so that the contents boil at one point only. Allow it to despumate (see p. 26) slowly for 6–8 hours, skimming off the grease, scum and foam from time to time whenever it rises. Occasionally throw in any pieces of rough scrap vegetables, scrap pieces of meat and bone, especially lean ham or bacon rinds, to increase its richness, and occasionally add further (cold) stock to allow for evaporation and help the refinement process. After 6–8 hours (or longer) strain into a fresh saucepan and reduce the whole by about a quarter, by fast boiling. Correct the seasoning.

If the sauce is not to be used immediately pour it into an enamel bowl and throw a small ladle of cold water over the surface to prevent a skin forming. It is unnecessary to follow the classic method of stirring continuously until it gets cold. It is no great disaster if a skin does form, for the crust can be lifted when you want some sauce and replaced afterwards.

Reducing by a quarter will not make your Espagnole thick enough to use as a sauce, but it is the right thickness for storing. Most sauces with a Brown or Espagnole base are further reduced by fast boiling to the desired consistency, which is nearly always a thin syrup, like pouring cream.

Second Recipe

This is a French method of cooking a large quantity of Espagnole, which some cooks may find more practical. It takes about 5 hours, $3\frac{1}{2}$ one day and $1\frac{1}{2}$ the next.

12 litres/$2\frac{3}{4}$ gallons Estouffade or brown stock
425 g/14 oz roux for liaison
255 g/9 oz carrot, chopped
125 g/5 oz onion, chopped
thyme
2 bay leaves
125 g/5 oz fresh pork (or bacon) back, or breast, fat, chopped
1 glass white wine
1 litre/2 pints tinned tomato purée

Bring to the boil 8 litres/2 gallons of stock. Thin down the roux with 1 tablespoon of the hot stock in a bowl, then add to the stock in the pan, whisking hard. Stir or whisk until it comes back to the boil, then lower heat and simmer.

Make a *mirepoix* of the vegetables and herbs. Sauté the pork fat with the vegetables till they begin to colour. Then drain them free of all fat in a colander, add the *mirepoix* to the sauce and deglaze the *mirepoix sauteuse* with a glass of white wine. Reduce this to half a glass by rapidly boiling and add this too to the sauce. Wedge the saucepan so that the contents boil at one point only and despumate for 1 hour, skimming every now and then.

Strain the sauce into a clean saucepan, pressing lightly on the *mirepoix* to extract juices. Add 2 more litres/4 pints stock, bring back to the boil, then slowly simmer and despumate for another 2 hours. Finally strain the sauce again into an earthenware bowl and stir occasionally till it cools. Leave in a cold larder overnight.

Next day remove congealed fat and pour the sauce into a heavy or thick-bottomed saucepan with 2 more litres/4 pints stock, 1 litre/2 pints tinned tomato purée (not concentrate), or equivalent of fresh tomatoes. (If you use tinned purée cook it in the oven first for a little till it browns, which removes the acidity.) Bring the sauce to the boil on a high heat stirring all the time, then lower heat, wedge saucepan and despumate for one more hour, skimming carefully when necessary. Strain it for the last time, and stir occasionally till it is quite cold. If the sauce is not perfectly smooth, it can be whirled in a liquidizer for a minute before straining.

Of course there are many other and quicker ways of preparing an Espagnole; I give three of them on pp. 70–1.

A Note on Demi Glace

It will be seen that many of the following recipes call for Espagnole Sauce OR Demi Glace (Half Glaze). Demi Glace is a completed Espagnole Sauce which has been strengthened by the addition of a second lot of good brown stock and then reduced once more to perfection. When a recipe calls for Espagnole, Demi Glace or full glaze, it is really a question of strength and thickness which you choose (and of time available!). The recipe for Demi Glace can be found on p. 47. A quick, but good, Demi Glace of a more modern kind is given on p. 70.

THE DERIVATIVES OF *ESPAGNOLE SAUCE*

BERCY BRUN

Lightly sauté 100 g/4 oz chopped shallots in a saucepan in a little butter, then moisten with white wine and meat glaze and reduce. When reduced, add 500 ml/1 pint Espagnole and garnish with diced poached, beef marrow and chopped parsley. Do not add lemon juice, as you would for a white Bercy (see p. 34). Serve with grilled meat.

BOURGUIGNONNE

To 500 ml/1 pint Espagnole or Demi Glace Sauce add 10 tablespoons Burgundy wine. Garnish with small glazed onions, sautéed, diced bacon, and mushrooms. Finish with chopped parsley.

BRESSOISE

To 500 ml/1 pint Espagnole or Demi Glace add 3 finely chopped shallots, 3 tablespoons purée of chicken livers. Simmer for 30 minutes. Strain and finish with the juice of an orange.

BROGLI

Reduce 500 ml/1 pint of Espagnole with 10 tablespoons sherry and a little mushroom liquor. Despumate from time to time. Finish with a little diced cooked ham.

CHAMPIGNONS, aux, I

225–375 g/½–¾ lb mushrooms
3 tablespoons clarified butter
1 shallot, finely minced or 1 clove garlic finely minced
about 250 ml/½ pint Espagnole
juice of ½ lemon
salt and pepper

Trim off the root end of the mushroom stems, wash the mushrooms thoroughly, and chop them up fairly fine. Sauté them in hot, clarified butter with the shallot or garlic, stirring until they are brown. Do not let the butter turn black, as it is then very indigestible. Lift the mushrooms with a skimmer to a clean saucepan. Add three times their quantity of Espagnole and the lemon juice. Heat, stir and correct seasoning before serving.

CHAMPIGNONS, aux, II

Garnish a Velouté, Béchamel or Espagnole with cooked, sliced, button mushroom heads and blend with a purée of mushrooms or mushroom essence.

CHASSEUR, au An Espagnole or Demi Glace garnished with sautéed, minced mushrooms and chopped shallots; moistened and reduced in white wine, with a little brandy, tomato purée and game juices from the roasting pan added. Finish with some butter swirls and chopped parsley.

CHATEAUBRIAND Put 50 g/2 oz chopped shallots, 50 g/2 oz mushrooms (parings, stalks), a sprig of thyme and a bay leaf into 250 ml/½ pint of dry white wine and reduce by half. Strain through muslin cloth and add 500 ml/1 pint Espagnole or 250 ml/½ pint Demi Glace. If Espagnole is used the sauce must then be reduced to desired thicker consistency before finishing with 75 g/3 oz Maître d'Hôtel Butter and a little chopped tarragon, cayenne pepper and lemon juice.

CHEVREUIL, au Sauté in a little butter 2 onions and 100 g/4 oz ham, cut in fine strips. Moisten with a little tarragon vinegar; add 500 ml/1 pint Espagnole or 250 ml/½ pint Demi Glace, 10 tablespoons wine and 4 tablespoons red currant jelly. Reduce to the desired consistency. Serve with roe deer, venison or mutton cutlets. This sauce can also be made more elaborately with a Poivrade base, see p. 48.

DUXELLE An Espagnole or Demi Glace blended with tomato purée, with the addition of a little sautéed onion and shallots that you have reduced in a spoon or two of white wine. Finish with chopped parsley and Dry Duxelles (see p. 23).

GENOISE An Espagnole or Demi Glace reduced in the same manner as Sauce Génevoise (p. 52). Flavour with anchovy essence and mushroom essence. Finish with chopped parsley.

DEMI GLACE or HALF GLAZE An Espagnole reduced to perfection by the addition of equal proportions (or less) of good brown stock (be sure to reserve some brown stock for this purpose when you are making an Espagnole whose destiny is Demi Glace) over a fierce heat. If you feel the Espagnole or brown stock is not strong enough, the addition of meat glaze, or jellied gravy, or veal broth, or even proprietory makes of good meat extracts, is quite permissible. When it has reached its finished consistency, the liquid should be almost syrupy and it should readily adhere to a spoon. Reduction should go on until this consistency is reached; the sauce should be carefully stirred towards the end of reduction and the heat lowered, to avoid catching – but to begin with, it should boil briskly over a fierce heat. Strain through a fine sieve or whirl in a liquidizer and then strain and finish with about 10 tablespoons good sherry to each 500 ml/1 pint sauce. The addition of a little mushroom liquor before reducing is also an improvement. *For derivatives of Demi Glace see p. 49.*

HUSSARDE Lightly stew 100 g/4 oz minced onions and shallots in a little butter. Moisten with 10 tablespoons white wine, and reduce by half. Add 500 ml/1 pint Espagnole, 3 tablespoons tomato pureé, a small bouquet garni; then 50 g/2 oz raw lean ham and a little crushed garlic. Simmer for 30 minutes. Take out the ham; rub the remainder through a sieve and finish with 2 tablespoons grated horseradish and a garniture of small pieces of the diced ham and chopped parsley.

ITALIENNE Lightly stew in a little olive oil 50 g/2 oz chopped shallots and the same quantity of mushroom parings and stalks. Moisten with about 10 tablespoons white wine. Add 10 tablespoons tomato purée and reduce the whole by about one third. Add this to 500 ml/1 pint Espagnole and allow to simmer for 15 minutes. Sieve, and finish with seasoning, lemon juice and nutmeg.

MADEIRA (MADERE) Put 1 large tablespoon meat glaze into a stewpan, pour in 500 ml/1 pint Madeira wine, add a pinch of pepper and reduce by half. Pour 1 litre/2 pints Espagnole into the wine and meat glaze reduction and continue to boil until the sauce is of a nice creamy consistency. Pass the sauce through a fine sieve.
For derivatives of Madeira see p. 52.

OLIVES, aux An Espagnole flavoured with Madeira wine and garnished with julienne of olives. Serve with duck or fowl.

PARISIENNE An un-reduced Espagnole, with the addition of a little meat glaze and lemon juice. Serve with grilled meat.

PAUVRE HOMME An Espagnole blended with a *Sugo di Pomodoro* (see p. 117) or good tomato ketchup, anchovy essence, vinegar and pepper. Serve with grilled fish.

POIVRADE This is an elaborate sauce for tournedos and noisettes as well as for game. It is one of the greatest if you have the time and devotion to make it properly. Sauté and brown well about ½ kilo/1 lb *mirepoix* of vegetables: carrots, onions, celery. Add 5 tablespoons vinegar and about 250 ml/½ pint marinade, ideally the one you have steeped the meat or game in. Reduce by two thirds and add 500 ml/1 pint Espagnole or Demi Glace. Simmer for a further 45 minutes, putting in 3 or 4 crushed peppercorns after about 30 minutes. Strain well and add a further 250 ml/½ pint marinade, then allow to simmer and despumate again for a further 15 minutes. Whirl for a minute in a liquidizer, then strain again and finish with 50 g/2 oz butter.
For derivatives of Poivrade see p. 52.

GAME POIVRADE The perfect sauce to be served with all kinds of game: make the same way as Poivrade but add game trimmings when frying the *mirepoix*, and moisten with game stock and marinade.

ROBERT   Lightly sauté 2 medium onions in a little butter. Moisten with 5 table-spoons white wine, 2 tablespoons vinegar and reduce by a good third. Add 500 ml/1 pint Demi Glace or 1 litre/2 pints Espagnole and keep reducing until the required consistency is obtained. Finish with a little meat glaze, 1 teaspoon mustard and a little caster sugar.

ROMAINE   An Espagnole or Demi Glace with the addition of currants, sultanas and *pignole*, diluted and reduced in white wine vinegar, then strained.

SICILIENNE   An Espagnole reduced with Marsala wine. Garnish with sliced onions, lightly sautéed in butter just before serving. Serve with grilled or roast beef cuts.

VERJUS, au   Crushed unripe green grapes, cooked in stock and sherry; reduced and blended with Espagnole and finished with 50 g/2 oz butter. Serve with roast duck or pork.

ZOUAVE   An Espagnole or Demi Glace mixed with Tomato Sauce and blended with the reduced liquor of 2 or 3 tablespoons chili vinegar, in which you have cooked a little chopped garlic, tarragon and mustard.

Sauces derived from DEMI GLACE *(see p. 47)*

Tomato Demi Glace or Sauce Niçoise   For each ½ litre/1 pint of Espagnole add about 10 tablespoons tomato purée, then reduce to Demi Glace consistency, i.e. till it coats the back of a spoon.

Algérienne   To a Demi Glace add 10 tablespoons white wine; garnish with diced tomatoes and add a suspicion of garlic. Serve with chicken sauté and large joints.

Bigarade   To 250 ml/½ pint Demi Glace add the strained and de-greased braising stock of the duck or duckling, and reduce; add the juice of 4–5 oranges and 1 lemon; reduce again to the desired consistency, and garnish with julienne of blanched orange and lemon zest. Red currant jelly is optional. Serve with braised duckling.

Bordelaise Rouge   Stew 75 g/3 oz minced shallots, 2 bay leaves, a little thyme and pepper in 250 ml/½ pint red wine; reduce by half. Add 250 ml/½ pint Demi Glace; simmer for 20 minutes, despumating occasionally. Meanwhile poach 50 g/2 oz beef marrow for 3–4 minutes in a little of the stock. Drain and dice. Strain the sauce through a fine sieve and finish with a little dissolved meat glaze, lemon juice, and the diced, poached beef marrow. Serve with grilled meats.
For derivatives of Bordelaise Rouge see p. 53.

Castelaine   Flavour a Demi Glace with pimento and lemon juice. Garnish with chopped sautéed, or boiled, lean ham.

Catalane	To a Demi Glace add 10 tablespoons white wine, sautéed mushrooms, small glazed onions, cooked, chopped chestnuts, chipolatas and diced tomato. Serve with chicken sauté.
Czarine, à la	A Demi Glace garnished with chopped capers, gherkins and chopped bleached raisins.
Doria	A Demi Glace flavoured with lemon juice and garnished with diced, cooked cucumber. Serve with chicken sauté or trout.
Epigrammes, aux	Blend chestnut purée with a Game Demi Glace.
Gratin, au	To 10 tablespoons fish fumet and 5 tablespoons white wine, add 75 g/ 3 oz chopped shallots and reduce by half. Add to a Demi Glace and finish with 2–3 tablespoons Dry Duxelles (see p. 23) and chopped parsley. Serve with egg or fish dishes.
Huîtres à Brun, aux	The same as Sauce aux Huîtres with a Béchamel base but using Demi Glace in place of Béchamel or Normande.
La Vallière	A Demi Glace with the addition of game essence and sour cream. Garnished with a fine julienne of truffles and mushrooms.
Lyonnaise	Sauté 75 g/3 oz finely chopped onion in a little butter, add 10 tablespoons white wine and the same of vinegar. Reduce this almost completely, then add $\frac{3}{4}$ litre/$1\frac{1}{2}$ pints of clear Demi Glace; simmer for a further hour, and strain.
Marchand de Vin, au	Lightly sauté in a saucepan 50 g/2 oz chopped shallot in a little butter. Moisten with 10 tablespoons claret, add a little meat glaze and reduce by half. To this add 250 ml/$\frac{1}{2}$ pint Demi Glace. Simmer for 5 minutes and strain.
Marigny	Blend into a Demi Glace tomato purée and mushroom liquor; add 8 tablespoons white wine and reduce by a quarter.
Matelote Brune	See page 36 for Matelote Blanche but use Demi Glace in place of Velouté and red wine in place of white.
Mironton	Blend an onion and tomato purée into a Demi Glace. Flavour with vinegar and prepared mustard.
Moëlle, à la	The same as Bordelaise Rouge (p. 49), using white wine instead of red. Garnish with diced marrow, chopped parsley, chervil, chive and tarragon.
Périgourdine	A Demi Glace enriched with foie-gras purée and garnished with sliced truffles. Serve with eggs, bouchés, etc. For serving with tournedos, etc., omit foie-gras.

Piccadilly A Demi Glace blended with Anchovy Butter and flavoured with shallots and mustard.

Piment A Demi Glace blended with tomato purée and well seasoned with pimentos and cayenne pepper.

Piquante Put into a saucepan 10 tablespoons white wine, 10 tablespoons vinegar and 75 g/3 oz chopped shallots, and reduce by half. Add 500 ml/1 pint Demi Glace. Bring to the boil and reduce again by one third. Garnish with about 50 g/2 oz chopped gherkin and capers and 1 teaspoon mixed, finely chopped chervil, tarragon and parsley.

Poivrade This can be made with Demi Glace or Espagnole. The recipe is given on p. 48.

Porto A Demi Glace with the addition of 5 tablespoons port wine just before serving.

Réforme Mix together equal quantities Demi Glace and Poivrade, garnish with 25–50 g/1–2 oz julienne of gherkins, mushrooms, truffles, tongue and hard-boiled egg white. This is Soyer's famous sauce called after the Reform Club where he created it.

Salmis Stew a *mirepoix* of vegetables with some game carcasses and trimmings in a little butter. Moisten with red or white wine and reduce. Add Demi Glace together with a small bouquet garni. Strain and finish with 50 g/2 oz butter.

Tortue, à la To 250 ml/½ pint veal stock add a small sprig sage, sweet marjoram, thyme, basil, coriander, rosemary, bayleaf, 50 g/2 oz mushrooms (parings or stalks) and 25 g/1 oz parsley. Infuse for 30 minutes over gentle heat. Two or 3 minutes before straining the infusion add 4 crushed peppercorns. Strain through a muslin cloth and add, away from the heat, 250 ml/½ pint Demi Glace and the same of Tomato Sauce, 5 tablespoons sherry, a little truffle essence and a good pinch of cayenne pepper.

York, d' A Demi Glace with the addition of red currant jelly, port wine, orange juice and a little ground cinnamon. Garnish with julienne of blanched orange zest. Serve with boiled ham and roast or pickled pork.

Zingara Demi Glace or Madeira Sauce blended with tomato purée, garnished with mushrooms, julienne of truffle, ham and tongue; finish with a little cayenne pepper.

Sauces derived from MADEIRA SAUCE *(see p. 48)*

Alexandra A Madeira Sauce garnished with asparagus heads. Served with chicken sauté.

Archiduc Blend *foie-gras* purée with a Madeira Sauce, garnish with brunoise of carrot, and truffle. Serve with duck or duckling.

Financière, à la A Madeira Sauce blended with truffle essence.

Génevoise A Madeira Sauce reduced with fish essence and red wine; flavour with anchovy essence and garlic; finish with a little butter, so obtaining a mellow and more palatable flavour.

Nancy A Madeira Demi Glace enriched with chicken purée. Serve with grilled beef.

Périgueux To 500 ml/1 pint Madeira Sauce add 250 ml/½ pint good veal stock, 2 tablespoons truffle essence and meat glaze. Reduce by one third. Garnish with chopped truffles.
For derivatives of Périgueux see opposite.

Richmont A Madeira Sauce garnished with minced morels, previously tossed in butter and chopped parsley, to which thin slices of truffle are added. Serve with eggs. An inferior version uses cèpes. Russian dried morels can sometimes be bought in Soho and reconstituted and they are excellent.

Rossini A Madeira Sauce garnished with slices of truffle and foie-gras. Serve with poultry and grilled tournedos.

Sauces derived from Poivrade *(see p. 48)*

Cerises, aux or Badoise To a Poivrade add 2 tablespoons cream and cherry glaze. Garnish with stoned cherries. Serve with roebuck.

Conti To a Game Poivrade add 3 tablespoons white wine and blend with a little lentil purée. Garnish with julienne of tongue. Serve with roe deer.

Diane A Poivrade finished with cream.

Grand Veneur Add an equal volume of game stock to a Poivrade and reduce to a third. Add 2 or 3 tablespoons red currant jelly and finish with 10 tablespoons cream. Serve with venison.

Moscovite A Poivrade with an infusion of juniper berries. Garnish with grilled sliced almonds and currants swollen in warm water. Finish with a glass of Marsala.

Nesselrode A Game Poivrade blended with chestnut purée. Serve with roe deer.

Nora A Poivrade with addition of red currant jelly, Worcestershire Sauce, meat glaze and lemon juice.

Pignole A Poivrade enriched with cream and chopped garlic.

Viennoise A Poivrade blended with orange juice and reduced. Finish with paprika pepper and a little cream.

Sauces derived from Périgueux *(see opposite)*

Continental A Périgueux enriched with collops of foie-gras and julienne of truffle. Serve with eggs.

Masséna A Périgueux garnished with diced cooked beef marrow and artichoke hearts.

Sauce derived from Bordelaise Rouge *(see p. 49)*

Rouennaise Mix four raw duck's livers which have been sieved to a fine purée into a Bordelaise or Madeira Sauce. Heat for only a few minutes so that the livers do not become overcooked. Sieve, and add pepper, lemon juice and a reduction of shallots in white wine.

---

3 BUTTER BASED SAUCES AND BUTTER AND EGG BASED SAUCES

a) BUTTER BASED SAUCES

Melted, or Drawn, Butter Sauce
Beurre à la Vierge, or Sauce Mousseuse
Beurre Noisette
Beurre Noir (Black Butter Sauce)
Beurre, or Sauce, à la Meunière
Beurre Polonaise
Beurre Blanc
Beurre Blanc Béarnais
Sauce au Beurre, dite Bâtarde
For the traditional English Butter Sauces see Chapter 3.

b) EGG AND BUTTER BASED SAUCES

i) SAUCE HOLLANDAISE
Sauce Hollandaise I
Sauce Hollandaise II
VM's Hollandaise Sauce
Alice B Toklas's Hollandaise (au Beurre Noisette)

VARIATIONS OF *SAUCE HOLLANDAISE*
Chantilly or Mousseline   *Hubert*
Maître d'Hôtel II   *Maltaise*   *Marguéry*

ii) *SAUCE BEARNAISE*
Frozen Béarnaise

VARIATIONS OF *SAUCE BEARNAISE*
Bâtarde (cold)   *Choron*   *Foyot*
Paloise   *Sully*

This is really an international family of sauces. Sauce Hollandaise is claimed as a native by both the Low Countries and by France, which calls it Sauce Isigny. However, some of the plain or butter sauces may well have originated in England, for, long before the French Revolution modified and enriched our cooking through the influence of the emigré chefs and the Paris *sauciers*, London was famous for Fish Dinners in its clubs and taverns on the Thames, most of which were accompanied by delicate drawn, or melted, butter sauces, served plain or as a vehicle for other ingredients such as capers, oysters, parsley, egg, anchovy, shrimp, crab, truffles, etc.

NOTE: It is best to make all butter sauces with previously clarified butter. See p. 23.

a) BUTTER BASED SAUCES

Melted, or Drawn, Butter Sauce

50–65 g/2–2½ oz best fresh butter
about 2 tablespoons water
about 1 large teaspoon flour

Put the butter into a very clean saucepan, with the water. Dredge in the flour and shake it over a steady heat, one way, until it boils. Then pour it into your sauceboat and serve. See also p. 77 for a more detailed and lively recipe.

Beurre à la Vierge or Sauce Mousseuse

100–125 g/4–5 oz clarified butter
pinch of salt
tablespoon lemon juice
2 tablespoons very cold water
1–2 tablespoons whipped cream

Melt the butter, which has been softened into a paste, in an earthenware bowl or pan that has been rinsed out with boiling water and carefully dried. Season with a pinch of salt and work with a wire whisk until it froths well; add the lemon juice and cold water little by little while you continue whisking. The whipped cream may be added just before serving. This sauce is usually used with plain boiled fish or asparagus.

NOTE: Do not confuse Sauce Mousseuse with Mayonnaise Mousseuse, p. 62.

Beurre Noisette

125 g/5 oz clarified butter

Heat the butter in a clean enamelled pan until it foams and then slowly turns a golden nut brown. That is all; at this stage it is called Beurre Noisette and can be used as a simple sauce for soufflés, rissoles, egg or white meat dishes. It is very good with a cauliflower or a cheese soufflé.

Beurre Noir (Black Butter Sauce)

50–75 g/2–3 oz clarified butter
2 tablespoons *dry* parsley, chopped
1–2 tablespoons wine vinegar

Heat the butter in a frying pan until it is quite dark, but be careful it does not burn. Throw the parsley into it and fry until crisp. If the parsley is not completely dry it will burn black. Pour it on to the eggs, fish, brains, or whatever dish you are preparing *au beurre noir*. Then, while the frying pan is still hot, pour into it 1–2 generous tablespoons wine vinegar. Swill it round and let it get hot and reduce a little then pour this too, after the black butter, over the dish. Capers should be added for brains and fish dishes. A tablespoon of Worcestershire Sauce can be added when you are frying eggs and croûtons in *beurre noir*. Sit the eggs on the croûtons, sprinkle with parsley, pour the rest of the sauce over and you have an egg dish, *Oeufs au Beurre Noir*.

Beurre, or Sauce, à la Meunière

100 g/4 oz butter
1 lemon
2 tablespoons very finely chopped parsley

Melt the butter in a double boiler and to this add the juice of the lemon and the parsley.

Beurre Polonaise

75 g/3 oz breadcrumbs
1 tablespoon minced onion or shallot (optional)
125 g/6 oz butter
1 hard-boiled egg

Brown the breadcrumbs in the oven with a few flakes of the butter. Sauté the onion in the rest of the butter until transparent, then add the breadcrumbs and chopped hard-boiled egg. Use as a topping for vegetables, especially cauliflower, or sautéed chicken.

Beurre Blanc

1 glass white wine (Muscadet, Vouvray, an Anjou or similar good dry white wine)
salt and pepper
1 tablespoon shallots, finely minced
255 g/9 oz unsalted butter
lemon juice

This recipe was given to me by the Chef de Cuisine of the British Embassy, Paris, M. Jean Viané.

Put the wine, seasoning and shallots into a small pan and reduce over a fierce heat until there is only a spoonful of wine left. Put the butter into another pan and sink this into a warm, but not hot or boiling, bain-marie. Beat it with a whisk till it is soft but not melted. Gradually add to it the cooled-down wine and shallots, whipping all the time. If the butter looks like melting completely, remove it immediately from the bain-marie so that it does not melt any more and continue beating away from the heat until it becomes frothy and creamy and goes white. It is a fairly slow and tricky operation and needs patience. The finished sauce should be just runny, and homogenous. It should not be stiff or melted. Lastly add a squeeze of lemon and a little salt, according to taste.

Beurre Blanc Béarnais

1 glass dry white Jurançon wine
2 shallots, very finely chopped
pepper
2–3 tablespoons double cream
85 g/3½ oz unsalted butter, chilled and cut into small cubes
salt
lemon juice

Put the wine and shallots, seasoned with pepper, into a small saucepan and bring to the boil. Cook for a few moments. Before the liquid evaporates completely, add 1 tablespoon cream and thicken the sauce over very moderate heat by whisking in the butter, one small piece at a time. Work rapidly, making sure each piece is completely absorbed before adding the next. If the mixture heats too quickly, lift the pan off the heat. When all the butter has been absorbed, add the rest of the cream, stirring it in well with the wire whisk. Season with salt and lemon juice.

**Sauce au Beurre,
dite Sauce Bâtarde
or Mock Hollandaise**

25 g/1 oz butter
25 g/1 oz flour
500 ml/1 pint boiling water
pinch of salt
3 egg yolks
10 tablespoons cream
1 tablespoon lemon juice
50–100 g/2–4 oz softened butter

Make a roux with the butter and the flour. Do not cook but beat to a smooth paste, then pour the boiling water over the mixture all at once, add the salt and whisk briskly. Beat up the egg yolks in the cream in a bowl off the heat, then add the hot sauce to the eggs and cream, a few drops at a time to begin with, then in a steady stream. Pour back into the saucepan, bring to the boil, whisking hard, and boil for 5 seconds only. Remove from heat again, add the lemon juice, correct seasoning, strain, and then beat in the softened butter, a spoonful at a time, and away from the heat. Serve immediately it is ready.

b) EGG AND BUTTER BASED SAUCES

i) SAUCE HOLLANDAISE

A really wonderful sauce and it is well worth mastering the technique of making it, though this is a very personal matter which varies from chef to chef. It is a technique broadly similar to the one used in making Mayonnaise, but you use butter instead of oil and the mixture is hot, or rather warm, instead of cold. Like mayonnaise, there is always the danger of an Hollandaise curdling, or the egg and butter mixture rejecting emulsion, and it must be carefully made – more off than on the heat, with very hot rather than boiling water (and very little of it) at the bottom of the bain-marie, so that the upper part does not touch the water below. A round-bottomed enamel saucepan and a flat wire whisk are the best implements. Once made, an Hollandaise or a Béarnaise will keep perfectly well over warm water on a cool corner of the stove while you are preparing other food. The two sauces vary only slightly in consistency and ingredients. The technique for making them is the same, and if you can make one, the other is easy. Here then are four recipes for Hollandaise, one or all of which I hope will work for you.

Sauce Hollandaise I

This is sometimes called Sauce Isigny by the French, who insist that it was invented in Normandy.

2 tablespoons wine vinegar
pinch of salt
4 egg yolks
1 tablespoon cold water
225 g/8 oz butter, melted
lemon juice
cream (optional)

If possible, use an enamel saucepan or bowl with rounded bottom. Reduce the wine vinegar and salt in it to about half a tablespoonful by fast boiling. Take the saucepan off the heat and cool it completely. Meanwhile beat up the egg yolks together with the cold water and add to the reduced vinegar and salt when nearly cold. Put the pan back on to a very gentle heat or lower it into a double saucepan or bain-marie, in which there is only a small amount of very hot, but not boiling, water, beating it continually with a wire whisk until it becomes a thick homogenous cream. Then add the warm butter very slowly at first, as in Mayonnaise, while you continue whisking over the same gentle heat. Make sure every drop, then every spoonful, of butter is absorbed before you add the next – use a little jug. You can increase speed when you have formed a good base, but be patient and don't push it.

If the sauce gets too thick, a spoonful or two of hot water can be added. Season well and add the lemon juice to taste. If cream and other ingredients are to be added as in Sauce Mousseline, Marguéry etc, do so now, but do not heat up again after the addition of lemon juice or cream, or the sauce is likely to curdle. If it should curdle, don't despair, throw in a lump of ice, take off the heat and beat like mad till it is smooth again, when you can remove the ice-cube. And if this does not work, simply put another yolk into a clean basin and add the curdled sauce drop by drop, whipping as before. Finally sieve and keep just warm in a cool bain-marie.

Sauce Hollandaise II

Makes 375 ml/¾ pint
225 g/8 oz best, unsalted, clarified butter
3 tablespoons good, white wine vinegar
2 tablespoons water
3 large egg yolks
cold water
½ lemon
salt and pepper

Melt the butter gently and set aside. Mix the wine vinegar and water in the top of a double boiler and reduce over direct heat to 1 table-spoonful. Let it cool to the point where you can put your finger in it without discomfort, then add the egg yolks, which you have separated without leaving any trace of egg white. Mix well, thus reducing the risk of the heat later scrambling the egg yolks. Add 1 teaspoon of the medium cool, clarified butter. Place the pan over just simmering water on moderate heat, and from now on never stop stirring. Add the butter bit by bit as you see the sauce thickening, the heat making an emulsion of egg and butter. For safety's sake you should keep a little cold water near at hand; at the slightest sign of curdling add a little cold water and remove the pan from over the heat, stirring vigorously. It is the same technique as mayonnaise, but using melted butter instead of oil.

When all the butter has been added, remove from the heat altogether and add the juice of ½ lemon and season to taste. The sauce must not be reheated, and is served lukewarm otherwise it curdles.

Very experienced cooks thoroughly familiar with their stoves can make Hollandaise without a double boiler. This is a challenge worth taking up. But to add arrowroot or cream, is slightly sacreligious, unless it is to make a derivative sauce, or to hold an Hollandaise which has to be kept waiting.

A good version of an Hollandaise type sauce with arrowroot is Mrs Stanley's Julia Sauce, see p. 79.

VM's Hollandaise Sauce

3 egg yolks
1 tablespoon cold water
100 g/4 oz soft butter
¼ teaspoon salt
1 teaspoon lemon juice or to taste

Combine egg yolks and water in the top of a double boiler and beat with a wire whisk over hot (not boiling) water until fluffy.

Add a few teaspoonfuls of softened butter to the mixture and beat continually until the butter has melted and the sauce starts to thicken. Care should be taken that the water in the bottom of the boiler never boils. Continue adding the butter, bit by bit, stirring constantly. Add the salt and lemon juice. For a light texture, beat in a tablespoon of hot water if desired.

**Alice B Toklas's
Hollandaise Sauce
(au Beurre Noisette)**

4 yolks of eggs
pepper and salt
¼ lb browned butter
¾ cup shelled hazelnuts

This recipe is not for beginners but is quite delicious.

Put the yolks of eggs and a little pepper and salt in a small saucepan over the lowest possible flame. Stir continuously with a wooden spoon, adding drop by drop ¼ lb browned butter. Put ¾ cup shelled hazelnuts in the oven. When they are warm remove from oven and roll in a cloth until all the skins are removed. Pound them in a mortar to a powder, adding from time to time a few drops of water to prevent the nuts from exuding oil. Rub through a sieve or whirl in an electric grinder. Replace in mortar and add 1 cup water. Mix with wooden spoon. When perfectly amalgamated add in tiny quantities to the egg yolks in the saucepan, stirring continuously. If contents of pan become too hot, remove a moment from flame and add a small quantity of butter to cool the mixture before replacing over flame. When all the butter has been incorporated remove from flame and slowly stir into the sauce 1 tablespoon vinegar.

VARIATIONS OF *SAUCE HOLLANDAISE* (see p. 56)

*Chantilly
or Mousseline*

Hollandaise gently mixed with stiffly whipped cream; correct seasoning. Not to be confused with Mayonnaise Chantilly, see p. 61.

Hubert

Hollandaise garnished with blanched, chopped muscat grapes.

Maître d'Hôtel II

To 500 ml/1 pint Hollandaise Sauce add 1 tablespoon chopped parsley and a little grated nutmeg. Correct seasoning. For Maître d'Hôtel Butter see p. 64.

Maltaise

Hollandaise into which is blended a little blood orange juice and a julienne of blanched orange zest. Especially suitable for serving with asparagus.

Marguéry

Hollandaise flavoured with a fish fumet and a purée of oysters.

ii) *SAUCE BEARNAISE*

1 teaspoon chopped shallots
50 g/2 oz tarragon, chopped
75 g/3 oz chervil
a little white pepper
a pinch of salt
4 tablespoons good white
wine vinegar
1 tablespoon water
5 egg yolks
155 g/6 oz butter, melted
1 teaspoon minced chervil
and chopped tarragon
cayenne pepper

This is the perfect sauce to eat with steak and you will receive more compliments for it than any other.

Put the shallots, tarragon, chervil, white pepper, salt, vinegar and water into a saucepan. Reduce the vinegar and water by two thirds slowly. Take off the heat and allow the pan and its contents to cool to lukewarm. When quite cool, add the egg yolks, beating briskly with a wire whisk, then put the saucepan back on a gentle heat or bain-marie and add the melted butter to the yolks gradually, stirring and whisking continuously. Whisk the sauce briskly, so as to ensure the cooking of the eggs, which by gradual setting effects the liaison of the sauce. When the butter and eggs are smoothly combined and the sauce is thick, rub it through a sieve and finish with 1 teaspoon more minced chervil and chopped tarragon leaves. Correct the seasoning and add a pinch of cayenne. The sauce should be only tepid when served. It freezes perfectly. Never let it overheat or it will turn. Use with grilled poultry or meat, or with Roast Ribs of Beef for a special Sunday treat.

Frozen Béarnaise Freeze Béarnaise Sauce in an orange juice can. When frozen hard remove and slice with a deep freeze knife. Store frozen slices in plastic bags until ready for use. Defrost but do not reheat. Place a round of Béarnaise on a hot *filet mignon*. The heat of the steak will do the trick.

VARIATIONS OF *SAUCE BEARNAISE* (see opposite)

Bâtarde A cold Béarnaise flavoured with fish essence and blended with tomato purée and Anchovy Butter. Not to be confused with Sauce au Beurre, dite Bâtarde, see p. 56.

Choron A Béarnaise into which is blended a little thick tomato paste.

Foyot A Béarnaise finished with a thread of meat glaze.

Paloise A Béarnaise using mint in place of tarragon. Serve with leg of lamb.

Sully A Béarnaise into which is blended a little Anchovy Butter.

4 OIL AND EGG BASED SAUCES

MAYONNAISE SAUCE

Classic Mayonnaise

VARIATIONS OF *MAYONNAISE SAUCE*

Aïoli	*Albert or Albertine*	*Andalouse (Niçoise)*
Bulgarienne	*Caboul or East India Mayonnaise*	
Epicurienne	*Espagnole Mayonnaise*	*Génoise*
Gribiche	*Livournaise*	*Maximilian*
Mayonnaise Chantilly	*Mayonnaise Collée*	*Mayonnaise Escoffier*
Mayonnaise Italienne	*Mayonnaise Mousseuse*	
Mayonnaise à la Russe	*Mousquetaire*	*Rémoulade*
Russian Mayonnaise	*Tartare I and II*	
Verte or Vert-pré (Green Mayonnaise)		
Lady Dudley's Sauce Verte		*Vin Blanc Mayonnaise*

MAYONNAISE SAUCE

This is the most useful and varied of all cold sauces. Its chief ingredients are oil and yolk of egg, and, unless it is made in fairly large quantities, it requires time and a good deal of patience. But the larger the quantities, the quicker the emulsion, for you have more egg yolk to absorb the oil, and, once a firm base is achieved, the rest is easy. So it is practical to make 500 ml/1 pint or more of mayonnaise at a time

and keep the surplus in a cool larder. Here are some other points
to watch:

* all ingredients should be at room temperature
* take eggs out of the fridge well in advance
* warm bowl and oil, if necessary
* always beat egg yolks till they are thick
    and sticky, before you start adding oil
* always beat one way, i.e. clockwise

Don't be impatient for the first 4 or 5 minutes: the oil should be
added literally drop by drop to begin with, then teaspoon by teaspoon,
till you have a base, after that much more quickly. The maximum
amount of oil one egg yolk will absorb is about 155 g/6 fl oz, but it
is safer to say 100 g/4 fl oz, till you are an expert.

About Oils: There are several different types of oil which may be used when
making mayonnaise or other sauces which require oil:

olive – virgin or refined
nut – walnut or peanut
seed – sunflower (arrachide) and maize

It is largely a question of taste and habit which you use. Personally
I prefer walnut or arrachide or very refined olive oil for mayonnaises;
virgin olive oil – a strong tasting, pale green first-press oil – for
Mediterranean sauces and for ones that are to be served with fish or
mixed with tomatoes; arrachide or very refined golden olive oil for
salad dressings, as it is much lighter. Peanut and maize oils are inferior
in taste and should mostly be used for deep frying and sautéeing.

Classic Mayonnaise

3 egg yolks
salt and pepper
1½ teaspoons mustard powder
500 ml/1 pint olive oil
very little tarragon vinegar
squeeze of lemon juice

Break the egg yolks into a mortar or small bowl. Add a little salt,
pepper and a heaped teaspoon mustard powder. Stir well before adding any oil at all. At first the oil must be stirred in drop by drop, then
a little more each time as the mayonnaise gets thicker. Stir steadily but
not like a maniac. From time to time add a very little tarragon vinegar,
and at the end a squeeze of lemon juice and seasoning. Should the
mayonnaise curdle, break another yolk into a clean basin and add the
curdled mayonnaise very gradually. It will come back to life miracul-
ously. The seasoning at the end of making a mayonnaise is very
important and must be done with nice judgement and care.

VARIATIONS OF *MAYONNAISE SAUCE*

Aïoli Sauce

6 cloves of garlic
pinch of salt
pinch of white pepper
3 egg yolks
375 ml/¾ pint olive oil
1⅓ tablespoons lemon juice
1 tablespoon tepid water

Press into a mortar 6 cloves of garlic, add a pinch of salt, pepper and
1 egg yolk. With the pestle reduce these ingredients to an emulsion.
Add the other egg yolks. Mix well with a wooden fork or spoon, or
the pestle, or a wire whisk. Add the olive oil drop by drop, incorpor-
ating it well before you add more. When you have a good base add
⅓ tablespoon lemon juice and then add the oil more briskly. When it
becomes firm again add ½ tablespoon tepid water. Continue to add
oil, lemon juice and tepid water till the oil is all used up. Then taste
and correct seasoning carefully.

Albert or *Albertine*	Add to 250 ml/1 pint Mayonnaise (made with lemon juice instead of vinegar), 100 g/4 oz peeled, freshly boiled shrimps; then, just before serving, 4 tablespoons whipped cream and 2 teaspoons anchovy essence. Taste and correct seasoning carefully. For cold fish or cold *oeufs mollets* on a bed of lettuce.
Andalouse also called *Niçoise*	Add to a Mayonnaise 10 tablespoons thick, cold, tomato purée. Garnish with 2 or 3 red peppers cut into a fine julienne, or alternatively sweet capsicums or cayenne pepper. For cold boiled fish.
Bulgarienne	Blend about one third cold tomato purée to Mayonnaise. Add 2 tablespoons liquefied meat extract and the same of chopped, cooked celery.
Caboul or *East India Mayonnaise*	Pound and sieve a clove of garlic and mix it with 25 g/1 oz curry powder and a little olive oil, then carefully mix into the Mayonnaise, a little at a time.
Epicurienne	A Mayonnaise mixed with cucumber purée, aspic, chopped sweet chutney and gherkin.
Espagnole Mayonnaise	To a Mayonnaise add 3 tablespoons finely chopped lean cooked ham and a suspicion of garlic.
Génoise	To a Mayonnaise add 2 tablespoons previously blanched and pounded pistachios and almonds and one third of the volume of cold Béchamel. Finish with a little green herb purée and lemon juice.
Gribiche	Begin the Mayonnaise in the same manner as with Aïoli adding an additional teaspoon mustard. When it is made, garnish with finely chopped gherkin, capers, chervil and tarragon, using the hard-boiled egg whites cut in a fine julienne. Garlic is used to taste – it need not be as strong as in Aïoli.
Livournaise	Sieve 6 hard-boiled egg yolks, add a pinch of grated nutmeg and pepper; 4 or 5 pounded and sieved anchovy fillets (or 1 teaspoon essence). Now add 500 ml/1 pint olive oil gradually, in the same manner as for Mayonnaise, using tarragon vinegar to taste; finish with 1 teaspoon chopped parsley. Serve with cold meat and meat salads.
Maximilian	A Tartare Sauce (see p. 62) blended with cold tomato purée and flavoured with finely chopped tarragon leaves.
Mayonnaise Chantilly	Sometimes a lighter Mayonnaise is called for; for this use lemon juice instead of vinegar and add 1 teacup whipped cream to the finished mayonnaise, but only immediately before serving. It is then called Chantilly. Do not confuse this with Sauce Chantilly or Mousseline which is an Hollandaise.

Mayonnaise Collée   Add to a Mayonnaise 250 ml/½ pint cold, barely melted, thick, jelly of aspic made from the stock constituting the dish. Use for coating or masking. Put back in fridge immediately to set.

Mayonnaise Escoffier   To a Mayonnaise add 2 tablespoons finely shredded horseradish and 1 tablespoon mixed, finely chopped chervil and parsley.

Mayonnaise Italienne   To a Mayonnaise add 2 tablespoons diced, cooked calves' brains, 1 teaspoon chopped parsley, and a little lemon juice.

Mayonnaise Mousseuse   This is a light Mayonnaise similar to Chantilly but with a stiffly beaten egg-white folded into it, just before serving.
     Lemon juice and/or a good wine vinegar can be used for either Mousseuse or Chantilly. Both are good for cold salmon and for asparagus. Do not confuse with *Sauce Mousseuse* or *Beurre à la Vièrge*, see p. 54.

Mayonnaise à la Russe   A Mayonnaise blended with caviare purée, the creamy part of the lobster, mustard and Escoffier Sauce – which sounds like overdoing it to me.

Mousquetaire   Reduce in white wine 1 tablespoon finely chopped shallot. When cold add to the Mayonnaise Sauce and garnish with a little chopped chives. Finish with cayenne pepper.

Rémoulade   For 2 cups of sauce, mix together 1½ cups Mayonnaise, 1 teaspoon Dijon mustard, 2 tablespoons chopped sour gherkins, 2 tablespoons capers, 2 tablespoons finely chopped parsley, 2 tablespoons fresh (1 tablespoon dried) tarragon, 1 tablespoon fresh finely chopped (½ tablespoon dried) chervil, ½ teaspoon anchovy paste (optional), salt and pepper to taste.

Russian Mayonnaise   Blend with the Mayonnaise about 2 tablespoons mixed capers, gherkin and grated horseradish and a squeeze of lemon juice. Finish with a very little fine caster, or icing, sugar.

Tartare I   To a basic Aïoli Sauce add 2 tablespoons finely chopped onion, chives, tarragon, chervil, gherkin, capers and parsley.

Tartare II   Start with 2 hard-boiled egg yolks, and 1 raw one; proceed as for Classic Mayonnaise, then add herbs, gherkins and capers as in Tartare I.

Verte
or Vert-pré
Green Mayonnaise   Put the yolk of 1 egg in a bowl with 1 teaspoon salt and ¼ teaspoon pepper. Stir well. Add 2 tablespoons olive oil, drop by drop, constantly stirring. When it begins to stiffen add a few drops of lemon juice and pour in the oil more quickly. It will require ¾ cup of oil and the juice of ½ lemon. This Mayonnaise must be particularly firm.
     Take a small handful of cress, spinach, chervil and tarragon, boil them in unsalted water for 2 minutes, drain and put under a cold-water tap to cool and freshen, then press out all the water. Pound in

a mortar until they are reduced to a pulp that can be strained through a fine muslin. They should make about $\frac{1}{4}$ cup of purée. Add gradually to the Mayonnaise. The greens will give not only an attractive colour but a delicious flavour.

Lady Dudley's Sauce Verte

Make a good Mayonnaise Sauce. Add to it 2 tablespoons stiffly whipped cream then chop a small onion and pass it through a fine sieve together with a small piece of curry paste. Blanch a good handful of chervil, pound and pass this also through the sieve. When quite cold add this purée to the Mayonnaise slowly. Keep stirring over ice all the time you are mixing it in, but it must not become frozen. The onion and curry are only put in in very small quantities to bring out the delicate flavour of the chervil.

Vin Blanc Mayonnaise

Flavour the Mayonnaise with a good Chablis or Sauternes wine.

5 COMPOUND BUTTERS

Anchovy Butter
Beurre Bercy
Garlic Butter
Green Butter
Lobster Butter
Shrimp Butter
Maître d'Hôtel Butter
Marchand de Vin Butter
Watercress Butter
Hazelnut Butter or Beurre Noisette

Anchovy Butter

50 g/2 oz salted anchovy fillets pounded with 75 g/3 oz butter and sieved.

Beurre Bercy

2 shallots, chopped
125 ml/¼ pint white wine
75 g/3 oz softened butter
50 g/2 oz beef marrow, diced, poached and well drained
a few sprigs of parsley
lemon juice
pepper and salt

Boil shallots with the white wine and reduce almost to nothing. Allow to cool a little. Add the butter and stir till smooth. Add the marrow and parsley and season with lemon juice, pepper and salt. Good with steaks.

Garlic Butter

Pound 25 g/1 oz garlic, mix with 100 g/4 oz butter and pass through a fine sieve. Mould into sausage shape, chill, wrap in foil, and use as required. It is excellent between slices of a French loaf gently heated in the oven, or with a potato baked in its jacket or in the centres of grilled mushrooms on toast.

Green Butter Spinach leaves, parsley, chervil, tarragon and watercress in equal quantities. Blanch them, steep them in cold water and thoroughly dry them. Pound with a little blanched shallot, capers, gherkin, anchovy fillets and a little garlic. To each 25 g/1 oz of purée add 2 hard-boiled egg yolks, seasoning, 375 g/12 oz butter and 5 tablespoons olive oil. Pass the whole through a fine sieve.

Lobster Butter Pound the creamy parts of a lobster with hard-boiled eggs and coral, with equal parts of butter. Pass through a fine sieve.

Shrimp Butter This is made much the same way, except that you use the whole shrimp.

Maître d'Hôtel Butter Scald a few sprigs of parsley. Dry them well. Chop enough to fill 2 tablespoons. Work them into 100 g/4 oz butter in a bowl. Squeeze a large lemon and work its juice into the butter too. Roll the butter on a marble slab into a long sausage, wrap it in foil. Refrigerate and chop off bits from one end as you need them, to garnish steaks, fish, etc, or melt it gently on a hot plate and pour it over the dish you have prepared. It can then be called *à la meunière*.

Marchand de Vin Butter Reduce 125 ml/¼ pint of red wine and 1 teaspoon chopped shallot to one quarter. Add 25 g/1 oz meat glaze, melt, cool, incorporate 100 g/4 oz butter, juice of ¼ lemon and 25 g/1 oz chopped parsley. This can be rolled up and refrigerated like Maître d'Hôtel Butter.

Watercress Butter Blanch and dry some watercress, and pound with an equal quantity of butter. Pass through a fine sieve.

Hazelnut Butter or Beurre Noisette Pound a handful of slightly roasted and skinned hazelnuts to a cream with a few drops of water. Mix together with about the same quantity of butter.

THE CLASSIC FRENCH SAUCES

2 THE QUICKLY OR MORE SIMPLY MADE CLASSICS

Quickly made is, I am afraid, somewhat optimistic. It is impossible to make some of the grand Classic Sauces quickly, but in this section I have tried to find versions that are reasonably simple and practical for the smaller kitchen and that, while retaining their character, can be made with the minimum time and trouble. Several recipes are given for the same Foundation sauce in the hope that one will be found to suit every life and cooking style.

A fortnightly or monthly sauce-making day would ensure supplies of Espagnole and Velouté for even the most gourmet larder, and this is, without doubt, the most practical way for the ordinary cook to tackle the Classic sauces, as the alternatives – the recipes that do not use these Foundation sauces – often take longer to make and are less satisfactory in the end than the recipes that use stored Espagnole and Velouté.

A good standby, if the Foundation sauces are not used, is a bowl of Meat Glaze, see p. 20. It will last a long time as you use it sparingly and it is an excellent and easy way of enriching sauces, stews, braises, gravies etc.

1 THE WHITE SAUCES

a) *VELOUTE* AND ITS DERIVATIVES
Quick Allemande
Quick Allemande without Velouté
Poulette
Lady Dudley's Supreme
Sauce Suprême without Velouté

b) *BECHAMEL* AND ITS DERIVATIVES
Aurore
Cardinal
Crevettes, aux
Quick Sauce Mornay
Lady Dudley's Good Sauce Soubise

c) OTHER QUICK CLASSICS
Crème

Louisa Rochfort's Sauce Crème
Normande
Mrs Stanley's Vin Blanc or *White Wine Sauce*

a) **VELOUTE SIMPLE**   It must be remembered that Velouté is not strictly speaking a sauce
         or VIN BLANC   on its own but the first stage in the preparation of Allemande or
Suprême Simple Sauces, and that the Stock it is made with must
correspond with the dish it accompanies, see p. 15.

Makes 1 litre/2 pints Velouté   Make a white roux with the butter and flour and do not let it colour.
50 g/2 oz clarified butter   Add the cold stock, gradually bring to the boil, beat out any lumps
60 g/2¼ oz flour   and then simmer, placing the saucepan in a pan of water or bain-marie
1 litre/2 pints white stock   for another 30–45 minutes. Season very lightly. Strain through muslin
(veal, chicken or fish)   or strainer, and it is ready.
NOTE: Asparagus stock (or the water in which you have cooked
Asparagus) makes very good Velouté, especially if you enrich it at
the end with 2 egg yolks beaten up in a little cream.

DERIVATIVES OF *VELOUTE SAUCE*

Quick Sauce Allemande   To 500 ml/1 pint veal or chicken Velouté add 25 g/1 oz butter and
also called Sauce Blonde   work in 2 egg yolks. Do not allow to boil after the yolks are added
and Parisienne   or it will curdle.

A Quick Allemande   Melt the butter in a thick pan. Add the flour, stirring all the time,
without Velouté   over a medium heat, being careful not to let it brown. Cool, then add
40 g/1½ oz butter   the hot stock gradually, still stirring continuously. Cook for 10
40 g/1½ oz flour   minutes on a gentle heat. Sauté the mushrooms in a little butter and
500 ml/1 pint chicken stock   add. Season with salt and pepper and cook for a further 5 minutes. Add
50 g/2 oz fresh mushrooms, sliced   the lemon juice and remove from heat. Put the egg yolks in a heated
3 egg yolks   bowl with a few tablespoons of double cream and pour the sauce
juice of ½ lemon   gradually on to them as you stir. Strain the sauce if you wish but it is
salt and pepper   quite nice with the mushrooms through it.
cream to taste

Poulette   This is made from ¾ litre/1½ pints Allemande simply by reducing it by
half or two thirds, and adding a little mushroom essence; and then, off
the heat, a little butter, more lemon juice if necessary, and finely
chopped parsley.
NOTE: The Allemande recipe without Velouté (above) is quite suitable
provided you strain it.

Lady Dudley's Suprême   Put one and a half pints of very clear poultry stock and a quarter of
a pint of mushroom cooking liquor into a saucepan. Reduce to two
thirds; add one pint of poultry Velouté; reduce on an open fire,
stirring with the spatula the while and work in half a pint of good
cream, added little by little. When the sauce has reached the desired
consistency, strain it through a sieve and add another quarter of a pint
of cream and two ounces of best butter. Stir from time to time and
keep the pan well covered.

Sauce Suprême without Velouté

35 g/1½ oz butter
35 g/1½ oz flour
375 ml/¾ pint chicken stock
125 ml/¼ pint mushroom liquor
salt and pepper
1 small bay leaf
1 shallot
1 teaspoon lemon juice
125 ml/¼ pint cream
1 egg yolk (optional)

Melt the butter. Add the flour and cook for a few minutes only. Stir in the stock and mushroom liquor, whisk until the sauce boils. Add the bay leaf and shallot. Simmer for 20 minutes. Skim and add the lemon juice and cream. Sieve through muslin or fine nylon before use. The yolk of an egg is often added with the cream to this sauce. Reheat very gently and do not boil.

b) BECHAMEL SAUCE also called WHITE SAUCE or CREAM SAUCE in America

1 litre/2 pints milk
1 small onion, peeled
6 peppercorns
bouquet garni
50 g/2 oz clarified butter
60 g/2¼ oz flour

Put the milk on to boil with a small peeled onion, 6 peppercorns and a bouquet garni (thyme, bay leaf, parsley stalks, small blade of mace) and simmer for 5 minutes, without colouring. Cool. Strain milk and combine with cool roux, stirring all the time. Bring back to the boil and when boiling take off the heat and beat out any lumps. Return to heat and simmer gently for at least 20 minutes. Wedge pan if you wish. If you have to let it wait or wish to store the sauce, butter the top to prevent a skin forming. See also p. 33.

QUICK BECHAMEL SAUCE

25 g/1 oz clarified butter
25 g/1 oz cornflour
salt and pepper
50 g/2 oz cream (optional)
375 g/¾ pint hot milk

Melt butter over low heat, add cornflour, salt and pepper. Stir well to blend. Cook for about 5 minutes stirring continuously. Do not let it colour. Remove from heat and cool. Pour on hot milk all together or, if you like, a cup at a time, stirring vigorously. Bring to the boil and when it boils take off the heat and beat out any lumps. Put back on heat and simmer gently on a low heat, stirring continuously, for 15–20 minutes. Take off heat and add cream. It will make 500 ml/1 pint sauce. Butter top if you have to let it wait before serving.

DERIVATIVES OF BECHAMEL SAUCE

Aurore

More than the flavour, what matters in this sauce, is the colour and its effect on the eye.

To a Béchamel enriched with double cream add either tomato purée or paprika and/or vegetable dye. The colour should be a beautiful pink, like the dawn it is named after.

Cardinal

500 ml/1 pint Velouté or Béchamel
5 tablespoons mushroom liquor
salt, pepper and nutmeg
juice of ½ lemon
25 g/1 oz butter
15 g/½ oz lobster coral, finely chopped or 25 g/1 oz Lobster Butter
1 dessertspoon meat glaze

Reduce the sauce with the mushroom liquor; season with salt, pepper and nutmeg. Add the lemon juice and whisk in the butter and lobster coral or Lobster Butter. Strain through a fine sieve. Return to the stewpan and add the meat glaze. Stir until smooth and stand the pan in boiling water (bain-marie) to keep hot until required. If not red enough, add a little vegetable dye.

Crevettes, aux

100 g/4 oz Shrimp Butter (p. 64)
500 ml/1 pint Béchamel Sauce
enriched with 100 g/4 oz cream
2 teaspoons mild Hungarian
paprika

Combine Shrimp Butter with Béchamel and colour with paprika.

Quick Sauce Mornay

Boil 500 ml/1 pint Béchamel Sauce with 125 ml/$\frac{1}{4}$ pint stock of the dish you are cooking, vegetable or chicken. Reduce by a good quarter and add, off the heat, 50 g/2 oz grated Gruyère cheese and 50 g/2 oz grated Parmesan cheese. Put the sauce back on the heat for a few minutes and stir well until the cheeses are melted. Finish away from the heat with 50 g/2 oz butter added by degrees. If you wish a very rich sauce, cool and then combine with a liaison of egg yolks and cream off the heat. Reheat but do not boil. Serve with chicken or eggs.
NOTE: **Mornay for Fish Dishes:** use 125 ml/$\frac{1}{4}$ pint fish liquor instead of the light stock.

Lady Dudley's Good Sauce Soubise

Stew in butter two pounds of finely minced onions, scalded for 4–5 minutes and well drained. This stewing of the onions in butter increases their flavour. Then add one pint of thick Béchamel Sauce. Season with salt and a teaspoonful of powdered sugar. Cook gently for half an hour; rub through a sieve and complete the sauce with one tablespoon of cream and two ounces of butter. Correct seasoning, reheat gently and it is ready. Do not hurry this sauce. It should take 40 minutes to one hour to make. You can let the sauce simmer without harming in a bain-marie.

c) OTHER QUICK CLASSICS

Crème

Heat 50 g/2 oz butter and 50 g/2 oz fresh double cream in a double boiler. Stir until thick. Season with salt and ground black pepper. Serve hot with roast chicken, veal or fresh sautéed trout.

Louisa Rochfort's Sauce Crème

2–3 egg yolks
500 ml/1 pint good cream
50 g/2 oz fresh butter
a very little flour
salt
cayenne
juice of 1 lemon

Beat up the raw yolks of egg; put them into a saucepan with the cream. Add the butter into which you have kneaded a teaspoon of Vienna (i.e. fine white) flour. Stand the saucepan in a bain-marie and stir well with a wooden spoon until it becomes thick and creamy. Then add the salt, a grain or two of cayenne pepper and a few drops of lemon juice*. Pass through a fine sieve and serve. Excellent with Eggs Benedict, sweetbreads of fine quality poached fish.
* This sauce is very similar to Elizabeth David's famous Sauce Messine which originates in Auricoste de Lazarque's *La Cuisine Messine* but in their recipe fresh herbs and shallots and lemon peel are infused in the cream sauce and more lemon juice is added just before serving. Lady Clark of Tillypronie gives three versions of 'Venetian Sauce' (a difficult one to pin down exactly) which is also much the same.

Normande If you have poached a fish in a fumet of onion, herbs, mushrooms stalks, fish stock, white wine and lemon juice you can make a rich sauce for it thus: thicken the liquid in which the fish has been cooked with 1 tablespoon butter and 1 dessertspoon flour mixed together (*beurre manié*). Let it cook for about 10 minutes or till it loses the taste of flour. If possible now add a little oyster or mussel or even scallop liquor and cook for a few minutes, then allow to cool. Meanwhile beat up 3 egg yolks in 125 ml/¼ pint cream, and add to liquid. Return to the saucepan and heat up, beating and stirring, till it is smooth and thick. But DO NOT LET IT BOIL once the egg yolks have been added. A few mussels, shrimps, prawns, or scallops heated up and tossed in a little butter should garnish the dish.

Mrs Stanley's Vin Blanc or White Wine Sauce

1 medium onion
50 g/2 oz butter
1 tablespoon flour
125 ml/¼ pint white wine
125 ml/¼ pint fish stock
juice of ½ lemon
2 egg yolks
2 tablespoons double cream
salt and pepper

Chop the onion finely and cook in the butter until translucent. Work in the flour, add the wine and the fish stock and bring to the boil. Allow to simmer for 5–10 minutes and add the lemon juice. Strain. Beat the egg yolks and cream together, and, off the heat or in a double boiler, add the sauce to them with seasoning. Allow to thicken over a gentle heat for a few minutes. For fish, crab, etc.

2 THE BROWN SAUCES

THE BROWN FOUNDATION SAUCE: ESPAGNOLE
ESPAGNOLE ORDINAIRE
VM's QUICK ESPAGNOLE FROM BEAUFORT
ESPAGNOLE SAUCE
DEMI GLACE
MRS EMSLIE'S DEMI GLACE
RICH BROWN SAUCE, an alternative to ESPAGNOLE
PLAIN BROWN SAUCE

DERIVATIVES OF BROWN FOUNDATION SAUCES

Bercy	*Bigarade*	*Bordelaise I and II*
Brown Mushroom	*Quick Sauce Chasseur*	
Chasseur Sauce	*Chevreuil*	
Devil Sauce Dressing		*Genoese*
Italienne	*Alice B Toklas' Sauce Italienne*	
Languedocienne	*Madeira*	*Madère*
Marchand de Vin	*A Kind of Périgueux*	
Piquante	*Poivrade*	*A Kind of Poivrade*
Réforme, à la	*Richelieu*	*Robert*

THREE VERSIONS OF THE FOUNDATION SAUCE: *ESPAGNOLE*

ESPAGNOLE ORDINAIRE

Makes ¾–1 litre/1½–2 pints
Time taken 2½–3 hours

a little chopped ham or lean bacon
1 onion, roughly chopped
1 carrot
50 g/2 oz butter
6 peppercorns
a little parsley
thyme
½ bay leaf
50 g/2 oz mushroom parings and stalks
100 g/¼ lb cooking tomatoes
1 tablespoon tomato purée
50 g/2 oz browned flour (see p. 21)
1½ litres/3 pints Brown Stock
1 tablespoon sherry

Sauté the ham or bacon, onion and carrot in the butter. Add peppercorns, parsley, thyme, bay leaf and mushrooms. When mushy add the tomatoes and tomato purée and allow to cook for a further few minutes. Next throw in the browned flour, stirring vigorously to avoid lumps, then gradually add the stock, beating and stirring continuously until it boils, and you have beaten it completely smooth. Then draw the saucepan away from the heat and wedge it (see p. 44), allowing it to despumate slowly for about 2 hours, occasionally skimming and adding occasional spoonfuls of cold stock to allow for evaporation and to bring impurities and acids to the surface. Strain, put into a clean saucepan, and reduce again, by about one quarter to one third.* Correct seasoning and finish with a large tablespoon sherry.
* When it is thick enough to coat the back of a spoon it has reached the Demi Glace stage.

VM's SAUCE ESPAGNOLE FROM BEAUFORT

4 tablespoons butter
4 tablespoons chopped streaky bacon
1 large onion, chopped
½ cup sliced mushrooms
1 small carrot, chopped
4 rounded tablespoons plain flour
1 tablespoon tomato purée
1 pint good brown stock
½ teaspoon mixed herbs
peppercorns, mace
salt and pepper
¾ tablespoon Madeira or sherry

Melt butter in saucepan and fry chopped bacon gently. Add onions, mushrooms and carrot and fry till lightly browned. Add flour and fry gently to rich golden brown. Stir in tomato purée, stock, mixed herbs and spices. Season to taste. Simmer for 40 minutes. Skim and sieve. Re-heat sauce, check seasoning and add Madeira just before serving – but boil it up for a minute or two first, to 'burn off' the alcohol.

ESPAGNOLE SAUCE

50 g/2 oz raw ham, diced
1 small onion
½ small carrot
a stick of celery
6 mushrooms
2 tomatoes
100 g/4 oz butter
bouquet garni
2 cloves
6 peppercorns
1 litre/1 quart good stock
½ glass of sherry
75 g/3 oz flour
1 teaspoon lemon juice

Fry the ham and vegetables in 25 g/1 oz butter. Add the herbs and spices. Pour in the stock and wine. Cook gently for an hour. Melt remainder of butter, mix in the flour and cook till of a good brown colour. Stir in the strained stock. Whisk over the fire until it boils. Cook gently for at least half an hour. Skim off the butter as it rises. Add the lemon juice and strain through muslin or a fine nylon sieve.

DEMI GLACE SAUCE

250 ml/½ pint Espagnole or brown sauce
125 ml/¼ pint consommé or gravy

Reduce to rather less than 250 ml/½ pint. Skim well. Season if necessary.

MRS EMSLIE'S DEMI GLACE

This is Cataldi's Glaze and first stock mixed – nothing else.

RICH BROWN SAUCE
an alternative to ESPAGNOLE

100 g/4 oz mushrooms, including stalks, coarsely chopped or sliced
1 small onion
1 small carrot, chopped or sliced
3 sticks celery, chopped or sliced
1 rounded tablespoon butter
1 rounded tablespoon flour
250 ml/½ pint stock, or beef bouillon to which you have added some roasting pan meat jelly or a spoonful of Meat Glaze
8 tablespoons Madeira, or brown sherry, or port
1 bouquet garni
salt and black pepper
knob of butter

Cook mushrooms, onion, carrot and celery in the butter for 5 minutes or till vegetables are coloured and mushy, but be careful not to burn. Then stir in the flour and brown this roux slightly. Add the cold stock gradually to make a sauce. Simmer for 20 minutes. Stir in the wine and simmer for another 5–10 minutes. Season well, and, just before serving, beat in knob of butter, which gives the sauce a shiny look and an extra good flavour.

PLAIN BROWN SAUCE

1 small onion
a piece each of carrot, turnip and celery
50 g/2 oz butter
35 g/1½ oz flour
2 cloves
6 peppercorns
a bunch of herbs
a blade of mace
500 ml/1 pint stock
salt and pepper

Fry the vegetables in the fat lightly. Add the flour and cook till of a nut brown colour. Put in the herbs and spices. Stir in the stock and boil for 10 minutes. Season and strain.

DERIVATIVES OF BROWN FOUNDATION SAUCES

Bercy (without Espagnole)

3 or 4 shallots, finely chopped
3 tablespoons white wine
2 tablespoons meat glaze or natural gravy jelly from a roast
salt and pepper
25 g/1 oz fresh butter
lemon juice
fresh parsley

Put the shallots into a small pan with the wine and reduce it by fairly fast boiling to half its original quantity. Stir in the meat glaze or gravy, season, beat in the butter, add a squeeze of lemon juice and a little chopped parsley. This is a simplified version of one of the Classic French Sauces for steak, eggs, fish and grills. When used for fish, the meat glaze should be replaced by concentrated fish stock.

Bigarade

Peel the rind of a bitter orange very thinly, leaving some of the white pith. Cut these strips into small shreds, and throw them for a minute or two into scalding water, then drain the shreds and put them into a bain-marie, with a little glaze and some well-reduced Espagnole or Rich Brown Sauce and half to one third of the orange, divided into segments and skinned. Bring to the boil, and boil thoroughly for a few minutes, then cool, and add a little best butter in swirls, just before serving.

Bordelaise I

Put into a vegetable pan 50 g/2 oz very finely minced shallots, 250 ml/½ pint good red wine, a pinch of mignonette pepper (milled white pepper) and bits of thyme and bay leaf. Reduce the wine by three quarters and add 250 ml/½ pint much reduced Espagnole or Rich Brown Sauce. Allow the sauce to simmer for 30 minutes. Skim from time to time and then strain through a sieve. When dishing it up, finish with 2 tablespoons dissolved meat glaze, a few drops of lemon juice and 100 g/4 oz beef marrow, cut into slices and poached in gently boiling water or stock. This sauce may be finished with butter swirls to the extent of about 75 g/3 oz per 500 ml/1 pint which makes it smoother, but less clear. It is very good served with grilled meats.

Bordelaise II

250 ml/½ pint dry red wine
(Burgundy is best)
2 tablespoons shallots, minced
bay leaves
thyme
6 peppercorns
no salt, or very little
2 tablespoons butter
2 tablespoons flour
1 tin beef consommé or strong
brown stock
1 teaspoon tomato paste
1 tablespoon meat glaze or
2 tablespoons jellied gravy
100 g/4 oz beef marrow

Simmer red wine, shallots, bay leaves, thyme and peppercorns until wine is reduced by half. Strain and reserve. Melt butter, stir in flour and cook for 3–4 minutes, until roux is thickened. Add the consommé or brown stock and tomato paste and stir until the sauce is smooth. Stir in the strained wine and meat glaze and continue to stir over the heat until well blended. Meanwhile poach the marrow in a separate pan in a little of the consommé for a few minutes only, reserving some large slices for a garnish, then dice the remainder and add to the sauce just before serving.

Brown Mushroom

3 tablespoons butter
½ tablespoon vegetable oil
2 tablespoons shallots, minced
250 g/½ lb fresh mushrooms, sliced
1 glass dry vermouth
1½ tablespoons tomato paste
1½ tablespoons Espagnole or
Rich Brown Sauce
4 tablespoons mixed parsley, chives
and tarragon

Melt 1 tablespoon of butter with the oil. Sauté shallots and mushrooms. Add vermouth and reduce until almost dry. Add tomato paste and Brown Sauce. Simmer a few minutes. Just before serving add remaining butter and herbs. Serve with egg timbales, sautéed veal escalopes etc.

Quick Sauce Chasseur

1 tablespoon minced shallots
3 tablespoons minced mushrooms
1 tablespoon butter
3 tablespoons tomato purée
½ pint consommé madrilène
2 tablespoons wine (white or red)
1 teaspoon minced parsley
1 tablespoon tarragon vinegar

Fry shallots and mushrooms in butter; add tomato purée, consommé and wine, and simmer for a few minutes. Just before serving add parsley and tarragon vinegar. This makes an excellent sauce for fish.

From Admiral Joe Williams and the US Submariners cookbook *Dolphin Dishes*.

Chasseur Sauce

Chop 2 shallots and cook them well in a little olive oil. Then moisten them with some good white wine (Sauternes) or sherry. Reduce well, then add equal quantities of tomato and brown sauce (Espagnole or Rich Brown Sauce). Mince some mushrooms and put in the sauce, also a small pinch of cayenne pepper, and let these ingredients cook for 10 minutes. At the time of serving add a little chopped parsley.

Chevreuil
(without Espagnole)

2 glasses red wine
2 tablespoons vinegar
2 tablespoons sugar
½ lemon, peeled and diced
4–5 tablespoons red currant jelly
2 tablespoons butter or lard
2 tablespoons flour
1½ glasses stock mixed with pan juices
a good pinch of pepper

Put into a saucepan: 1½ glasses of the red wine; the vinegar, sugar and lemon. Mix the jelly into this preparation and boil until it is reduced by half. Meanwhile prepare a brown roux with the butter and flour, add the stock and the rest of the wine, and cook slowly for 20 minutes. Mix the two preparations, add the pepper and put through a fine sieve and reheat.

Devil Sauce Dressing

1 good tablespoon mustard
4 tablespoons chili vinegar
1 tablespoon horseradish, grated
2 bruised shallots
1 teaspoon salt
a few grains cayenne, or a very small pinch, if you like it hot
1 teaspoon salt
½ teaspoon black pepper
1 teaspoon sugar
1 teaspoon chopped chili peppers, optional
2 raw egg yolks to bind

This is not really a sauce but a dressing and comes from Alexis Soyer's *Culinary Campaign*, a splendid account of the Crimean War, through which he cooks his way with great verve and enthusiasm.

Rub any devilled food with the combined ingredients.

Soyer's instructions are to 'broil slowly at first and end as near as possible to the Pandemonium Fire'.

Genoese Sauce

1 shallot or small onion
1 tiny piece of garlic
bouquet garni
35 g/1½ oz butter
½ glass Madeira or port wine
250 ml/½ pint Brown Sauce
¼ teaspoon anchovy essence
2 teaspoons chopped parsley
salt and pepper

A rich sauce for fish

Fry the onion, garlic and bouquet garni in 25 g/1 oz of the butter for a few minutes. Add the wine and sauce, then simmer for 20 minutes. Skim and put through a fine sieve. Reheat with the anchovy essence, parsley and seasoning. Remove the pan from the fire and gradually add the rest of the butter. The Brown Sauce should be made with fish stock.

Italienne
(without Demi Glace)

50 g/2 oz shallots, minced
a little olive oil
75–100 g/3–4 oz mushroom
parings and stalks, finely chopped
1 tablespoon finely chopped ham
1 tablespoon finely chopped parsley
1 bay leaf
a pinch of finely chopped thyme
a sprig of sweet basil, chopped
½ glass dry white wine
100 ml/4 fl oz tomato purée
250 ml/½ pint Rich Brown Stock
or gravy, strengthened, if possible,
by glaze
lemon juice
nutmeg

Chop or mince the shallots very finely and sweat them in olive oil till soft, but not coloured. Add the mushrooms, ham and parsley, cook for 3 or 4 minutes, then add the other herbs and wine. Now add the tomato purée, boil up and reduce by one third. Lastly add the cold stock; let it all come to a boil again, simmer for 15 minutes more, add lemon juice, correct seasoning, strain and serve. Serve with fish, calves' brains, rissoles, etc. Some people prefer to omit ham if the sauce is to accompany fish.

Alice B Toklas'
Sauce Italienne
(for braised lettuce)

Coarsely chop one-third cup mushrooms. Place mushrooms in saucepan over low heat with 2 tablespoons olive oil and 2 tablespoons butter, 1 tablespoon chopped onion and ½ tablespoon chopped shallot. Mix well and add one-third cup HOT dry white wine. Cover and simmer for 10 minutes, add ¼ cup tomato purée, ¼ teaspoon salt. Add ¼ cup butter in small pieces. Melt and mix by tipping the saucepan in all directions. Do not allow to boil.

As its creator says, this is a change – indeed a violent one!

Languedocienne

4 bulbs garlic
125 g/5 oz ham
1 large onion
a few sprigs parsley
3 tablespoons olive oil
1 tablespoon flour
1 large glass dry white wine
1 large glass stock, reinforced
if necessary
1 sprig thyme
2 bay leaves
salt and milled pepper
gravy from the joint

This sauce is for garlic addicts only.

Peel the garlic. Cut the ham into very small pieces, chop the onion and the parsley. Heat the oil in a thick-bottomed pan and gently sauté the ham, the onion, and the parsley; cook until the onion is translucent. Add the flour and stir briskly. Add wine, stock, thyme, bay leaves, salt and pepper. Simmer for 25 minutes. Add garlic and cook for 10 minutes. At last moment add the gravy from the joint which has been roasting while you were preparing the sauce. Strain into a hot sauceboat or leave unstrained if you wish.

Madeira
(without Espagnole)

50 g/2 oz small onions or shallots,
finely chopped
2 tablespoons mushroom stalks and
peelings, chopped
1 tablespoon ham, chopped
125 ml/¼ pint port wine
125 ml/¼ pint Madeira wine
125 ml/½ pint Rich Gravy
or Brown Stock, if possible,
enriched with meat glaze
2 teaspoons tomato ketchup
or paste
salt, black pepper

Sauté onions, mushrooms and ham in butter until brown, dust with flour and cook till brown, stirring vigorously. Pour off extra fat, add port and Madeira, boil up and reduce by half. Add gravy, tomato ketchup and seasonings and simmer for 10 minutes. Strain through a sieve. Reheat and swirl in 2 or 3 flakes of butter.

Madère

Add Madeira wine to taste to a much reduced, almost thick, Demi Glace Sauce; warm it up gently and serve.

Marchand de Vin Sauce for Steak
(without Espagnole)

2 tablespoons butter
4–5 shallots, finely chopped
375 ml/¾ pint dry red wine
½ bay leaf
¼ teaspoon dried thyme
4 sprigs parsley
2 teaspoons meat glaze combined with 3 tablespoons hot water
155 g/6 oz soft butter
1 tablespoon lemon juice
1 teaspoon flour
2 tablespoons finely chopped fresh parsley

Melt the 2 tablespoons butter in an enamelled saucepan over moderate heat. When the foam subsides, cook the shallots, stirring constantly, for 2 minutes, or until they are soft but not brown. Pour in wine, add the bay leaf, thyme and parsley sprigs and simmer over moderate heat until reduced to half (10–15 minutes). Strain it into a bowl, then return it to the saucepan, adding the thinned-down meat glaze; bring to a boil and simmer on a low heat. Meanwhile cream the 155 g butter until fluffy and beat in the lemon juice, flour and parsley. Set aside, and start cooking your steak. When the steak is à point, transfer to a heated platter and season. Now pour the reduced wine mixture into the steak skillet and bring to boil over moderate heat, stirring constantly. Remove from the heat and blend in the creamed butter mixture, 2 tablespoons at a time. To serve, slice the steak and offer the sauce separately.

Enough for 8 helpings of steak.

A Kind of Sauce Périgueux
(without Espagnole)

2 tablespoons shallots, finely chopped
1¼ tablespoons butter
1 tablespoon flour
500 ml/1 pint clear brown stock, or tinned consommé
salt and pepper to taste
50 g/2 oz smoked ham, Bayonne, Prosciutto or similar, chopped
½ tablespoon dark rum
2 truffles, finely chopped
1 tablespoon foie-gras

Sauté the shallots in the butter, shake in the flour and cook until they are a rich brown. You must stir constantly so that the roux will not stick to the saucepan or burn, but just colour. Add the stock, season with salt and pepper, and bring to a boil. Add the chopped ham and continue boiling until the sauce is reduced to half. Remove from stove, strain through a sieve, put it back in the saucepan and stir in the rum. Now reduce the heat, for the sauce must not be allowed to boil after the truffles go in, since this would kill their delicate flavour. Put in the truffles, followed by the creamed foie-gras. Leave on the stove until the truffles are well heated. If you are making this sauce to accompany a roast (it is excellent on beef), stir in the juice of the meat at the last moment before serving.

Piquante
(without Espagnole)

In oil, butter or dripping fry a sliced onion until it is golden, then add a wineglass of vinegar and 500 ml/1 pint stock of whatever meat the sauce is to be served with. Add herbs, a crushed clove of garlic, salt and pepper, and simmer until the sauce is a good consistency. A few minutes before serving, add 1 tablespoon each of capers and chopped gherkins.

Poivrade and Game Poivrade

To 500 ml/1 pint Espagnole or Rich Brown Sauce, add chopped shallots that have been boiled for 10 minutes in good white wine vinegar. Add also a pinch of cayenne and black pepper, freshly ground. Warm to serve. If the sauce is to be served with game that has been marinated, the liquid of the marinade, boiled up and reduced, should be added to the sauce, then the mixture should be strained through muslin. Other variants call for the addition of red currant jelly, the blood of the animal and 1 tablespoon, or less, of Worcestershire Sauce.

A Kind of Poivrade
(without Espagnole)

Add to the butter and juices in which meat has been roasted a good pinch of black pepper, a small glass of wine vinegar and 2 minced shallots. Reduce this by rapid boiling, then add 2 tablespoons meat glaze or meat jelly or ½ glass strong Brown Stock; boil up and reduce again; lastly add half a glass of red wine and reduce once more.

Réforme, à la

25 g/1 oz butter
1 onion
35 g/1½ oz ham, cooked
bay leaf
¼ clove garlic
mixed herbs
2 tablespoons tarragon or chili
vinegar
250 ml/½ pint brown sauce or
Demi Glace
4 tablespoons stock
1 tablespoon tomato paste
½ tablespoon red currant jelly
½ oz mushrooms chopped
1 hard-boiled egg
1 gherkin (and/or Indian green
pickle)
2 whole mushrooms

Melt the butter, slice the onion and cook slightly. Add 1 oz chopped lean ham, bay leaf, garlic and a pinch or two of herbs. Cook for 10 minutes and then add the vinegar and boil 1 minute. Now put in the brown sauce, the stock and tomato paste. Bring to the boil, simmer for 10 minutes, skim and allow to reduce until fairly thick. Add the red currant jelly and chopped mushrooms. Check seasoning and when the jelly has melted pass the sauce through a sieve. When ready to serve bring to the boil again, take off the fire and add the white of the hard-boiled egg cut into thin strips about ½ inch long, also the remaining ham cut into strips, the sliced gherkin and 2 blanched mushrooms also cut into strips. Keep warm and do not boil again.

For 5–6 lamb cutlets.

The original recipe was created by Alexis Soyer for the Reform Club and is quoted in Mrs Christopher Morris's biography.

Richelieu
(without Espagnole)

2 shallots
8 sweetbreads, chopped
8 cêpes, if not fresh, then
reconstituted dried ones
5 mushrooms, sliced
2 tablespoons butter
½ glass sherry
250 ml/½ pint brown gravy
or strong stock
salt and pepper

Sauté the shallots, sweetbreads, cêpes and mushrooms in butter for 5 minutes. Add sherry and gravy or stock. Season to taste and let it simmer for 3 minutes. Serve over steak.

Sauce Robert

1 large onion or 5 oz shallots,
minced fine
a little melted butter
½ glass dry white wine or French
wine vinegar
2 teaspoons Dijon mustard
2 teaspoons prepared English
mustard
1 good teaspoon meat glaze
250 ml/½ pint Rich Brown Sauce

Fry the onion in the butter. Add the wine and reduce a little. Stir in the mustard, glaze and sauce. Boil gently for 15 minutes. Skim off the fat. Strain and serve.

3 BUTTER BASED AND BUTTER AND EGG BASED SAUCES

a) BUTTER BASED SAUCES:
Melted, or Drawn, Butter
French Melted Butter
Gouffé's Melted Butter or, The Original White Sauce

b) BUTTER AND EGG BASED SAUCES
American 'No Fail' Hollandaise
Ice Box Hollandaise
Blender Hollandaise
Trianon
Mousseline
Moutarde
Mrs Stanley's Julia Sauce
Béarnaise

a) BUTTER BASED SAUCES

Melted, or Drawn, Butter

Time taken: 1 minute
100 g/4 oz best fresh butter
1 teaspoon flour
2–3 tablespoons hot water

Mix the butter and flour well together in a small basin, till quite smooth; then put paste into a very clean enamel saucepan with the hot water. Shake it round – always in the same direction, or it will become oily. Boil it quickly for 1 minute and serve.

This sauce depends to a great extent on the quality of the butter.

French Melted Butter

Time taken: 3 minutes
2 egg yolks
100 g/4 oz best fresh butter
250 ml/½ pint water, or less
squeeze of lemon

Beat the yolks of 2 very fresh eggs well in a bowl off the heat; then melt the butter and water in a small enamelled saucepan. Bring to the boil and pour it instantly onto the beaten eggs, stirring them quickly round while you pour on the butter. Put the mixture back into the saucepan shake it over the heat for a minute, but do not let it boil. Then squeeze a little lemon juice into it, taking care no pips fall into your sauce, as they give a bitter flavour.

NOTE: These two recipes come from a Victorian English housewife's cookery book where they exist side by side, but they are quite different in character; the French version really being a sort of poor man's, or embryo, Hollandaise.

Yet another and splendidly English (in spite of its title) version of our traditional melted butter sauce comes from Dr Kitchener's *Apicius Redevivus or The Cook's Oracle* published in 1817. See p. 95.

Gouffé's Melted Butter or, The Original White Sauce

From Gouffé's Royal Cookery Book

75 g/3 oz butter
25 g/1 oz flour
1 pinch of salt
1 small pinch of pepper
250 ml/½ pint warm water

Put in a litre stewpan, first 25 g/1 oz of butter and 25 g/1 oz of flour. Mix the butter and flour to a paste. Add the pepper, salt and warm water. Stir over the fire, with a wooden spoon, till boiling – the sauce should be thick enough to coat the spoon. Then add the remaining butter, cut in pieces to accelerate its melting; take off the fire and stir till melted. The sauce is then ready. The foregoing quantities should produce about 1 pint of melted butter. In case the melted butter should be too thick, which is quite possible, some flours requiring more moisture than others, add a few tablespoons of water, according to circumstances, before putting in the cold butter.

As shown above, the great point for melted butter is, as soon as it has come to the boil, to take it off the fire, and add to it the cold butter which gives it its flavour.

b) EGG AND BUTTER BASED SAUCES

Here are three relatively simple ways of making Hollandaise.

American 'No Fail' Hollandaise

½ cup, or more, butter
2 level tablespoons lemon juice
4 egg yolks
¼ teaspoon salt
dash cayenne pepper
¼ cup boiling water (gives a light fluffy texture to sauce)

Divide the butter in 3 parts. Beat the lemon juice and egg yolks together, add 1 piece of butter and cook over gently simmering but not boiling water, stirring constantly until mixture begins to thicken. Remove from stove, add second piece of butter and stir rapidly, then add remaining butter and continue to stir until mixture is completely blended. Add salt, cayenne and boiling water. Return to double boiler and stir until sauce thickens. Cream can now be added if wished. NOTE: If possible, cook the sauce in a round-bottomed enamel sauce-pan or bowl with only a small amount of water in the bottom of a double boiler or bain-marie. Never let the water boil. If the sauce should curdle, add 2 tablespoons cold single cream or a piece of ice and beat like mad off the stove. As soon as sauce is smooth again remove ice.

Ice Box Hollandaise

1 cup unsalted butter and
3 tablespoons melted butter
4 egg yolks
salt
cayenne pepper
2 tablespoons or more lemon juice

Melt butter gently in a double boiler. Meanwhile beat the egg yolks in a warm basin until thick and sticky. Add salt, a grain or two, not more, of cayenne, and the 3 tablespoons of butter to the egg mixture a drop at a time. Continue to beat vigorously. You can do this with the bowl sitting on the kitchen table or in a bain-marie, to keep it warm – but not hot. Now add the remaining butter and lemon juice alternately, still beating. It should be served lukewarm, not hot, and if you have beaten successfully should be enough for 6–8 servings. It can be kept in a closed jar in the fridge for about 10 days. Good for serving with eggs, fish and vegetable dishes, particularly French (snapper) beans.

Blender Hollandaise

You can make a very passable Hollandaise in a blender if you follow this recipe:
Put 3 egg yolks, a few drops of lemon juice, seasoning and a tablespoon of water into a blender and whirl for a few seconds. Now pour in 6 oz of foaming hot butter, DROP by DROP, but in a steady trickle blending all the time at medium speed.* When it is all mixed in pour into a just warm bowl and whisk up very lightly with a wire whisk. Correct seasoning adding a grain or two of cayenne pepper and some more lemon juice if necessary.
Delicious with asparagus or artichokes.
* You will have to wear a plastic apron as it splatters.

Trianon

This is an Hollandaise to which you add at the same time as the table-spoon of lemon juice a good tablespoon of dry sherry. It is excellent with fish and an easy and little-known variation.

Mousseline and Moutarde

To a Sauce Hollandaise, add 3 or 4 tablespoons double cream off the heat and mix the two thoroughly. This is Sauce Mousseline. If to this you add Dijon or Tewkesbury prepared mustard, preferably the *nature* kind, of a light yellow colour, in the proportion to suit your taste, you have Sauce Moutarde (or Sauce Mousseline Moutarde).

Mrs Stanley's Julia Sauce

2 tablespoons tarragon vinegar
2 tablespoons white wine
1 slice onion
4 peppercorns
½ bay leaf
salt
½ teaspoon arrowroot
25 g/1 oz butter
4 egg yolks

A good and easy alternative to Hollandaise.

In a small pan boil the tarragon vinegar (or wine vinegar and a few tarragon leaves) the white wine, onion, peppercorns, bay leaf and a pinch of salt, until reduced by half. Mix the arrowroot with 3 tablespoons water in the top of a double boiler, strain in the reduced vinegar and wine, add the butter and bring almost to the boil with stirring, when the mixture will thicken. Allow to cool. Strain in the egg yolks. Put the boiler pan over barely simmering water, and whisk continuously until the sauce thickens and becomes smooth. If a few lumps begin to form, strain immediately into a warm boat.

This sauce keeps well on a hot-plate if another 12 g/½ oz butter is added in small lumps.

For beef, chicken, or fish.

Béarnaise

This is said to be the creation of the *chef de cuisines* of the Pavillon Henri IV at St Germain en Laye, and dates from about 1830.

It is really an Hollandaise Sauce with tarragon. Proceed as for Sauce Hollandaise, but increase the vinegar to 5 tablespoons and add to it 1 tablespoon chopped tarragon leaves, which remain in the sauce. Also, reduce the vinegar and water mixture much more slowly in order to make the infusion of the vinegar stronger. Use good white wine tarragon vinegar if possible. Shallot salt or even onion salt is preferable to ordinary salt in the final seasoning. The sauce should be served lukewarm or it will curdle.

4 OIL BASED SAUCES

Basic Vinaigrette (I)
Vinaigrette Sauce with Fines Herbes (II)
Vinaigrette III
French Dressing from New Orleans
Archiduc
Cold Ravigotte from America
Lady Keswick's Sauce Gribiche
Blender Mayonnaise
Blender Mayonnaise with Dill
Never Fail Mayonnaise
Mustard Mayonnaise
A Good Rémoulade from Tennessee

Basic Vinaigrette or French Dressing for Salads (I)

1 teaspoon salt
½ teaspoon freshly ground pepper
125 ml/¼ pint vinegar or lemon juice (or less if you like your dressing more oily than sharp)
½ teaspoon dry mustard
1 clove garlic, minced
1 scant teaspoon sugar (optional)
375 ml/¾ pint olive or walnut oil (or arrachide oil if you want a lighter dressing, see p. 60)

Put all ingredients except oil into a jar, screw the top on and shake until blended. Add gradually, between shakings, olive or walnut oil. Shake well before using. This will keep well in a cool place.

Vinaigrette Sauce with Fines Herbes (II)

Mix 1 tablespoon vinegar with 3–4 tablespoons olive oil and add 1 teaspoon mixed chopped parsley, tarragon, chervil and chives, ¼ teaspoon prepared mustard and salt to taste.

Vinaigrette Sauce (III)

375 ml/¾ pint olive oil
125 ml/¼ pint lemon juice
salt to taste
½ teaspoon dry mustard
freshly ground black pepper
1 tablespoon chopped capers
1 teaspoon pickles, finely chopped
½ teaspoon parsley, chopped
½ teaspoon chervil, chopped
½ teaspoon chives, chopped

Combine all the ingredients well and chill. Serve chilled.

French Dressing from New Orleans

1 small onion (or 2 shallots)
1 tablespoon chopped parsley or tarragon or fennel
1 clove garlic
2 whole eggs
¾ cup oil
¼ cup lemon juice (or wine vinegar)
1 tablespoon yellow mustard
1 tablespoon paprika (optional) or freshly ground black pepper
1 small teaspoon salt

Créole version of Sauce Vinaigrette aux Oeufs*

Chop the onion, herbs and garlic extremely fine. Mix with eggs, oil and lemon juice, mustard, paprika or black pepper, and salt. Blend well and let it stand a little before using. This Vinaigrette can be used on salads or seafoods or rice or chicken.
* Elizabeth David has a version of this sauce in *Summer Cooking*, without, naturally, the typically Créole paprika, in which she soft-boils the eggs and scoops out the yolks into the Vinaigrette which gives it excellent 'body' and a delicious taste.

Archiduc for Cold Asparagus Vinaigrette

250 ml/½ pint olive oil
125 ml/¼ pint vinegar
1 teaspoon fresh chives, minced
1 teaspoon fresh tarragon, minced
1 teaspoon parsley, minced
1 teaspoon fresh chervil, minced
1 teaspoon dry mustard
2 hard-boiled eggs, chopped

Mix all ingredients except hard-boiled eggs. When blended, add chopped eggs and stir well before serving.

Cold Ravigotte from America

3–4 shallots or 1 small onion
2–3 stalks celery
2 cloves garlic
1 sprig parsley
5 tablespoons hot mustard
2 tablespoons paprika
salt and pepper
⅓ cup vinegar
⅔ cup olive oil

Mince the onions, celery, garlic and parsley very finely. Add mustard, paprika, salt and pepper. Add vinegar and mix thoroughly, then gradually add olive oil. Refrigerate. You can marinate boiled shrimp and pieces of tunny in this sauce and serve on shredded lettuce with a garnish of lemon wedges, making a quick and easy starter.

Lady Keswick's Sauce Gribiche

Hard-boil 5 eggs. Remove yolks and pound them into a paste in a bowl or mixer. Add 2 pinches of salt (1 teaspoon) and a powerful grind of pepper, then 2 teaspoons of mustard. Add the oil, drop by drop at first, then faster (as in mayonnaise). Feed in ½–¾ pint of whichever kind you like best, arrachide, refined olive or walnut. Then add 4–5 tablespoons of best wine vinegar. Finally add 1 heaped tablespoon of chopped parsley, tarragon and chervil in equal parts, 1¼ tablespoons of capers, 3 small chopped sour gherkins and the whites of 3 hard-boiled eggs finely diced. Excellent with cold lamb's tongues that have been slowly cooked in broth until tender then chilled and sliced.

Blender Mayonnaise

1 egg
¾ teaspoon salt
½ teaspoon dry mustard
2 tablespoons lemon juice, strained
250 ml/½ pint olive or vegetable oil

Put egg, salt, mustard, lemon juice and half of the oil in blender. Place on medium speed, covered, for ½ minute. Uncover and pour in the rest of the oil in a fine stream. If blender clogs a bit as dressing thickens, use a rubber spatula to stir, being careful not to touch blender blades. Takes about 3 or 4 minutes.

Blender Mayonnaise with Dill

2 eggs
½ teaspoon dry mustard
1 teaspoon salt
½ teaspoon pepper
juice of 1 lemon
375 ml/¾ pint vegetable oil
125 ml/¼ pint sour cream
2–3 tablespoons chopped fresh dill
2 cucumbers, peeled, seeded and chopped

In electric blender, on medium speed, place eggs, mustard, seasonings and lemon juice. Blend for about 1 minute. Cover the blender jar with wax paper, secure with a rubber band and cut a small hole in the centre of the paper. Blending at medium speed, pour the oil through the hole in the paper as slowly as possible. When the blender clogs, sauce will be done. Mix in the rest of the ingredients by hand. Can be served with cold game and poultry or cold potatoes.

Never Fail Mayonnaise

1 whole egg or 2 yolks
¾ teaspoon dry mustard
1 tablespoon vinegar
1 teaspoon salt
¼ teaspoon pepper
½ pint or more olive oil
1–2 tablespoons lemon juice

Put egg, mustard, vinegar, salt and pepper in electric blender with three-quarters of the oil and blend on medium speed for 5 seconds. Then pour in remaining oil in a very fine, slow stream. Remove from blender when thick and add lemon juice.

Mustard Mayonnaise

250 ml/½ pint 'never Fail Mayonnaise' as above
1 teaspoon made mustard
½ teaspoon onion juice
juice of ½ lemon
salt

Mix all ingredients and serve.

A Good Rémoulade from Tennessee

1 pint olive oil
4 hard-boiled egg yolks
4 raw egg yolks
2 saltspoons each of salt, paprika, dry mustard, onion juice
juice of 2 lemons
a little minced parsley

Mash cooked yolks smooth with the mustard onion juice and paprika. Add raw yolks one at a time; then slowly add the oil, dripping it in and beating steadily. Add lemon juice, salt and a little minced parsley.

3

THE TRADITIONAL ENGLISH AND AMERICAN SAUCES

These sauces are mostly gathered from family recipes and old-fashioned cookery books. Many American recipes have been proudly handed down from mother to daughter since the days of the early colonists and can sometimes be more genuinely traditional than those found in their country of origin. In some recipes I have left the original 8 fl oz cup measures.

THE TRADITIONAL ENGLISH AND AMERICAN SAUCES

1 HOT SAUCES

Almond Sauce for Chicken Croquettes
Aubergine Sauce for Gratin of Chicken
A Good Béchamel Sauce from Tennessee
Theodora's Chicken Liver and Lemon Sauce
Grape Sauce for Chicken
18th Century Sauce for Fowls
Kentucky Pan-broiled Gravy
The Right Way to Make Bread Sauce
A Victorian Recipe for Bread Sauce
White Celery Sauce for Boiled Chicken or Turkey
Celery Sauce for Boiled Pheasant
Simple Cheese Sauce
Cheese Sauce
A Victorian Grill Sauce for Meat
Theodora's Anchovy, Egg and Herb Sauce for Beef Fillets (c 1850)
A Victorian 'Sauce Robert' for Rumps and Steaks
Juniper Sauce for Steaks or Kidneys
Creamed Mushroom Sauce
Rhoda's Cordon Bleu Mushroom Sauce
Mushroom and Madeira Sauce
Goodwood Sauce
Mrs Gore's Mushroom Sauce
A Victorian Mushroom Sauce
Honey-mint Sauce for Lamb
Sauce for Hot or Cold Roast Lamb
Marinade for Lamb Chops
Theodora's Prune and Blackcurrant Sauce for Boiled Mutton
Dr Kitchener's 1822 Recipe for Port Wine Sauce for Roast Mutton
Mustard Sauce for Baked Ham
Orange Sauce for Pork, Ham and Duck
Orange Raisin Sauce for Ham
Cherry Sauce for Hot Ham or Tongue
Theodora's Green Sauce for Ducklings
Tennessee Orange Sauce for Roast Duck
Virginian Raisin Sauce
Raisin Sauce

Red Wine Sauce
Wild Duck Sauce – First Life Guard's Recipe
*Spatchcock or Devil Sauce for Roe deer or Roast Pheasant or
 Turkey*
Theodora's Prune and Spices Sauce for Hare
Mrs Rundell's Currant Sauce for Venison and Roe deer (c 1840)
Hot Sauce for Venison
Dr Kitchener's Recipe for Melted Butter
Old Fashioned Parsley Sauce
Fennel Sauce
Old Fashioned English Egg Sauce
Virginian Chicken Liver and Lemon Sauce
Sour Cream Sauce
Theodora's Chestnut Sauce
Sorrel Sauce
Cream Curry Sauce
Admiral Ross's Indian Devil Mixture
Quick White Devil Sauce
Theodora's Devil Sauce
Devilled Butter for Devilled Bones
Indian Sauce for Salmon
Almond Butter for Grilled Trout
Anchovy Cream Sauce for Fish
Good Fish Sauce (c 1850)
Victorian Hen Lobster Sauce
Green Gooseberry Sauce for Mackerel
Rhoda's Cream Sauce for Halibut
Theodora's Scallop and Mushroom Sauce for Sole
Mustard Sauce for Grilled Herrings
Lemony Mustard Sauce
Mustard Cream Sauce – Hot or Cold
Old-fashioned Oyster Sauce for a Large Party
Victorian Cockle Sauce
Hollandaise Sauce from Tennessee
Watercress Sauce for Fish

Almond Sauce
for Chicken Croquettes

500 ml/1 pint creamy Béchamel
Sauce
1 teaspoon lemon juice
cayenne
⅓ cup stuffed olives, sliced
½ cup ground almonds

Add the other ingredients to the Béchamel Sauce. Serve very hot.

Aubergine Sauce
for a Gratin of Chicken

6 aubergines
250 ml/½ pint Béchamel Sauce
salt and pepper
155–225 g/6–8 oz cheese, grated
a little butter

Roast the aubergines in a medium hot oven or grill them over charcoal until they are soft. Skin them and mash them or whirl them in a liquidizer; season well, add the Béchamel and about the same quantity of cheese as you had aubergine pulp. Reheat till the cheese is melted and the sauce is bubbling hot. Pour over either sliced chicken or vegetables in a gratin dish. You can dot the top with butter and more cheese and brown the dish under a grill or in the oven.

A Good Béchamel Sauce
from Tennessee

Blend 1½ oz each of butter and flour; add 3–4 slices of onion and carrot, 6 boiled mushrooms, 2 parsley sprigs, 2 lemon slices, 2 bay leaves, 6 peppercorns. Add 1 pint of white stock and cook slowly for ½ an hour. Strain through a sieve, pressing hard, and add one cup of cream. Reheat gently, but do not boil.

Theodora's Chicken Liver
and Lemon Sauce

1 or 2 chicken livers
250 ml/½ pint chicken stock
grated rind of 1 lemon and the juice
salt and pepper
50 g/2 oz butter
1 level dessertspoon flour

Simmer the chicken livers in the stock and then mash finely. Add the rind of the lemon and season to taste. Melt the butter in a saucepan, stir in the flour and cook for a few minutes then add the chicken liver mixture and the stock. Stir very well and let it just bubble up. Finally add the lemon juice and serve hot.

This sauce, although originally intended for boiled chicken, is equally good over eggs *en cocotte* or veal fillets.

Grape Sauce for Chicken

40–50 g/1½–2 oz butter
40–50 g/1½–2 oz flour
pinch of salt
500 ml/1 pint chicken stock
2 tablespoons lemon juice
2 tablespoons sugar
½ cup double cream (optional)
2 cups seedless grapes

Melt the butter in a saucepan and blend in flour and salt. Stir until smooth. Gradually add the chicken stock, stirring constantly until smooth and thick. Stir in lemon juice and sugar. Correct seasoning. Add the cream and reheat, but do not boil, or it will curdle. Add grapes just before serving.

18th Century Sauce
for Fowls

Boil 250 ml/½ pint of cream with a blade of mace, 2 anchovies and a small bit of lemon peel and a little salt. Scald the livers of the fowls and bruise them very smooth with the yolks of 2 hard-boiled eggs and a little flour and butter. By degrees add these and a little chopped parsley to the cream and put it on the heat to thicken, but do not boil. Stir constantly.

Kentucky Pan-broiled
Gravy

This is an excellent sauce for roast chicken or roast veal.

Pour off all the fat except for 1 tablespoon from a roasting tin or pan in which you have just roasted chicken or veal. Lightly brown a finely minced onion or 2 shallots in this fat. Add ½–1 cup reduced chicken stock and 2–3 tablespoons white wine. Boil it all up together and deglaze the pan by scraping all the juices together. When ready to serve, turn up the heat and boil fast until it becomes syrupy; then immediately remove from heat, and stir in 1–2 tablespoons softened butter.

The Right Way to Make Bread Sauce

Put 500 ml/1 pint milk to boil with 1 onion and a few white peppercorns. Simmer gently for 30 minutes or more; then sieve and return it to the heat. Just before serving add 2 tablespoons of breadcrumbs, 10 tablespoons cream, salt and pepper and serve hot in a heated sauceboat.

A Victorian Recipe for Bread Sauce

1 onion
500 ml/1 pint milk
1 breakfastcupful of stale bread
a little mace, cayenne and salt
25 g/1 oz butter

Personally I think this produces a slimy bread sauce, but some people like it.

Peel and slice an onion, and simmer it in the milk until tender; then remove the onion from the milk. Break the bread into small pieces and put it into a saucepan. Strain the hot milk over it, cover it close, and let it soak for an hour. Then beat it up smooth with a fork, add the pounded mace, cayenne, salt, and the butter; boil it up, and serve it at once in a sauce boat.

White Celery Sauce for Boiled Chicken or Turkey

4 small, or 2 large, heads of celery
2 litres/4 pints water or stock
salt
250 ml/½ pint white gravy
(from chicken or veal)
a little butter and flour
a little nutmeg
250 ml/½ pint cream

This is a Victorian recipe.

Wash the celery and boil it in the water or stock and salt; when tender drain it on a sieve, and cut it in pieces about 3 cm/1 inch long. In the meantime, boil the gravy with the butter rolled in the flour (*beurre manié*) till it is thick and smooth, grate in the nutmeg, add it to the celery, and boil it up for a few minutes, then add the cream; just warm it again, serve it in a sauceboat, or pour it over boiled fowls or turkeys.

Celery Sauce for Boiled Pheasant

This sauce is equally good with roast pheasant.

Clean 4 sticks of celery, only using the heart. Chop it and put in a stewpan with a piece of butter the size of an egg, 1 quartered onion, 1 faggot of herbs, and 1 clove. Just cover with a light consommé. Let it cook gently until the celery is tender, drain it, reserving liquor, and pound it in a mortar, then pass through a fine sieve. Put the purée into a stewpan and thin it with an equal quantity of cream sauce and the reduced celery liquor.

Simple Cheese Sauce

3 tablespoons butter
3 tablespoons flour
1 teaspoon salt
¼ teaspoon pepper
375 ml/¾ pint milk
2 cups grated cheese, ideally half
Gruyère and half Parmesan
½ teaspoon Worcestershire Sauce

Melt butter over low heat, add flour, salt and pepper. Stir until well blended. Remove from heat. Gradually stir in milk and return to heat. Cook, stirring constantly until thick and smooth then add grated cheese and Worcestershire Sauce. Stir only until cheese has melted.

Cheese Sauce

2 tablespoons butter
1 teaspoon grated onion
2 tablespoons flour
12 fl oz single cream
¾ cup grated Cheddar cheese
dash of Worcestershire Sauce
pinch of cayenne
½ teaspoon paprika
salt to taste

This is an American recipe.

Melt butter over medium heat, add onion and cook until onion is golden. Stir in flour to make roux, cook for a few minutes and then add cream to make a cream sauce. Add cheese and remaining seasonings and stir only until cheese is melted.

A Victorian Grill Sauce for Meat

Half a teaspoon mustard, 1 tablespoon Harvey Sauce, 25 g/1 oz meat glaze, a few drops salad oil, a small piece butter about the size of a walnut, a pinch each of black pepper, cayenne and salt. Mix it all up on a plate, put the meat to be grilled in this mixture and grill under a fierce heat or over charcoal for a few seconds. Place the remainder of the sauce in a small stewpan to heat but not boil; dish the grill, pour the sauce over and serve.

Theodora's Anchovy, Egg and Herb Sauce for Beef Fillets (c. 1850)

2 hard-boiled eggs
4 anchovy fillets, pounded in a mortar
1 tablespoon mixed, chopped chives, parsley, tarragon and chervil
juice of 1 large lemon
black pepper
4–6 fillet steaks
25–50 g/1–2 oz butter

Mash up the eggs with the pounded anchovies and mix well with the herbs, lemon juice and pepper. Grill the fillets slightly under the time for perfect cooking. Put the sauce in an ovenproof dish, place the fillets on top, season them and then add a pat of butter to each fillet. Put into a hot oven for about 5 minutes, just until the butter has melted into the sauce. Be sparing with the salt on account of the anchovies.

A Victorian 'Sauce Robert' for Rumps and Steaks

Put a piece of butter, the size of an egg, into a saucepan, set it over the heat and when browning throw in a handful (about 100 g/¼ lb) sliced onions cut small. Fry them until brown, but do not let them burn. Add half a tablespoon of flour, shake the onions in it and give it another fry. Then put 4 or 5 spoons gravy into it and some pepper and salt and boil it gently for 10 minutes. Skim off the fat, add 1 teaspoon mustard, 1 tablespoon vinegar and the juice of ½ a lemon. Boil it all and pour it round the steaks. They should be of a fine yellow brown and garnished with fried parsley and lemon.

Juniper Sauce for Steaks or Kidneys

Pan-grill tender beef steaks or kidneys (lamb or veal). Remove; keep warm. In same pan, melt 2 tablespoons butter, brown 20 crushed juniper berries and a mashed garlic clove. Flame ¼ cup cognac in pan; add 1 cup beef stock; reduce to half, scraping pan. Serve over meat, it is particularly good with venison steaks.

Creamed Mushroom Sauce

1 cup coarsely chopped mushrooms
40 g/1½ oz butter
40 g/1½ oz flour
1½ cups milk
salt and pepper
pinch of nutmeg
2 teaspoons lemon juice
2 egg yolks, beaten

Brown mushrooms in butter, add flour and mix well. Stir in the milk and mix thoroughly before adding seasonings. Cook slowly until thick and smooth, stirring constantly. Take off the heat and cool a little. Add the lemon juice to the beaten egg yolks and beat again. Add to the sauce slowly and re-heat for about a minute, but do not boil. Serve at once.

Rhoda's Cordon Bleu Mushroom Sauce

Stew some sliced mushrooms (100 g/¼ lb or more) in 15 g/½ oz butter, covered. When tender add a tablespoonful of Worcestershire Sauce, then the juices from the steak. Season well with salt and freshly ground pepper, and lastly add 2 tablespoons double cream.

For use with roast or grilled steaks.

Mushroom and Madeira Sauce

¼ lb mushrooms
2 tablespoons butter
2 tablespoons flour
½–1 cup beef stock or canned consommé
1–2 tablespoons Madeira
pinch of salt
freshly ground pepper
1 teaspoon minced fresh tarragon or ½ teaspoon dried

Wipe mushrooms. Remove stems and chop finely. Slice caps. Melt butter and sauté stems and caps. After 3–4 minutes sprinkle in flour. Cook and stir gently for 2 more minutes. Pour in beef stock and add seasonings and Madeira. Taste and correct seasonings. Stir until thickened and smooth. Makes 1½ cups.

For hamburgers, left-over beef, game croquettes, etc.

Goodwood Sauce

100 g/4 oz mushrooms
milk
pinch of mustard powder
1 teaspoon Harvey's or Worcester sauce

Chop the mushrooms as finely as possible and cook for 5 minutes in a very small quantity of milk (barely enough to cover) in a lidded pan. Stir in the mustard powder and Harvey's or Worcestershire Sauce and simmer very gently until fairly thick. Serve with grills and fish.

Mrs Gore's Mushroom Sauce

2 rashers bacon
25 g/1 oz butter
200 g/½ lb mushrooms
12 g/½ oz flour
8 tablespoons white wine
½ clove garlic (optional)
1–2 tablespoons stock

Trim and chop the bacon, and cook in butter until nearly crisp. Add the chopped mushrooms, mix well and cook covered, with gentle heat for 2–3 minutes. Stir in the flour and add the wine, crushed garlic and a little stock. Season with pepper only. Simmer until the sauce is fairly thick. In lieu of stock a little sour cream can be added. For beef or chicken.

These two recipes come from Mrs Stanley's excellent book *English Country House Cooking*.

A Victorian Mushroom Sauce

500 ml/1 pint young mushrooms
coarse salt
1 blade of mace
a little nutmeg
40 g/1½ oz butter
a little flour
500 ml/1 pint cream

Rub off the tender skin from the mushrooms, with a rough cloth dipped every now and then in a little coarse salt; put them into the stewpan with the mace, nutmeg, the butter which has been rolled in a teaspoon of flour, and 500 ml/1 pint of good cream.* Put it over a clear fire and boil it up till sufficiently thick, stirring it all the time; then pour it round boiled fowls or rabbits.

* I would advise cooking mushrooms in butter, adding 40 g/1½ oz flour and making a roux which you cook for a few minutes before adding the cream.

Honey-mint Sauce for Lamb

½ cup water
1 tablespoon vinegar
1 cup honey, preferably clover
¼ cup chopped mint
½ teaspoon salt

Heat water and vinegar. Add honey, stir well; then add chopped mint and salt. Cook slowly for 5 minutes. It keeps indefinitely. Use it to baste lamb chops or roast during cooking, or serve with roast lamb in a sauce boat.

Sauce for Hot or Cold Roast Lamb

½ cup brown sugar
¼ cup butter
¼ cup apple jelly
½ cup tomato ketchup
3 tablespoons lemon juice
1 teaspoon cinnamon
½ teaspoon allspice
¼ teaspoon ground cloves
½ teaspoon pepper

Combine all ingredients and heat through in a double boiler.

Marinade Sauce for Lamb Chops

5 tablespoons dry mustard
1 tablespoon garlic vinegar*
½ teaspoon salt
¼ teaspoon paprika
5 tablespoons olive oil
juice of 1 lemon (optional)

Blend ingredients well and pour over chops an hour before grilling. Turn chops several times during the hour. Use a little marinade with pan juices to make hot sauce to serve with chops. Fiery but good. Improved by squeezing lemon juice over chops while grilling and into sauce.
* For home-made Garlic Vinegar: bring 250 ml/½ pint vinegar to a boil. Toss in several garlic buds. Let cool. Pour into bottle for later use.

Theodora's Prune and Blackcurrant Sauce for Boiled Mutton

1 cup prunes
125 ml/¼ pint red or white wine
1 pinch cinnamon
2 tablespoons sugar
1 cup mutton stock
2 tablespoons breadcrumbs
juice of 1 lemon
salt and pepper
1 cup blackcurrants washed and picked over carefully
½ tablespoon chopped parsley

This is an Edwardian recipe which may have an earlier origin.
    Soak and stone the prunes and cook them in the wine with a pinch of cinnamon and the sugar until they are well cooked. Then put through a sieve and add the mutton stock, breadcrumbs, lemon juice and seasonings. Add the blackcurrants, whole and raw, and the parsley. Bring to the boil and simmer for 3 minutes, no longer.

Dr Kitchener's 1822 Recipe for Port Wine Sauce for Roast Mutton

125 ml/¼ pint port wine
125 ml/¼ pint unflavoured mutton gravy
1 large tablespoon red currant jelly

Let it just boil up, and send it to table in a sauce boat.

Mustard Sauce for Baked Ham

1 cup brown sugar
½ cup flour
1 tablespoon dry mustard
1 teaspoon turmeric
wine vinegar, a little cold
and a little hot
2 tablespoons olive oil

Mix dry ingredients and moisten with enough cold vinegar to make a paste. Stir in hot vinegar to make the consistency of cream. Do not cook. Beat in olive oil. Serve cool with hot baked ham.

Orange Sauce for Pork, Ham and Duck

peel and juice of 1 orange
peel and juice of ½ lemon
1½ tablespoons sugar
2 tablespoons wine vinegar
½ tablespoon cornflour
¼ cup white wine or cider

Boil orange and lemon rind cut into thin strips for 10 minutes, then drain. Cook sugar with vinegar in a deep saucepan until it begins to turn brown. Remove from heat and add fruit juices. Return to heat and stir until caramelized sugar is dissolved. Then add cornflour mixed with wine and cook until slightly thickened. Stir in peel.

Orange Raisin Sauce for Ham

1 tablespoon flour
pinch of salt
½ cup brown sugar
½ cup orange juice
½ cup water
2 tablespoons vinegar
⅓ cup raisins

Mix the flour, salt and sugar, and cook in a saucepan until thickened. Stir in the orange juice, water and vinegar, and simmer gently for a few minutes; finally add the raisins.

Cherry Sauce for Hot Ham or Tongue

1 tablespoon red currant jelly
1 tablespoon mango chutney
2 tablespoons stock, if possible of
the dish
juice of 1 lemon
salt and pepper
10 tablespoons port
10 tablespoons red wine
juice of 3 oranges
1 cup stoned black cherries,
tinned if necessary

This sauce is also delicious with domestic or wild roast duck.

Mix all ingredients together except the cherries and boil gently for 30 minutes, or until reduced to about half. Strain through a sieve and then add the cherries. Simmer for a further 10 minutes and serve cold.

Theodora's Green Sauce for Ducklings

250 ml/½ pint spinach or sorrel water
10 tablespoons white wine
25 g/1 oz butter
1 tablespoon caster sugar
225 g/8 oz cooked puréed gooseberries or white grapes
salt

Add the spinach or sorrel water, white wine, butter and sugar to the gooseberries or grapes. Season to taste and boil them all up for at least 10 minutes on a fairly hot stove, so that there is not too much liquid. Serve hot.

Tennessee Orange Sauce for Roast Duck

To 1½ cups of thick, rich brown gravy, add the juice of three oranges and the grated yellow rind of one.

Virginian Raisin Sauce

1 large orange
1 large lemon
1 cup seeded raisins
¼ cup water
¼ cup vinegar
2 tablespoons sugar
1 heaped teaspoon dry mustard
1 tablespoon Worcestershire Sauce
dash of cayenne
8 allspice, 8 cloves, ½ stick cinnamon,
1 piece ginger: all tied in a
muslin bag

Thinly peel the rind from the orange and lemon and chop finely. Squeeze out the juice. Put both into a saucepan with all the other ingredients. Bring slowly to the boil over moderate heat and simmer very slowly for about 1 hour. Remove spice bag and serve hot in a sauceboat.

Raisin Sauce

1 cup soft brown sugar
1 heaped tablespoon flour
2 heaped teaspoons dry mustard
1 cup cider vinegar
2½ cups water
1 large apple, diced
1 cup raisins
pinch of salt

Blend sugar, flour and mustard. Add the liquids. Stir until dissolved and add apple, raisins and salt. Cook gently until the consistency of honey.

Red Wine Sauce

250 ml/½ pint red wine. Let it boil with a small pinch of pepper and a very small quantity of shallot until there is only about half a cupful left in the saucepan. Then add 3 tablespoons very rich brown stock. Let it simmer slowly. Add a walnut of butter and a pinch of salt to taste, stirring it with a spoon. The sauce must then be passed through a cloth. A good sauce for steaks.

Wild Duck Sauce – First Life Guards' Recipe

Squeeze ½ a lemon into a soup plate; add 2 teaspoons mustard and 1 teaspoon salt; mix them together; add a good deal of red and black pepper with 2 tablespoons port wine and 5 or 6 tablespoons gravy from the duck, or good stock; mix the whole till quite smooth, let it be heated and sent to the table hot. This sauce is also good for any kind of grill.

Spatchcock or Devil Sauce for Roe deer or Roast Pheasant or Turkey

This sauce is used with game that has been roasted in the ordinary way, taken off the bone and laid in a shallow entrée dish. After which the sauce is poured over it.

It is made of 250 ml/½ pint cream, the juices of the roast with as little fat as possible and 1 tablespoon Worcestershire Sauce. The dish is then garnished with straw potatoes.

If you wish to use a Devil Sauce for heating up cold breast of pheasant or turkey see Quick White Devil Sauce, p. 97.

Theodora's Prune and Spices Sauce for Hare

½ lb prunes
½ teaspoon cinnamon
a pinch of nutmeg
½ bottle sweet white wine
½ teaspoon ginger
salt and pepper

Soak the prunes and stone them. Cook them in the white wine with the spices and seasonings. When well cooked put it all through a sieve and serve hot.

Mrs Rundell's Currant Sauce for Venison and Roe deer (c. 1840)

Boil an ounce of dried currants in half a pint of water, a few minutes; then add a small teacupful of breadcrumbs, six cloves, a glass of port wine and a bit of butter. Stir it till the whole is smooth.

Hot Sauce for Venison

1 onion
1 carrot
2 sprigs parsley
2 sprigs thyme
1 bay leaf
½ pint consommé
1 wine glass sherry or port
½ lemon
1 stalk celery
1 tablespoon butter
1 tablespoon flour
cayenne, salt and black pepper to taste
½ glass currant jelly

Melt butter and blend in flour. Let it brown slowly. Add the consommé and boil well. Add the herbs, finely chopped vegetables and grated lemon peel. Cook slowly for an hour or longer. Add the wine and season with salt, pepper and cayenne. Cook about 10 minutes longer, then strain. Add the juices of the roasting pan and the currant jelly and cook for another 10 minutes. Serve hot.

Dr Kitchener's Recipe for Melted Butter

and his observations on it, from Apicius Redevivus *or* The Cook's Oracle, *by William Kitchener, MD, 1817.*

Keep a pint stew-pan for this purpose only.

Cut two ounces of butter into little bits, that it may melt more easily, and mix more readily; – put it into the stew-pan with a large tea-spoonful (i.e. about three drachms) of Flour, (some prefer Arrow Root, or Potato Starch), and two tablespoonsful of Milk.

When thoroughly mixed, – add six table-spoonsful of water; hold it over the fire, and shake it round every minute (all the while the same way), till it just begins to simmer, then let it stand quietly and boil up. It should be of the thickness of good cream.

Observations – This is the best way of preparing melted butter; – Milk mixes with the butter much more easily and more intimately than water alone can be made to do. This is of proper thickness to be mixed at table with Flavouring Essences, Anchovy, Mushroom, or Cavice [a white pepper from the South Sea Islands], etc. If made merely to pour over vegetables, add a little more milk to it.

N.B. If the BUTTER OILS, put a spoonful of cold water to it, and stir it with a spoon, – if it is very much oiled, it must be poured backwards and forwards from the Stew-pan to the Sauce-boat till it is right again.

LASTLY. – Observe, that in ordering the proportions of MEAT, BUTTER, WINE, SPICE, etc. in the following receipts, THE PROPER QUANTITY IS SET DOWN, and that A LESS QUANTITY WILL NOT DO; – and in some instances those Palates which have been used to the extreme of *Piquance*, will require additional excitement.

This may be easily accomplished by the aid of that Whip and Spur, which Students of long standing in the School of Good Living are generally so fond of enlivening their palate with, i.e. Cayenne and Garlic.

Old-fashioned Parsley Sauce

a bunch of parsley
125–250 ml/¼–½ pint melted butter
(see p. 77)

Wash the parsley thoroughly, boil it for 6 or 7 minutes till tender, then press the water well out of it and dry with a cloth. Chop it very fine. Make the melted butter as required and mix it gradually into the parsley.

Fennel Sauce

a small bunch of fennel leaves
a little salt
125–250 ml/¼–½ pint melted butter
(see p. 77)

Carefully strip the leaves of the fennel from their stems. Wash them very carefully and boil quickly, with a little salt in the water, till they are quite tender. Squeeze them till all the water is expressed; mince them very fine and mix with hot melted butter.

Old-fashioned English Egg Sauce

2 eggs
125 ml/¼ pint melted butter
(see p. 77)

Boil the eggs for 15 minutes, then drain and put in cold water to get cool. Shell them and cut them into small dice, put the minced egg into a very hot sauce tureen and pour over them the boiling melted butter. Stir the sauce round to mix the eggs with it and season with salt and ground pepper.

Virginian Chicken Liver and Lemon Sauce

the chicken livers
250 ml/½ pint melted butter
(see p. 77)
1 hard-boiled egg, chopped
the juice of a small lemon

Sauté the livers for a few moments only in the butter. Chop them up fine. Add the egg, the livers and the lemon juice to the drawn butter in a small pan. Heat, season and serve in a hot sauceboat.

Sour Cream Sauce

3 tablespoons butter
2 tablespoons flour
1 teaspoon salt
1 teaspoon pepper
2 cups thick soured cream
1½ tablespoons lemon juice

Melt the butter, add the flour, salt and pepper. Blend well. Remove from heat. Gradually stir in cream and return to heat for a few minutes only. Do not let it boil. Just before serving correct seasoning and stir in lemon juice.

Theodora's Chestnut Sauce

20 shelled chestnuts
6 button mushrooms
salt and pepper
25 g/1 oz butter
250 ml/½ pint consommé or stock or milk

This sauce can be used for roast turkey, hot ham or mutton cutlets.

Prick the chestnuts and remove both skins. Then boil them for 20 minutes. When they are soft pound them in a mortar until they are quite smooth. Put them in a saucepan with the butter, chopped mushrooms, pepper and salt, then pour over the consommé and mix it all very well. Heat up for about 4 minutes before serving.

Sorrel Sauce

225 g/8 oz sorrel
50 g/2 oz butter
cream to taste

Spine and wash the sorrel as if it were spinach. Then put into a saucepan without drying it. Do not add water. Pound it with a wooden spoon until it comes to the boil. Then simmer for about 3–5 minutes. It will then resemble a spinach purée. Strain through a sieve and return to the saucepan adding the butter and cream.

This sauce is quite delicious as a base for poached or cocotte eggs. If you wish a larger quantity for serving with white meat, thin it down with a little stock.

Creamy Curry Sauce

1 small onion or 3 shallots, chopped
25 g/1 oz butter
1 tablespoon curry powder,
as fresh as possible
garlic
salt
375 ml/¾ pint vegetable stock
50 g/2 oz cream
1 apple, chopped
½ tablespoon desiccated coconut
(optional)
green mango chutney

Soften the onion or shallots in the butter, add the curry powder, garlic, salt and stock. Cover and simmer for 30 minutes, adding more stock as necessary. Finish with cream, if desired.

The sauce can be varied by adding the apple at the beginning and coconut towards the end of preparation.

This is an ideal sauce for poached eggs laid on a bed of plain rice. Simply pour sauce over before serving and also pass separately. Serve green mango chutney separately or stir a little into the sauce.

Admiral Ross's Indian Devil Mixture

4 tablespoons cold gravy
1 tablespoon ketchup
2 teaspoons made English mustard
2 tablespoons butter
1 tablespoon curry paste
1 tablespoon vinegar
2 teaspoons salt

Mix all the above ingredients as smooth as possible in a soup plate, put with it the cold meat, or whatever you wish to devil. Stew it gently until thoroughly warmed, and then you will have a good devil. NOTE: Alternatively you can dip cold meats with the Devil Mixture then roll in breadcrumbs, dot with butter and grill.

Quick White Devil Sauce

250 ml/½ pint double cream
salt and pepper to taste
1 tablespoon Harvey's Sauce
1 tablespoon Escoffier Diable sauce

Whip up the cream and add salt and pepper: use a pinch of cayenne if you wish to hot it up. Then add the other sauces.

To use it, gently heat any left-over pieces of cold game, chicken or turkey in a very little stock in a casserole in the oven. When warmed through add the devilled cream and mix through. Put back in a slow to medium oven until it turns a little golden on top.

Theodora's Devil Sauce

100 g/4 oz butter
1 level tablespoon dry mustard
2 tablespoons breadcrumbs
1 teaspoon Worcestershire Sauce
1 teaspoon mushroom ketchup
salt and cayenne pepper

Mix all together very well, then spread on the cutlets, chicken legs, or whatever you are using, grill for a few minutes and then serve.

These last three sauces come from *The Art of British Cooking* by Theodora Fitzgibbon.

Devilled Butter for Devilled Bones

(A Boodles Club recipe)

50 g/2 oz butter, ½ tablespoon dry mustard, ½ tablespoon Worcestershire Sauce, 1 teaspoon Harvey's Sauce, a pinch of cayenne pepper and salt. Spread the mixture over the bones, particularly over the sawn off ends to prevent the marrow leaking, and grill under a hot grill.

Indian Sauce for Salmon

Skin and fry some onions with plenty of butter until soft and brown, then add 1 tablespoon curry powder and allow it also to fry. Next pour in either fish or meat stock and a sliced apple and tomato, and if wished, a little vegetable marrow or courgette and allow to stew to a pulp. Then add a few tamarinds, free from stones and skin, etc., and a little grated coconut. Finally rub the sauce through a sieve and serve either with grilled salmon or steak.

NOTE: The ideal way to give sauces a coconut flavour is to steep some grated coconut in water in a bowl for 30 minutes. Then put this liquid in a liquidizer; the result is coconut milk.

Almond Butter for Grilled Trout

3 tablespoons slivered almonds
½ cup butter
2 tablespoons pimento,
finely chopped (optional)
2 teaspoons parsley
2 teaspoons lemon juice
1 teaspoon salt

Sauté almonds in 2 tablespoons butter slowly until golden brown. Cream remaining butter and add almonds, pimento, parsley, lemon juice and salt. Mix thoroughly, and spread on trout just before serving.

Anchovy Cream Sauce for Fish

3 tablespoons melted butter
3 tablespoons flour
1 cup fish stock
1 teaspoon lemon juice
2 teaspoons anchovy paste
salt and cayenne
cream (optional)

Make a roux of butter and flour. Add 1 cup boiling stock and cook in a double boiler until this begins to boil, then add lemon juice and anchovy paste. Season to taste with salt and cayenne. Serve with baked or steamed fish. A little cream should be added just before serving.

Good Fish Sauce (c 1850)

Draw the gravy from good lean beef. Take 2 or 3 anchovies, some eschalots, horseradish and a little water, and when pretty well boiled, strain and add to the drawn gravy. Thicken all this with a little butter and flour, beating vigorously over heat. Cook some more and then add a little white wine and 1 tablespoon fresh single cream.

Victorian Hen Lobster Sauce

1 hen lobster with coral
⅔ of its weight of good cream
⅓ of its weight of fresh butter

Cut the lobster flesh in small pieces and pound the coral, mix it up with two thirds of good cream and one third of fresh butter. NO stock, fish-sauces, anchovies or essences to be used.

Green Gooseberry Sauce for Mackerel

a handful of green sorrel leaves
250 ml/½ pint green gooseberries
small piece of butter
25 g/1 oz sugar
pepper and salt
nutmeg

Spine and wash the green sorrel; cook it to a purée in a small pan without water. Boil gooseberries, drain them from the water and rub them through a sieve. Put the sorrel purée into a saucepan, allowing about a wineglass to the pulp obtained from the gooseberries. Add a piece of butter, a lump of sugar, pepper, salt and nutmeg. Make the sauce very hot and serve it up in a tureen.

Rhoda's Cream Sauce for Halibut

Fry a large piece of halibut in clarified butter slowly over moderate heat. Squeeze a whole lemon on to it while it is cooking. Remove fish and keep warm on serving dish. Add to the juices in the pan 250 ml/½ pint of cream and some more lemon juice, black pepper and salt. Simmer and stir together until the sauce thickens. Correct seasoning and pour over dish. That is all.

Theodora's Scallop and Mushroom Sauce for Sole

2 scallops
50 g/2 oz butter
250 ml/½ pint warm milk
1 level tablespoon flour
salt and pepper
50 g/2 oz mushrooms, chopped
1 tablespoon mixed chopped parsley and lemon thyme
50 g/2 oz cream (optional)

Cut the scallops into pieces and boil for 15 minutes in the milk with 25 g/1 oz butter. Strain but retain the milk. Melt the rest of the butter in a pan, mix in the flour and slowly add the milk the scallops were cooked in, stirring constantly. Season to taste, and add a little more milk if the sauce seems too thick. Now add the mushrooms, herbs and scallops and simmer over a low flame for 5–10 minutes. Finish with cream to taste, but do not reboil once cream is added.

Mustard Sauce for Grilled Herrings

½ tablespoon made mustard
(powder made up with tarragon vinegar)
½ tablespoon chili vinegar
1 teaspoon anchovy essence
500 ml/1 pint Béchamel Sauce
a few grains of salt
soft roes of herring (optional)

Add mustard, vinegar and anchovy to white sauce and warm up gently. The soft roes of herring may be cut up and added. They will make the sauce creamier. Be careful with the salt.

Lemony Mustard Sauce

50 g/2 oz butter
2 tablespoons flour
1½ cups boiling water
3 large egg yolks, beaten until light
juice of 1 lemon
½ large teaspoon *moutarde de Maille*
salt and cayenne pepper

Melt butter in a saucepan and stir in flour to make a smooth paste. Add boiling water slowly, stirring constantly to eliminate all lumps. Cool a little and off heat, stir in egg yolks, mixing thoroughly. Blend in lemon juice, mustard, a scant teaspoon salt and a liberal sprinkling of cayenne. This is good for fish, cauliflower, celery, Jerusalem artichoke or celery root salad.

Mustard Cream Sauce – Hot or Cold

1 tablespoon cornstarch (cornflour)
2 cups cream
½ cup sugar
1 teaspoon salt
2 egg yolks
2 tablespoons mustard powder
1 cup vinegar

Dissolve cornstarch in a little cream, and bring remaining cream to boiling point. Add dissolved cornstarch and cook until thick in a double boiler over hot water. Add sugar and salt. Beat up the egg yolks with the mustard powder and add to cream. Cook and stir until thickened, then add vinegar. Cook 1 minute more, stirring. Serve hot with fish or cold with seafood mousse or smoked fish hors d'oeuvres.

Old-fashioned Oyster Sauce for a Large Party

The quantities can be doubled or quadrupled as necessary

50 g/2 oz butter
40 g/1½ oz flour
2 dozen oysters
375–500 ml/¾–1 pint creamy milk
1 saltspoon salt
¼ saltspoon cayenne
1 clove
4 peppercorns
1 tablespoon Harvey's Sauce
juice of ½ lemon (optional)
50 g/2 oz cream (optional)

Mix the butter and flour in your stewpan, making a roux. Beard the oysters and put them into a separate little stewpan. Add the oyster beards and liquor to the roux, cook till thick and smooth, then add the milk by degrees, the salt, cayenne, clove and peppercorns. Boil it 10 minutes, stirring it all the time. Add Harvey's Sauce. Strain this liquor over the oysters. Make the whole hot, the oysters should just curl at the edges, but do not let it boil. Some people add the juice of a ½ lemon. Extra cream can be added just before serving and this makes a much richer sauce.

Quantities given are enough for 5 servings and can be doubled or quadrupled according to numbers. In Virginia a similar recipe is served as a main course with Virginia ham: a delicious combination.

Victorian Cockle Sauce

100 cockles
½ of liquor from cockles
225 g/8 oz butter
a little flour
2 tablespoons anchovy liquor
(or 1 of essence)
1 tablespoon mushroom ketchup
or Harvey's Sauce

Wash the cockles very clean, put them into a large saucepan, cover them close and stew them gently till they open. Strain the liquor through a sieve. Wash the shelled cockles in cold water and put them into a stewpan. Pour half the liquor on them with the butter and a little flour. Add the anchovy liquor and the ketchup. Boil the sauce gently until the butter is melted and it is thick and smooth.

Hollandaise Sauce from Tennessee

Cream ½ cup of butter; add 4 egg yolks, one by one, then the juice of ½ a lemon, ½ teaspoon of salt and a dash of cayenne – all off the heat. Put the mixture in a double boiler; beat with an egg beater, adding slowly 6 tablespoons of boiling water.

Cook to consistency of stiff custard, beating continually. Serve warm with snapper beans, broccoli, asparagus, cauliflower and even fish.

Watercress Sauce for Fish

1 bunch watercress, chopped
250 ml/½ pint fish stock
(Court Bouillon)
25 g/1 oz butter
1 tablespoon flour
pepper and salt
3–4 tablespoons cream

Cook the stalks of the watercress in the fish stock then strain, but keep the liquor. Melt the butter, add the flour, then the warm stock. Season to taste and stir well to avoid lumps. Finally add the cream and the watercress leaves.

THE TRADITIONAL ENGLISH AND AMERICAN SAUCES

2 COLD SAUCES

Cumberland Sauce for Hot Gammon or Ham
Quick Cumberland Sauce
Lady Dudley's Cumberland Sauce for Cold Beef or Ham
Cumberland Jelly
Orange Sauce for Ham à la Wombwell
'Hanoverian' Sauce
Tennessee Mint Sauce
Mint Sauce for Roast Lamb
Damson Sauce for Cold Venison
Gisborough Sauce
Cucumber Sauce
Cucumber Sauce with Sour Cream I
Cucumber Sauce with Sour Cream II
Mrs Crickmere's Ritz Sauce
Sauce Victoria
Lily MacLeod's Menarlo Sauce
Currant Orange Sauce
Virginian Sour Cream Sauce for Smoked Fish
Marinade Sauce for Lamb Chops
Aromatic Seafood Sauce from Virginia
A Delicate Sauce for Cold Curries
Curry Mayonnaise
Cold Curry Risotto Sauce
Half and Half Dressing
1000 Island Dressing
Green Goddess Dressing
Quick Sauce Verte
Green Pea Mayonnaise
Mayonnaise Sauce à la Farquhar
'Hot' Sauce for Shrimp Cocktails
Shrimp or Prawn Cocktail Sauce
A Good Sauce for Prawn Cocktails
Sauce for Crab Cocktails or Salads
Cucumber Mayonnaise
Gloucester Sauce
Cambridge Sauce
President Carter's Sauce

Joan's Salad Dressing
Boiled Dressing for Salads
A Butler's Salad Dressing
Caldy Manor Salad Sauce
Sauce for Potato Salad
Yellow Salad Dressing from Tennessee

Cumberland Sauce
for Hot Gammon or Ham
zest of ½ orange
zest of ½ lemon
2 chopped shallots
225 g/½ lb red currant jelly
2 tablespoons port
juice of ½ orange
juice of ½ lemon
⅛ teaspoon mustard powder
generous pinch of ground ginger
pinch of cayenne pepper

Blanch the orange and lemon zest (which has been cut to a fine julienne) and the shallots for 3 minutes. Drain. Pass the red currant jelly through a sieve, mix with the port, orange and lemon juice and season with the mustard, ground ginger and cayenne pepper. Finally add shallots and julienne of orange and lemon zest and leave to stand for several hours. Serve with game dishes, or all types of ham.

Quick Cumberland Sauce
1½ cups red currant jelly
1 teaspoon Dijon mustard
½ peeled orange, sliced (no pith)
3 cm/1 inch square orange peel,
zest only
3 slices onion

Place all ingredients in blender and blend until smooth.

Lady Dudley's
Cumberland Sauce
for Cold Beef or Ham
1 wineglass claret or port wine
2 tablespoons red currant jelly
a little Green Label Chutney
1 tablespoon Worcestershire Sauce
1 tablespoon Harvey's Sauce
3 oranges
1 lemon

Put the wine and jelly into a small stewpan to boil for 5 minutes, then add the chutney and sauces. Squeeze in the juice of the 3 oranges and the lemon, then strain and serve cold, adding the rind of 2 oranges finely cut *à la julienne*, taking care to cut away the white inside part of the peel.

Cumberland Jelly
2 oranges
1–2 lemons
225 g/½ lb red currant jelly
pinch of mustard powder
12 g/½ oz gelatine
4 tablespoons port

Grate the rinds of oranges and lemons, and add to the red currant jelly with their juices. Warm together with a pinch of mustard powder. Put in the gelatine with the (grocer's) port, bring almost to the boil and then after straining allow to set.

Orange Sauce
for Ham à la Wombwell

One root horseradish grated, 50 g/2 oz red currant jelly melted, 1 tablespoon mixed English mustard, the grated rind and juice of 2 oranges and 1 lemon, 1 tablespoon white vinegar. Mix all together and serve.

'Hanoverian' Sauce

from an early 19th century cookery book

Grate the rind of a Seville orange or lemon onto 1 tablespoon caster sugar. Squeeze the juice over, add ½ tablespoon dry mustard, 2 tablespoons olive oil and 2 tablespoons port wine. Mix all thoroughly and serve over cold meats, or cold wild duck.

As the name implies this is really a version of Cumberland Sauce.

Tennessee Mint Sauce

Mince 3 tablespoons fresh green mint. Add the grated rind of 1 lemon. Mix and spoon into a sauceboat. To ¼ cup white vinegar and lemon juice add as much sugar as it will absorb. Pour this mixture over mint in sauceboat and let stand 2 hours.

Mint Sauce for Roast Lamb

½ cup mint leaves (pressed down)
¾ cup boiling water
3 tablespoons sugar
6 tablespoons vinegar
¼ teaspoon paprika
¼ teaspoon salt

Chop mint leaves finely. Add boiling water and sugar. Cover and let stand 30 minutes. Strain and add the vinegar and seasonings.

Damson Sauce for Cold Venison

½ cup damson jam
¼ cup orange juice
¼ cup sherry
½ teaspoon prepared mustard
¼ teaspoon salt

Mix all ingredients together and serve.

Gisborough Sauce

1 tablespoon red currant jelly
1 orange
½ lemon
2 tablespoons port
1 teaspoon Harvey's Sauce
1 tablespoon Worcestershire Sauce
chutney
cayenne pepper
100 g/4 oz glacé cherries

Melt the red currant jelly with the juices of the orange and lemon, add the port, sauces and a couple of teaspoonsful of the runny part of chutney. Season with cayenne pepper. Bring to the boil and simmer for a minute or two; finally add the halved cherries and serve cold. For cold meats or game.

Cucumber Sauce

1 large cucumber
a little vinegar
salt and pepper
250 ml/½ pint double cream
1 tablespoon vinegar
dash of cayenne

Peel and slice cucumber. Marinate it in vinegar to which salt and pepper have been added. After an hour, drain carefully, over a sieve. Just before serving, whip cream until thick and add vinegar, salt and cayenne. Lastly, add drained cucumber and serve very cold. Can be served with hot or cold salmon.

Cucumber Sauce with Sour Cream I

500 ml/1 pint sour cream
3 tablespoons white wine vinegar
1 tablespoon lemon juice
1 teaspoon salt
2 teaspoons grated onion
1 tablespoon dried dill
1 cup peeled, de-seeded and diced cucumber
⅛ teaspoon cayenne

Mix all ingredients together thoroughly and chill. Serve with Salmon Mousse.

Cucumber Sauce with Sour Cream II

2 cucumbers, very thinly sliced
¼ cup snipped fresh dill
1 tablespoon celery seed
4 spring onions with leaves, minced
1 cup sour cream
dash of Tabasco
salt

Blend all the ingredients but salt and chill no more than 6 hours. Add salt to taste immediately before serving with hot or cold seafood, or boiled salmon.

Mrs Crickmere's Ritz Sauce

250 ml/½ pint double cream, whipped
½ teaspoon Worcestershire Sauce
½ teaspoon Harvey's Sauce

Combine and serve immediately with hot, fried, breadcrumbed sole (goujons of).

Sauce Victoria

1 cup double cream, whipped
1 tablespoon tomato ketchup
salt and pepper
1 teaspoon lemon juice
1 pimento, finely chopped

Add all ingredients to cream and mix carefully.

Serve immediately or there is a danger of it separating.

Lily MacLeod's Menarlo Sauce

125 ml/¼ pint double cream, whipped
1 tablespoon grated horseradish
1 tablespoon finely chopped cucumber (skin and pips removed)
1 very small shallot, very finely chopped
½ tablespoon tarragon vinegar
pepper and salt to taste

Drain the cucumber. Add all the ingredients to the cream. An excellent sauce for cold chicken, game or cold fish.

Serve at once or it may separate.

Currant Orange Sauce

Derived from an eighteenth-century recipe.

Break 1 cup red currant jelly in a basin. Add ½ cup finely chopped mint leaves along with ½ cup orange juice. Leave for at least 1 hour before serving. Use with cold veal, game or mutton.

The following sauces all use oil or mayonnaise as part of their ingredients. For a note on the use of different salad oils – olive, arrachide, groundnut or walnut – see p. 60. It is largely a question of taste which you use.

Virginian Sour Cream Sauce for Smoked Fish

1 cup sour cream
1 teaspoon lemon juice
½–1 tablespoon horseradish
grated onion to taste
2 teaspoons chopped chives
½ cup mayonnaise
¼ teaspoon dry mustard

Combine all ingredients. Mix well and pour over green bean salad or smoked fish. This is an excellent sauce for smoked haddock, eel, trout, sturgeon and mackerel.

Marinade Sauce for Lamb Chops

5 tablespoons dry mustard
1 tablespoon garlic vinegar*
½ teaspoon salt
¼ teaspoon paprika
5 tablespoons olive oil

Blend ingredients well and pour over chops an hour before grilling. Turn chops several times during the hour. The marinade can be boiled up, reduced mixed with pan juices and served as a sauce with the chops.
* GARLIC VINEGAR Bring 250 ml/½ pint vinegar to a boil. Toss in several garlic buds. Let cool. Pour into bottle for later use.

Aromatic Seafood Sauce from Virginia

½ cup olive oil
3 shallots
1 teaspoon Dijon mustard
1 teaspoon soy sauce
1 teaspoon tarragon
½ teaspoon black pepper
¼ cup Pernod
2 tablespoons lemon juice
few sprigs of parsley

Combine all ingredients in the blender and blend for 30 seconds. Makes approximately 1–1½ cups.

A Delicate Sauce for Cold Curries

1 dessert apple, sliced
4 shallots, chopped
50 g/2 oz butter
1 teaspoon coriander seed
1 good tablespoon curry powder
1 teaspoon flour
a few sultanas
a little liquid (coconut milk if possible)
homemade mayonnaise or a commercial brand of salad dressing
seasoning
lemon juice
1 teaspoon sugar (optional)

Fry apple with shallots in butter. Add coriander seed mixed with curry powder and flour and the sultanas and liquid. (Coconut milk* is best, but milk, water or vegetable liquor can be used instead.) Add the mixture to the apple and shallots a tablespoon at a time, using just enough to make a thick paste. Cool and mix this thickish paste with the mayonnaise or salad dressing. Correct seasoning, add lemon juice and, if liked, a little sugar.
* For coconut milk see note on p. 97.

Curry Mayonnaise

This sauce is also called *Jubilee Mayonnaise*, as it was first served in 1935 at a banquet for HM King George V and Queen Mary's Jubilee. It is a sauce for special occasions, as it takes a long time to make, but it can be prepared the day before. Ideal for serving with cold chicken, turkey, buffet dishes, rice salads, etc.

25 g/1 oz oil
50 g/2 oz onion, finely chopped
½ tablespoon curry powder
2 teaspoons tomato purée
4 tablespoons red wine
3 tablespoons water
1 bay leaf
1 teaspoon sugar
salt and pepper
2 slices lemon
squeeze of lemon juice
375 ml/¾ pint mayonnaise
2 tablespoons apricot purée
3 tablespoons double cream, lightly whipped

Heat the oil, add the onion and cook gently for 3–4 minutes. Add the curry powder and cook for a further 2 minutes. Add the tomato purée, wine, water and bay leaf. Bring to the boil and add sugar, salt, pepper to taste, and lemon slices and juice. Simmer, uncovered, for 5–10 minutes. Fish out the lemon and bay leaf and leave to cool. Add the mixture to the mayonnaise by degrees, with the apricot purée. Check the flavour and sweeten or season to taste. Stir in the cream and serve well chilled.

Cold Curry Risotto Sauce

½ cup minced onion
3 tablespoons curry powder
2–3 tablespoons vinegar
¼ cup soy sauce
1½ cups thick mayonnaise

This is another cold buffet sauce for chicken and sea food risottos.

Simmer the onion and curry powder in the vinegar and soy sauce for 3 or 4 minutes. Cool and when cold mix carefully into the mayonnaise. Combine with rice (cooked a few hours previously and thoroughly drained – overnight in fridge is practical) and chicken, shrimp, petit pois, pimento, what you wish. Finally correct seasoning and serve.

Half and Half Dressing

1 cup mayonnaise, lightly seasoned
1 cup French dressing
1 clove garlic, minced
1 teaspoon anchovies, mashed
½ cup Parmesan cheese, grated

Combine all ingredients and serve on tossed salads.

1000 Island Dressing

1 cup mayonnaise, lightly seasoned
¼ cup chili sauce
2 tablespoons sweet relish
2 tablespoons ripe olives, chopped
1 pimento, minced
juice of ½ lemon
dash Worcestershire Sauce
dash Tabasco Sauce

Combine and blend all ingredients.

Green Goddess Dressing

1 cup mayonnaise
1 clove garlic, minced
3 anchovy fillets, minced
¼ cup finely minced chives
or green onions
¼ cup minced parsley
1 tablespoon lemon juice
1 tablespoon tarragon vinegar
½ teaspoon salt
ground black pepper
½ cup cultured sour cream

Combine and blend all ingredients.

Quick Sauce Verte

1 cup mayonnaise
½ small garlic clove, pressed
1 tablespoon fresh dill
1 tablespoon chopped chives
or green onion tops
½–1 teaspoon prepared mustard
a little cooked spinach juice

Mix all the ingredients together.

Green Pea Mayonnaise

Cook, drain and sieve 100 g/4 oz fresh green shelled peas. When cold add this purée to Mayonnaise. Good with cold cutlets. Serve with a border made from whole cold, cooked peas mixed with a very little plain Mayonnaise. Hand Green Pea Mayonnaise separately.

Mayonnaise Sauce à la Farquhar

Take the yolks of three fresh eggs, free from the whites. Put them in a basin with a pinch of pepper, salt and mustard. Work this gently with a wooden spoon; then add drop by drop 1 pint or more of the very best olive oil. Stir this well; then add drop by drop a very small quantity of tarragon vinegar. The sauce should be smooth and very thick. Take two or more tablespoons of the above, according to the quantity of sauce required, and add to it about half a gill or more of whipped double cream. Mix lightly, and add to it four or more small onions, cut into halves. Allow them to remain in the sauce for about an hour to flavour it; then remove the onions. Mix the sauce again very lightly, and sprinkle with a pinch of very finely chopped parsley and chervil. This sauce is excellent served with grilled, or spatchcock chicken or game, or mutton cutlets breadcrumbed and served on a grid, also with cold leg of lamb cutlets.

'Hot' Sauce for Shrimp Cocktails

2 cups mayonnaise
2 tablespoons chili sauce
2 tablespoons anchovy paste
salt, red pepper and tabasco to taste
2 teaspoons onion juice
2 tablespoons very finely chopped celery

Mix all ingredients, except celery. Stir until well blended. Season. Chill. Add celery just before serving.

Shrimp or Prawn Cocktail Sauce

1 tablespoon paprika, or less
2 tablespoons tarragon vinegar
1 cup mayonnaise
½ cup double cream, whipped
2 tablespoons anchovy paste
2 tablespoons single cream

Dissolve the paprika in the vinegar and then mix with the other ingredients. Chill in fridge until ready to serve.

A Good Sauce for Prawn Cocktails (or shrimp or lobster)

2 egg yolks
250 ml/½ pint arrachide or refined olive oil
juice of 1 large lemon
2 tablespoons tomato paste
125 ml/¼ pint double cream, whipped
salt and pepper
1 tablespoon Worcestershire Sauce
Tabasco

Make a firm mayonnaise with the egg yolks and oil, loosen it with the lemon juice and then add the tomato paste and whipped cream. Season well, add Worcestershire Sauce and Tabasco to taste.

Into this sauce fold the picked prawns, 2 chopped hard-boiled eggs and 2 skinned, seeded, drained and chopped tomatoes. Pile mixture into long sundae glasses which you have quarter filled with shredded lettuce. Dust with pepper, garnish with a curl of lemon rind on the rim of the glass.

Sauce for Crab Cocktails or Salads

2 cups vinegar
2 tablespoons tarragon
2 cups mayonnaise
4 tablespoons horseradish, grated
4 tablespoons mustard
6 tablespoons brown sugar
1 tablespoon Worcestershire Sauce
1 scant teaspoon garlic salt

Boil vinegar with tarragon leaves until reduced to 2 tablespoons of liquid. Meanwhile combine the other ingredients. Strain reduced vinegar into mixture and chill overnight.

Cucumber Mayonnaise

To 1 cup Mayonnaise (or ½ cup Mayonnaise, ½ cup sour cream) add 3 tablespoons lemon juice, a dash of Tabasco Sauce, ¼ teaspoon curry powder (optional) and mix well together. Combine ½ cup peeled, deseeded, chopped and drained cucumber with mayonnaise mixture. Chill before serving. Good with cold salmon or trout.

Gloucester Sauce

A Mayonnaise Sauce to which sour cream is added; blend in a little Escoffier Sauce and some chopped fennel.

Cambridge Sauce

Pound together 6 hard-boiled eggs; add 4–6 anchovy fillets, 2 tablespoons capers, chervil, tarragon and chives. Lastly add 2 tablespoons mustard and mix into 250 ml/½ pint of Mayonnaise. Season with cayenne pepper. Sieve and whisk again until quite smooth. Finish with 1 teaspoon chopped parsley.

President Carter's Sauce

Purée 4 or 5 bananas with about 75 g/3 oz peanut butter. Pass through a fine sieve and mix with Mayonnaise.

Not as strange as it sounds. In fact, rather a new and interesting flavour.

Joan's Salad Dressing
1 tablespoon dry mustard
1 tablespoon sugar
1 teaspoon salt
1 teaspoon flour
1 egg
1 teacup good quality vinegar
1 teacup milk

Mix the dry ingredients with the egg to a smooth paste. Add the vinegar and milk and cook in a double boiler (or in a basin over a saucepan of boiling water) until it thickens. Stir while it cools and pour into a screw-top jar. It will keep quite well in a cool larder or fridge.

Boiled Dressing for Salads
1 teaspoon each flour, dry mustard, salt and sugar
10 tablespoons water
5 tablespoons malt vinegar
5 tablespoons tarragon vinegar
1 tablespoon salad oil
1 egg

Mix the dry ingredients with a little of the water to a smooth paste. Bring the rest of the water along with the vinegars to boiling point and thicken with the paste. Boil together for 5 minutes. Add the salad oil and let it cool a little, then stir in the beaten egg and reheat but do not allow to boil.

A Butler's Salad Dressing

Pound well the yolks of 2 hard-boiled eggs. Mix in slowly, and by degrees, 1 saltspoon each of sugar, salt, mustard and pepper, then the yolks of 2 raw eggs, along with 1 teaspoon anchovy essence, 1 teacup salad oil, 1 tablespoon chili vinegar and 3 tablespoons common vinegar. This should turn out like thick cream.

Caldy Manor Salad Sauce
1 mashed hard-boiled egg
1 teaspoon Harvey's Sauce
or mushroom ketchup
1 teaspoon olive oil
2 tablespoons thick cream
little mustard, pepper and salt

Beat all ingredients together and chill.

Sauce for Potato Salad

4–6 anchovy fillets
125 ml/¼ pint olive oil
1 tablespoon chopped parsley
juice of ½ lemon

Soak the anchovy fillets in milk for an hour. Drain. Pound them in a mortar and add the olive oil. When smooth add lemon juice to taste, and chopped parsley. (The whole process can be done most easily by whizzing the anchovy fillets and the olive oil in the liquidizer, then adding the lemon juice and chopped parsley.) Prepare immediately before pouring over the still-warm potatoes, and then chill.

Yellow Salad Dressing from Tennessee

Thicken ½ cup of white vinegar in a double boiler with yolks of 6 eggs, which you have beaten up, add a pinch of salt and paprika.

Chill and beat into this ½ cup of olive oil and ½ cup of cream, whipped solid.

THE TRADITIONAL ENGLISH AND AMERICAN SAUCES

3 BOTTLED SAUCES FOR THE STORE CUPBOARD

Lord Sandys' Sauce
The Original Harvey's, but more correctly, *Mrs Comber's Sauce*
The Quorn Hunt's Recipe for Harvey's Sauce
American Apple Chutney
American Cranberry Sauce
Chutney de la Guardia
Delhi Sauce
Government Sauce
Grape Catsup from Tennessee
Mango Chutney
Mustard Relish
New England Chili Sauce
Tomato Catsup from Tennessee

Lord Sandys' Sauce,
the original recipe for
Worcestershire Sauce

This has been known for over 100 years as Worcestershire Sauce. Its manufacture is no longer confined to one firm, but Lea and Perrin are the original makers. The story is that it was given to the founder of the firm as an unconsidered trifle by the second Baron Sandys of Worcester, who picked it up when he was in India. Its possibilities were not realised until 1838 when its owners began to make it on a large scale and the business developed so tremendously that Mr Lea, the head of the firm, died a millionaire.

25 g/1 oz capsicum
225 g/8 oz shallots
4 drachms cinnamon
155 g/6 oz garlic
50 g/2 oz cloves
50 g/2 oz nutmeg
1 drachm cardamon
500 ml/1 pint soy sauce
1 litre/2 pints mushroom ketchup
4 litres/1 gallon brown malt vinegar

Bruise the shallots and garlic and boil for one half hour. Add the remainder of the ingredients and let them boil for another half hour in a closed saucepan. Let the whole remain covered over for a month. Strain through a fine sieve and bottle the sauce. (The spices when drained off may be boiled in a few pints of vinegar which they will flavour, and which will be most useful for making pickles when once more strained through a hair* sieve.)
* fine

The Original Harvey's,
but more correctly,
Mrs Comber's Sauce

Captain Charles Combers (born 1752), a member of the Quorn Hunt, when on his way to Leicestershire once stopped, as was his wont, to dine at The George at Bedford, then kept by a man named Harvey, where he ordered a steak, and when it was served Combers requested Harvey to let his servant bring from his buggy a quart bottle which contained an admirable sauce. Combers poured some of it onto his plate and (having) mixed it with the gravy of the steak he asked Harvey to taste it, and the host pronounced it to be a most excellent relish. 'Well, Mr Harvey,' said Combers, 'I shall leave the bottle with you to use till my return, only be careful to reserve enough for me.' One can imagine that Mr Harvey did not waste his time during the Captain's absence. Here is the recipe for which he, and not the good Mrs Combers, became unjustly famous.

The Quorn Hunt's Recipe for Harvey's Sauce

12 anchovies
1 oz cayenne pepper
6 tablespoons soy sauce
6 tablespoons walnut pickle
3 garlic bulbs
¼ oz cochineal
2 shallots
1 gallon vinegar

Chop the anchovies very small, bones and all.
Add the cayenne pepper, soy sauce and walnut liquor.
Chop, but not too small, the 3 bulbs of garlic and add them.
Add the cochineal and the shallots, chopped but not very small.
Finally add one gallon of vinegar.
Let it stand 14 days. Stir it well twice or three times every day, then pass it through a jelly bag. Repeat this till it is perfectly clear, then bottle it and tie a piece of bladder over each cork.

Mr Harvey, having made a considerable fortune from Captain Comber's mother's sauce, eventually sold the recipe for an annuity of £400 or £500 a year, which was very intelligent of him because gastronomes have since discovered that it originally came from a book called *The Compleat Servant Maid* which was published in 1677 and from which no doubt Mrs Comber learnt it! The recipes are almost identical.

American Apple Chutney

2 quarts apples, cut in small pieces
2 lb granulated sugar
2 cups seeded raisins
½ cup strong vinegar
⅓ teaspoon ground cloves
1 cup ground pecan nut meats
rind of 2 oranges, finely chopped

Boil all the ingredients together until apples and nuts are tender. Place in sterile jars and scald. Delicious with chicken or game.

American Cranberry Sauce

1 lb cranberries
3–4 large red apples, cored, but not peeled
about 6 oz liquid honey

Put cranberries and apples into an electric food mill or liquidizer. Whirl till they are a smooth purée, then add honey to taste. Do not cook.

Chutney de la Guardia

½ cup sliced mangoes
1 cup cider vinegar
¼ cup salt
1¾ cups sugar
2 garlic cloves, minced
1 cup seeded raisins
½ cup sliced pineapple
1 tablespoon dried, ground,
chili peppers
5 lb tomatoes, peeled and diced
½ cup dry currants
½ cup almonds
¼ cup minced ginger root
OR 3 tablespoons powdered ginger

Combine all the ingredients in a saucepan. Bring to a boil and cook over low heat for one hour, or until very thick. Stir frequently. Cool and pack in sterile 500 ml/1 pint jars.

Delhi Sauce

3½ kilos/7 lb ripe tomatoes, skinned
and cleaned
1 kilo/2 lb sugar
100 g/4 oz salt
1 litre/2 pints malt vinegar
1 kilo/2 lb raisins
100 g/4 oz garlic
100 g/4 oz root ginger, pounded
and ground up together
25 g/1 oz red chilis

From the days of the British Raj.

This is a most excellent sauce to make when tomatoes are cheap. It goes with curry and any highly flavoured dish. A by-product of the sauce is an excellent chutney. Boil all the ingredients together in a large saucepan, and then allow to simmer gently for at least an hour. Strain off the liquid and bottle as the sauce. The solid matter forms the chutney.

Government Sauce

3 quarts peeled and chopped
fresh tomatoes
2 quarts peeled and chopped
tart apples
10 medium onions, sliced
2 cups vinegar
2 cups sugar
2 tablespoons salt
2 tablespoons ground cloves
2 tablespoons ground cinnamon
1 teaspoon black pepper
cayenne to taste

This is the universal Tomato Ketchup at its best: it comes from Washington DC.

Cook all ingredients together in large enamelled kettle or jam pan until mixture thickens. Seal at once in small jars.

Serve with meat or baked beans.

Grape Catsup from Tennessee

Pop the pulp from 12 lb of very ripe grapes and put in one vessel; put skins in another with water to cook soft. Run pulp through sieve; mix. Add 5 lb of sugar. Add spice, cloves, cinnamon and nutmeg (tied in muslin) to taste, and 1 quart of vinegar. Boil 5 minutes.

Serve with fowl.

Mango Chutney

4 lb mangoes
¼ lb green ginger
2 tablespoons white salt
2 lb raisins
¼ lb garlic
3 lb brown sugar
2 oz yellow chilis
1 bottle vinegar

Slice firm peeled mangoes into small pieces. Cut ginger finely; mince garlic. Put all ingredients in a large jam pan. Let boil gently for 3 or 4 hours, stirring frequently. When chutney is thick enough to coat a spoon, remove from fire and pour into sterilized jars. Wax and cover with a lid.

Mustard Relish

2 oz mustard seed
½ oz powdered mustard
1 tablespoon sugar
2 tablespoons vinegar
1 teaspoon Worcestershire Sauce
1 teaspoon Harvey's Sauce
1 teaspoon salt
1 tablespoon olive oil
a few drops of Tabasco
or other hot sauce

Blend mustard, sugar and salt. Add vinegar and remaining ingredients. Mix thoroughly, until it is a smooth paste.

New England Chili Sauce

24 large ripe tomatoes
6 large green peppers
4 large onions
3 tablespoons salt
¾ cup sugar
3 cups vinegar
1 tablespoon cinnamon
1 tablespoon powdered cloves
a few dashes of cayenne or Tabasco
or 1 fresh *hot* pepper

Peel tomatoes. Put peppers and onions through a coarse food chopper. Add other ingredients and bring slowly to a boil. Reduce heat and simmer for about 4 hours or until very thick. Bottle when cold. Good with roast loin of pork or fish. Excellent for baked beans.

Tomato Catsup from Tennessee

Cook two pecks of ripe tomatoes, one large onion, one garlic clove, 2 hot red pepper pods, and 4 sweet green peppers until soft. Rub through a sieve to remove seed and skin (or emulsify in blender). Cook again. When mixture begins to thicken, add salt to taste (about one cup) and one cup of sugar.

Tie in a muslin bag 3 sticks of cinnamon, 1 oz mace, 2 tablespoons each of white mustard and celery seed, 2 teaspoons each of white pepper and grated horseradish, cloves and spice.

Drop into catsup and simmer until quite thick. Add one quart of fine vinegar and boil five minutes. [Remove herbs.] Put up in bottles. Seal tight while hot.

THE
TOMATO SAUCES

THE TOMATO SAUCES

1 TOMATO PUREE SAUCES

**FRENCH TOMATO PUREE SAUCE, also called
  PROVENÇALE or FONDUE DE TOMATE
SAUCE PORTUGUAISE
FRENCH TOMATO SAUCE DERIVATIVES:**
  Sauce Américaine
  Sauce Alphonse XIII
ITALIAN SUGO DI POMODORO *the classic recipe*
**QUICK EVERYDAY TOMATO SAUCE
CREOLE SAUCE I and II
CREOLE SAUCE FOR EGGS
HOT CREOLE SAUCE FOR FISH
MEXICAN TOMATO SAUCE
SALSA FRIA HOT SAUCE
UNCOOKED TOMATO SAUCE**

Tomato sauces belong to the Mediterranean. One form or another of *sugo di pomodoro* exists all round the Mediterranean littoral and has become a central part of the cuisine. In fact one sometimes wonders how its inhabitants coped before the introduction of the tomato plant from the Americas in the 15th century by Spanish and Portuguese merchants and venturers. That this event was much appreciated is evident by the names given to it: *Pomo d'oro* (golden apple) in Italy, *Paradis* (Paradise) in Dalmatia, etc. Europeans soon adapted it to a multitude of uses, creating sauces usually a lot milder and more subtle than those found in its country of origin where Créole and Mexican tomato sauces are almost always very hot and spicy.

I have also included in this section other Italian and Mediterranean sauces to eat with pasta or fish, with and without a tomato base. They may not be strictly classical, but seem to fit in here best. Tomato sauce should never be thickened by flour, but by long, slow cooking. The exceptions to this rule are some of the Créole tomato sauces in which a small amount of browned or baked flour is used to darken and thicken the sauce. Unless the tomatoes are very ripe and sun-sweetened, a hefty pinch of sugar is always necessary to correct their acidity.

FRENCH TOMATO PUREE SAUCE, *also called* **PROVENÇALE** *or* **FONDUE DE TOMATE**

Peel, de-pip, drain and chop 12 fine large tomatoes. Put them in a heavy pan in which you have heated 250–375 ml/$\frac{1}{2}$–$\frac{3}{4}$ pint of oil to smoking point. Season well with salt, pepper and a good pinch of fine sugar. Add a clove of garlic, crushed, and a teaspoon of chopped parsley. Cover the pan and let the tomato melt by very gently simmering on a low heat for about 30 minutes.

SAUCE PORTUGUAISE

Chop a large onion finely. Sauté it in oil in a heavy pan on a fierce heat. When the onion is translucent add 875 g/1$\frac{3}{4}$ lb peeled, de-pipped, drained and chopped tomatoes, a small clove of garlic (crushed), pepper, salt and a little sugar. Simmer the sauce gently for about 30 minutes over a low heat, then add a large spoonful of tomato concentrate, enough of the tinned tomato juice to make the quantity required, 4–6 tablespoons melted meat glaze and 1 tablespoon finely chopped parsley.

FRENCH TOMATO SAUCE DERIVATIVES

Sauce Américaine

A tomato purée sauce blended with Lobster Butter (p. 64) and finished with a little chopped chervil and tarragon. Serve with boiled white fish or lobster.

Sauce Alphonse XIII

A tomato purée sauce garnished with a julienne of fried aubergine (egg plant) and pimento. Serve with grilled lemon sole.

ITALIAN SUGO DI POMODORO *the classic recipe*

4 rounded tablespoons minced prosciutto fat (this raw Italian ham can be bought at most delicatessens) or minced smoked bacon fat
2 tablespoons best olive oil
1 tablespoon butter
3 large white onions, coarsely chopped
4 large fresh basil leaves, minced or 1 tablespoon dried sweet basil
2 tablespoons dry white wine or vermouth
12 large ripe plum tomatoes, peeled and diced
a large pinch of sugar
freshly milled black pepper
$\frac{1}{2}$ teaspoon salt

Sauté the finely minced fat in the oil and butter until it is crisp but not too brown. Add onions, herbs and wine. Simmer for 5–6 minutes. Add the tomatoes and sugar and stir together with a wooden spoon. Simmer together for half an hour, stirring frequently. Season well and correct the seasoning. Raise the heat and cook off any excess water from the tomatoes.

OPTIONAL: If you want a rich sauce you can now add 375 ml/$\frac{3}{4}$ pint of chicken or veal broth and $\frac{1}{2}$ tablespoon tomato paste, but if you like your *sugo* light, this is not necessary (and it will need another 1–2 hours cooking). This recipe should make about 2$\frac{1}{2}$ litres/3 pints of *sugo*, but as it deep-freezes well, it is practical to make more than you need at a time and freeze the rest.

QUICK EVERYDAY TOMATO SUGO

about 1 kilo/2 lb canned tomatoes
4 tablespoons olive or salad oil
1–1½ large onions, finely chopped
1 clove garlic, crushed
1 can (155 g/6 oz) tomato paste
375 ml/¾ pint chicken or veal stock
or water with a chicken cube added
2 sprigs parsley
1 teaspoon salt
3 teaspoons sugar
1 teaspoon dried oregano leaves
½ teaspoon dried basil leaves
¼ teaspoon white pepper

Purée tomatoes in liquidizer. In hot oil in a large skillet simmer onion and garlic until just beginning to colour (about 5 minutes). Add tomato paste, stock, parsley, salt, sugar, oregano, basil and pepper. Mix well and bring to boiling point. Reduce heat and simmer, covered, for 1 hour, stirring occasionally.

CREOLE TOMATO SAUCE I

1 litre/2 pints canned tomatoes
2 tablespoons minced onion
2 tablespoons sweet green pepper,
chopped
1 teaspoon salt
1 teaspoon sugar
8 cloves
3 bay leaves
1 teaspoon thyme
pinch of mixed spice

Cook all ingredients until soft then put through a sieve, pressing hard so as to get all the pulp. Either continue simmering until thick, or add 1 tablespoon flour lightly browned in the oven and rubbed into 1 tablespoon butter. Finally add a dash of cayenne. Cook until thick and all the floury taste has gone.

CREOLE TOMATO SAUCE II

2 cups onion, diced
2 cups celery, diced
4 cloves garlic
2 cups green peppers, chopped
1½ kilos/3 lb canned tomatoes,
crushed or put through mouli
1 cup water (or tomato juice)
2 bay leaves
¼ teaspoon thyme
4 tablespoons chopped parsley
⅛ teaspoon red chili powder
salt and pepper to taste

Sauté onion, celery, garlic and pepper in olive oil. Add tomatoes, water and all other ingredients and simmer about 1–2 hours, covered. The vegetables should all be browned a little when you sauté them; Créole sauces are darker than Italian tomato sauce, and hotter.

CREOLE SAUCE FOR EGGS

2 onions, chopped
a small clove garlic, very finely
minced
1 tablespoon breadcrumbs
1 tablespoon butter
6 ripe tomatoes, chopped
cayenne, salt and pepper to taste
2 tablespoons ham, minced

Sauté onions, garlic and breadcrumbs in butter until brown. Add the tomatoes and seasoning. Blend well and let simmer for at least 30 minutes. Add the ham just before spooning into an omelet or pouring over poached or scrambled eggs.

HOT CREOLE SAUCE FOR FISH

1 green pepper, blistered and
chopped
1 onion, chopped
1 clove garlic, crushed
1 cup celery, chopped
2½ tablespoons butter
2 tablespoons flour browned
in the oven
6–8 large tomatoes
1 cup stock
2 tablespoons parsley, ½ bay leaf,
½ teaspoon thyme
1 teaspoon salt
1 teaspoon sugar
dash of Tabasco and cayenne

Blister the pepper by rolling it round a hot electric plate. This will bring out its flavour. Sauté the vegetables in the butter till translucent. Add browned flour, stir well and simmer till smooth and the floury taste has disappeared. Add all other ingredients except the Tabasco and cayenne and simmer till sauce is thick. Sieve and finish with Tabasco and cayenne to taste.

MEXICAN TOMATO SAUCE

¾ cup drained, canned tomatoes
or about 3 large fresh tomatoes,
skinned, quartered, peeled
and de-seeded
6 tablespoons chili sauce
2 teaspoons prepared mustard
3 tablespoons grated or prepared
horseradish
¾ teaspoon salt
¼ teaspoon pepper
few grains cayenne
¾ teaspoon curry powder
6 tablespoons vinegar
1 teaspoon onion juice
1 clove garlic, crushed
1 teaspoon dried herbs
or 1 tablespoon fresh herbs

Simmer all ingredients except herbs in a saucepan until fairly thick. Strain the mixture and add the herbs.

SALSA FRIA

3 large tomatoes
4 tablespoons wine vinegar
1 green pepper, minced
1 teaspoon fresh cilantro
(coriander), chopped (optional)
2 onions, minced
3 cloves garlic, minced
½ teaspoon oregano
3 small HOT peppers, minced
1 teaspoon Tabasco sauce

Salsa Fria or Hot Sauce appears on almost every table in Mexico. It is delicious with all grilled foods or on crisp fried tortillas.

If fresh tomatoes are used, place directly over a high gas flame till skin chars and blisters. Peel off skin. Cut tomatoes in halves, remove stem ends, and with your hands, squeeze out juice and seeds. Do the same with the peppers.

If tinned tomatoes are used, drain them well, and squeeze out excess liquid and seeds.

Chop tomatoes coarsely. Add all remaining ingredients. Put into a clean quart jar and cover tightly. Store in refrigerator. Salsa Fria keeps for a month or so.

To make up Guacamole, which is almost the national dish of Mexico, chop 1 or 2 ripe avocados coarsely, season with salt and stir in 2 or 3 tablespoons Salsa Fria.

UNCOOKED TOMATO SAUCE

3–4 large tomatoes
1 small onion
2 tablespoons olive oil
2 teaspoons vinegar
2 tablespoons made mustard
1 tablespoon chopped parsley
2 egg yolks

Pour boiling water over the tomatoes, skin, take out the seeds, drain and chop. Mix together with the chopped onion, the olive oil, a very little vinegar, and made mustard. Force through a sieve, season with salt and pepper and add the parsley and the egg yolks. Allow the sauce to stand for at least half an hour before serving with cold meat, when it will have thickened.

THE TOMATO SAUCES

2 ITALIAN AND MEDITERRANEAN SAUCES FOR PASTA AND RICE

RAGU or SALSA BOLOGNESE – The classic recipe
RHODA'S BOLOGNESE
A QUICKER RAGU BOLOGNESE
SUGO DI CARNE   ITALIAN MEAT SAUCE
MRS STANLEY'S SAUCE HELENE
SUGO WITH MUSHROOMS
MARINARA SAUCE
SALSA ALLA MERETRICE   HARLOT'S SAUCE
SALSA VERDE   GREEN SAUCE FOR SPAGHETTI
PESTO SAUCE
PESTO ALLA GENOVESE
SALSA ALLE VONGOLE   CLAM SAUCE
SALSA DI NOCI   WALNUT SAUCE
SALSA DI NOCI AL PROSCIUTTO
SALSA DI FEGATINI   CHICKEN LIVER SAUCE
SALSA DI TONNO   TUNNY FISH SAUCE
*SALSA DI LINGUA E PROSCIUTTO   HAM AND
    TONGUE SAUCE*
SALSA DI PROSCIUTTO
PROSCIUTTO AND CREAM SAUCE
*SALSA DI GAMBERI   PRAWN SAUCE WITH PINE
    NUTS*

RAGU
or SALSA BOLOGNESE
The classic recipe

This sauce, which is the classic tomato and meat sauce which accompanies Spaghetti Bolognese, is a very distant relation to what one is sometimes outrageously served in Italian restaurants under that name. I doubt if they would recognise each other if they met. As it is a sauce with a great many ingredients I have put an * beside those which may not be available to you and without which a passable Bolognese can still be made, but try to keep to the real thing. It is worth the extra effort and this sauce is very easily made once the ingredients are lined up.

3 tablespoons chopped bacon
3 tablespoons butter
4 tablespoons chopped prosciutto fat
(ordinary smoked bacon can be substituted)
2 small carrots, chopped
2 small white onions, chopped
2 celery stalks, chopped
a sprig of fresh basil,
or dried basil and a sprig of fresh parsley including stalk
225 g/8 oz beef mince, as lean as possible
100 g/4 oz chopped veal (increase quantity of chopped pork if veal not available)
100 g/4 oz chopped lean pork
250 ml/½ pint chicken broth
250 ml/½ pint dry white wine
or 1 wineglass dry vermouth or dry sherry
3 large ripe tomatoes, peeled and diced
½ tablespoon tomato paste
a pinch of sugar
1 teaspoon salt
a generous amount of milled black pepper
1 clove
225 g/8 oz fresh mushrooms,*
finely sliced
3 raw chicken livers,* finely chopped
500 ml/1 pint hot water
125 ml/¼ pint double cream

Cook the bacon in the butter till soft; add the prosciutto and simmer for 2 minutes. Add vegetables and cook until they are soft. Stir in the three meats and simmer till they are half cooked, and the beef still pink. Stir in the broth and wine, raise the heat slightly and cook until the sauce thickens, stirring constantly. Blend in the tomatoes, tomato paste and sugar. Add seasoning and spices. Stir well, taste and correct seasoning. Add the water, stir and cover the pan; simmer over a low heat for 1 hour, raising the lid and stirring frequently. Now blend in the mushrooms and chicken livers. Raise the heat and cook uncovered for 5 minutes. Just before using the sauce, blend in the double cream, stirring the mixture for the last time. It makes about 1½ litres/ 2½ pints.

NOTE: ½ kilo/1 lb of pasta will feed six people if it is to be a first course, or if they are dainty eaters. It will feed four people if they are Italian, or hungry. To every ½ kilo/1 lb of spaghetti serve 375 ml/¾ pint of Bolognese Sauce, and 100 g/4 oz of grated Parmesan cheese.

RHODA'S
BOLOGNESE

2 large onions, finely chopped
1 tablespoon oil
1 tablespoon butter
3 tablespoons bacon and chopped meats, uncooked or cooked:
beef, pork or veal
2 cloves of garlic, minced
1 tablespoon Italian tomato paste
225 g/8 oz tin plum tomatoes
pepper, salt, bay leaf, pinch of sugar

Fry the onions in butter and oil mixture until translucent. Add the other ingredients, bacon and meat first, and simmer for 45 minutes– 1 hour till the juices are more or less absorbed and the sauce fairly thick.

A QUICKER RAGU BOLOGNESE BOLOGNESE MEAT SAUCE

12 g/½ oz butter
50 g/2 oz unsmoked bacon, finely chopped
75 g/3 oz onion, finely chopped
50 g/2 oz carrot, finely chopped
1 stick celery, finely chopped
2 tablespoons double cream or 25 g/1 oz butter
225 g/8 oz neck beef, finely minced
6 tablespoons white wine, or 1 wineglass dry sherry
250 ml/½ pint stock or water
1 level tablespoon tomato paste
salt and pepper
grated nutmeg

Melt the butter in a saucepan and over gentle heat fry the bacon, onion, carrot and celery until tender and golden, about 10 minutes. Add the meat and stir until brown, then add the wine and allow to bubble briskly for a minute or two. Stir in the stock, tomato paste, and salt, pepper and grated nutmeg to taste. Bring to the boil, cover the pan and simmer gently for at least 45 minutes, stirring occasionally. Remove from the heat, check seasoning and stir in the cream or butter.

NOTE: Serve with any type of hot, freshly cooked pasta, which in Bologna would traditionally be *tagliatelle*. Mix a little of the sauce with the pasta and serve the rest on top. Pass grated Parmesan separately.

SUGO DI CARNE ITALIAN MEAT SAUCE

25 g/1 oz lard or butter
50 g/2 oz onion, finely chopped
1 clove garlic, crushed (optional)
225 g/8 oz fresh minced beef*
1 level tablespoon tomato paste
salt, pepper and sugar to taste
4 leaves fresh basil or ¼ teaspoon of dried
225 g/8 oz tin peeled tomatoes
a little water (if necessary)

Melt the lard or butter in a saucepan and fry the onion and garlic gently until golden. Add the minced beef, and stir and cook for several minutes. Stir in the tomato paste, the salt, pepper and sugar to taste and the fresh or dried basil, and finally the tinned tomatoes and their juice. Cover the pan and simmer very gently for at least 30 minutes, if possible longer, stirring from time to time and adding a little stock or water if the sauce becomes too thick. Serve with pasta, rice or potato gnocchi.

* If a more hearty sauce is required the meat, which should be steak, can be cut into pencil thick strips and increased slightly in quantity.

MRS STANLEY'S SAUCE HELENE

1 onion
1 clove garlic
3 large tomatoes
155 g/6 oz pork sausage meat
75 g/3 oz chicken or veal (raw)
1 gill white wine
bay leaf and thyme
75 g/3 oz cream cheese

Cook the chopped onion and garlic in butter, add the peeled and seeded tomatoes, sausage meat and minced raw chicken or veal. Cook for a few minutes, pour on the white wine, add herbs and seasoning, and allow to simmer on a low heat for 30 minutes. Remove the bay leaf and thyme and stir in the cream cheese. A few stoned, chopped, black olives can be added.

SUGO WITH MUSHROOMS

2 cloves garlic
2 tablespoons olive or salad oil
225 g/8 oz fresh mushrooms, sliced
225 g/8 oz minced pork
225 g/8 oz minced veal
1 tin (1 kilo/2 lb) tomatoes
75 g/3 oz tomato paste
2 teaspoons sugar
3 teaspoons salt
¼ teaspoon pepper

Sauté garlic in hot oil in a heavy skillet until just golden, then remove. Add mushrooms, pork and veal to oil, and cook, stirring occasionally for 10 minutes. Add tomatoes, tomato paste, sugar, salt and pepper. Bring to boiling then reduce heat and simmer, covered, and stirring occasionally, for 1 hour.

MARINARA SAUCE

6 tablespoons olive oil
50 g/2 oz butter
3 large cloves of garlic, crushed
16 fresh parsley sprigs, leaves only
½ teaspoon salt
¼ teaspoon freshly ground pepper
1 kg 225 g/2½ lb peeled tomatoes
1 tablespoon dried oregano
8 anchovy fillets, chopped
2 heaped tablespoons tomato paste
100 g/4 oz tinned minced clams
(optional)

Combine olive oil and butter in a saucepan and heat, chop garlic and parsley together and add to the pan. Cook slowly for 5 minutes, then add salt and pepper. Drain the tomatoes and chop the solid parts. Add the chopped tomatoes and oregano to the sauce and cook slowly for 30 minutes. Add anchovies, clams if used, and tomato paste, stir well, and remove from the heat. At the end of cooking taste for salt and add some if necessary, but remember, the anchovies will make the sauce salty. Serve over macaroni, spaghetti, hard-boiled or scrambled eggs.

SALSA ALLA MERETRICE HARLOT'S SAUCE

2 cloves garlic, minced
2 tablespoons olive oil
8 anchovies, cut into pieces
1 kg 75 g/2 lb 3 oz can tomatoes
8 stuffed green olives, sliced
8 pitted black olives, sliced
1 teaspoon capers
1 teaspoon dried basil
¼ teaspoon dried red pepper

Sauté garlic in oil until soft; add the anchovies. When anchovies have broken apart, add the tomatoes, simmer for 10 minutes. Blend in olives, capers, basil and red pepper. Simmer in uncovered pan for 10 minutes or until sauce has thickened. Serve on vermicelli.

SALSA VERDE GREEN SAUCE FOR SPAGHETTI

375 g/12 oz unsalted butter
1 tablespoon olive oil
½ clove garlic, minced
2 small white onions, minced
a large bunch of fresh parsley,
finely chopped

Combine butter and oil in pan over low heat. When butter is melted, stir in garlic and onions and sauté until onions are soft. Stir in parsley quickly. It should come to about 50 g/2 oz or 2 cupfuls. Pour over cooked, drained pasta, toss until well mixed and serve immediately. Enough for ¾ kilo/1½ lb pasta to serve 8 people as a first course. Pass grated Parmesan separately.

PESTO SAUCE

50 g/2 oz Parmesan and/or Sardo
cheese, grated
4 tablespoons parsley, finely
chopped
1 clove garlic, crushed
1–2 teaspoons dried basil leaves
½ teaspoon dried marjoram leaves
4–6 tablespoons olive or salad oil
¼ cup walnuts or pine nuts,
blanched and finely chopped

With wooden spoon, cream Parmesan, parsley, garlic, basil and marjoram until well blended. Gradually add oil, beating constantly (it can be made in a blender or 'Magimix'). Add nuts, mix well. Toss with hot spaghetti to coat well.

PESTO ALLA GENOVESE

50 g/2 oz fresh basil*
2 cloves garlic, peeled
¼ teaspoon salt
1 tablespoon Parmesan cheese, grated
1 tablespoon Sardo cheese, grated
3–4 tablespoons olive oil
*Fresh basil is essential for this traditional Genovese sauce.

Weigh the basil leaves after stipping from the stalks, chop roughly then pound in a mortar with the garlic and salt until reduced to a thick paste. Stir in the cheeses. Add the oil, little by little, stirring all the time until the sauce has the consistency of a purée. Use as required or spoon into a jar, cover with a thin layer of oil and keep in the refrigerator for up to a week. In Genoa pesto is served on freshly cooked pasta, particularly with spaghetti or *trenette*, a long thin local pasta. A little pesto is also stirred into the traditional Genovese minestrone.

NOTE: Pesto in tins is available from Italian food stores, but so is Sardo cheese which enables you to make the real thing.

SALSA ALLE VONGOLE CLAM SAUCE

200 g/7½ oz minced clams
4 tablespoons salad or olive oil
50 g/2 oz butter
2–3 cloves garlic, crushed
2 tablespoons parsley, chopped
½ teaspoon dried oregano
1½ teaspoons salt
freshly ground black pepper

Drain clams reserving 170 ml/6 fl oz liquid. In a skillet, slowly heat oil and butter. Add garlic, crush it with back of a spoon and sauté it until golden. Remove from heat. Discard garlic. Stir in clam liquid, then oregano, parsley, salt and pepper. Bring to boiling point. Reduce heat and simmer uncovered for 10 minutes. Add clams. Simmer for 3 minutes. This should be enough for 225–300 g/10 oz spaghetti. Cook the spaghetti *al dente*, butter it and toss it well in half the sauce. Serve the remainder spooned on top of individual servings.

SALSA DI NOCI WALNUT SAUCE

50 g/2 oz shelled walnuts
about 125 ml/¼ pint single cream
salt and pepper
leaves from 2 sprigs of marjoram, very finely chopped

Coarsely chop or grind the walnuts then pound to paste in a mortar. Stir in the cream little by little to form a sauce the consistency of thick cream. Season to taste with salt and pepper and add the marjoram leaves. Alternatively put all the ingredients into an electric blender at medium speed for about 2 minutes. Serve the sauce on freshly cooked ribbon pasta (such as *taglierini* or *tagliatelle*) previously dressed with butter.

NOTE: 1) About 25 g/1 oz parsley may be used instead of marjoram and the resulting sauce will then be prettily speckled with green.
2) The pink part of prosciutto can also be chopped very finely and added to the sauce, when it is called *Salsa di Noci al Prosciutto*.

SALSA DI FEGATINI CHICKEN LIVER SAUCE

40 g/1½ oz butter
50 g/2 oz unsmoked streaky bacon, chopped
50 g/2 oz onion, finely chopped
50 g/2 oz mushroom, finely chopped
225 g/8 oz chicken livers
1 level tablespoon flour
2 tablespoons Marsala or sweet sherry
1 level tablespoon tomato paste
250 ml/½ pint chicken stock
salt and pepper to taste

Put 25 g/1 oz butter and the bacon, onion and mushrooms into a saucepan and cook over gentle heat for 10 minutes. Chop livers finely, having first discarded any hard tissues or discoloured parts. Add livers and flour to mixture, increase the heat and stir for 1–2 minutes only, until the livers change colour. Add the wine and bubble briskly until almost evaporated, add tomato paste, then stock. Add seasoning, cover, and simmer gently for about 30 minutes. Stir in remaining butter and serve with green noodles, potato gnocchi or boiled rice.

SALSA DI TONNO TUNNY FISH SAUCE

40 g/1½ oz butter
1 155 g/6 oz tin tunny fish
½ tablespoon parsley, chopped
165 ml/⅓ pint chicken or fish stock
and 2 level tablespoons tomato paste
or 165 ml/⅓ pint tomato juice
ground black pepper
capers (optional)

Melt the butter in a small saucepan, add the tunny fish and parsley and stir until the fish is well broken up. Cook gently for a few minutes, stirring occasionally. Add the stock and tomato paste and a little ground pepper. Simmer for 5 minutes. Serve hot with pasta. A few capers are sometimes added to this sauce.

SALSA DI LINGUA E PROSCIUTTO HAM AND TONGUE SAUCE

75 g/3 oz cooked tongue
75 g/3 oz cooked ham
250 ml/½ pint Béchamel Sauce
100 g/4 oz double cream

Cut the cooked tongue and cooked ham into thin strips. Add to the Béchamel Sauce and heat gently for 5 minutes. Stir in cream at the last minute. Correct seasoning. Serve on freshly cooked ribbon pasta (such as *fettuccine*) previously dressed with butter. Be careful to keep sauce, pasta, plates, etc., very hot.

SALSA DI PROSCIUTTO

100 g/4 oz sliced prosciutto
1 tablespoon olive oil
50 g/2 oz unsalted butter

Cut the ham into 1-cm/¼-inch squares. Heat the olive oil and the butter in a saucepan, add the prosciutto and over very gentle heat cook for 4–5 minutes, stirring now and then. The ham should not brown. Pour this simple but delicious sauce over hot pasta or boiled rice, stir, and sprinkle generously with grated Parmesan cheese.

PROSCIUTTO AND CREAM SAUCE

Cut 6 thin slices of prosciutto or Parma ham into narrow julienne strips; throw them into a large warm bowl in which you have melted 2 tablespoons butter. Add 1 egg yolk and 4 tablespoons double cream, mix together well, then turn into the bowl 500 g/1 lb of carefully strained fresh green noodles that you have just cooked *al dente* in 7 litres/14 pints of fast boiling, salted water. Mix and toss and grind black pepper over, and *ecco! è pronto la colazione. . . .*

SALSA DI GAMBERI PRAWN SAUCE WITH PINE NUTS

1 small onion, chopped
1 tablespoon oil
1 tablespoon butter
1 tablespoon parsley, chopped
100 g/4 oz cooked shelled prawns
15 g/½ oz pine nuts

Melt the onion in the oil and butter. Add the parsley and the prawns. Roast the pine nuts in the oven for a few minutes, pound them in a mortar and add them to the prawns. Add 5–6 tablespoons warm water and simmer very slowly for 15 minutes. The sauce can either be sieved or served as it is with rice, eggs or fish.

100 g/¼ lb of shelled prawns is equivalent to approximately 500 ml/1 pint unshelled. Frozen prawns are not recommended. In Bari and southern Italy the prawns are fat and fresh and grilled over charcoal, which makes them particularly succulent.

5

SAUCES
FROM ALL OVER

These are more original and less traditional
sauces collected by me from many countries
and sources. They are grouped under the names
of their country of origin.

SAUCES FROM ALL OVER

1 HOT SAUCES

AUSTRIA
Caper Sauce
Dill Sauce
Hot Horseradish Sauce
Sauce for Potatoes

ENGLAND
Mrs Clissold's Creamy Parsley Sauce
Mrs Dimbleby's Brandy and Orange Sauce
Mrs Dimbleby's Cream Curry and Nut Sauce
Mrs Dimbleby's Juniper Berry Sauce
Mrs Dimbleby's Curried Mushroom Sauce
Mrs Dimbleby's Tarragon and Caper Sauce
Mrs Stanley's Sauce Landaise
Mrs Stanley's Sauce Nenette
Mrs Stanley's Parsley Sauce
Mrs Stanley's Tarragon Sauce
Truffle Sauce from Dorset

FRANCE
Alsatian Brandy and Cream Sauce
Mademoiselle de Rothschild's Sauce Aurore or Rothschild Sauce
Mrs David Bruce's Cream Sauce
Sauce Moutarde Dijonnaise
La Rouille

GERMANY
Cream Sauce for Hare or Roe Deer
Hot Potato Salad Sauce

HUNGARY
Paprika Sauce

ITALY
La Bagna Cauda

POLAND
Sos Koperkowy
Shura's Sauce Polonaise

RUSSIA
Julian Amery's Sauce for Shashlik of Salmon or Sturgeon
Smitane Sauce
Hot Sour Cream Sauce

SCOTLAND
Mrs James Young's Barbecue Sauce for basting Roast Chicken
VM's Hazelnut Sauce for Sauté of Chicken
Lady Victoria Wemyss's Tomato Sauce

SPAIN
Salsa Verde Española

SWEDEN
Dill Sauce

UNITED STATES OF AMERICA
Chicken Barbecue Sauce I
Chicken Barbecue Sauce II
Ferocious Barbecue Sauce
Richmond Barbecue Sauce for Pork or Spare Ribs
Texan Barbecue Sauce
Admiral Ralph Stevens' Sauces for Submariners: Barbecue
    Sauce
Three Sauces for Barbecued Spare Ribs of Pork:
    1) Marinade
    2) Roasting Sauce
    3) Chinese Mustard Sauce
Oriental Marinade
Jamaican Sweet Sour Pineapple Sauce
Teriyaki Sauce
Mustard Butter Sauce

AUSTRIA

Caper Sauce

Brown half a tablespoon flour in a little butter. When pale brown and smooth, combine it with 250 ml/½ pint cool stock. Bring to the boil, and stir briskly to beat out any lumps. Simmer for 10–15 minutes, then add a lavish amount of capers, some finely chopped lemon peel, and finish with a few tablespoons of sour cream, off the heat.

Dill Sauce

Dill is very popular in Austria and is extensively used as a flavouring for sauces and dishes. One tablespoon of chopped dill is added to a sauce made with stock and thickened with a little flour browned in butter, or it is sometimes added to a plain butter sauce.

Hot Horseradish Sauce

Put a few tablespoons of stock in a small saucepan, bring to the boil, and add about 1 tablespoon of white bread without the crust broken into small pieces, and mix well. A tablespoon of finely grated horseradish is then stirred in, with 3 or 4 tablespoons of sour cream and a good pinch of saffron. Simmer for a few minutes and it is ready for use. When served with fish, fish stock is used instead of meat stock.

Cold horseradish sauce is also prepared with grated horseradish, grated apples, cream and lemon juice.

Sauce for Potatoes

butter
1 tablespoon finely chopped onion
flour
125 ml/¼ pint stock
1 or 2 tablespoon vinegar
the peel of 1 large lemon, cut in 3 or 4 large strips
1 bay leaf
salt and pepper
a few freshly boiled potatoes

Melt some butter in a saucepan and fry the chopped onion till it begins to brown. Sprinkle with a little flour, and when this browns add the hot stock gradually, and finally the vinegar, lemon peel, bayleaf and a seasoning of salt and pepper. Simmer for half an hour. Add the hot boiled potatoes, cut into small cubes, and simmer for 5 minutes. Remove the bay leaf and lemon peel, and serve.

ENGLAND

Mrs Clissold's Creamy Parsley Sauce

2 large handfuls of parsley, chopped
375 ml/¾ pint cream

Put the parsley in a saucepan, season it, cover it with cream and cook it very slowly by the side of the stove for 2 hours. Strain and serve. (There must not be any parsley left in the sauce.) It can be served with white fish or a roast chicken that has been stuffed with heads of parsley.

Mrs Dimbleby's Brandy and Orange Sauce for Sautéed Kidneys

2 large onions
1 dessertspoon oregano or rosemary
juice of ½ lemon
juice of ½ orange
1–2 tablespoons brandy
4–5 fl oz single cream
2 oz butter

Melt the butter and cook the kidneys. Add to this the onions, chopped into small slices. Stir in the herbs and lemon and orange juice and simmer very gently for about 10 minutes. Then stir in the brandy and finally, just roughly, the cream.

This should be enough for 6–8 sautéed kidneys.

Mrs Dimbleby's Cream Curry and Nut Sauce for serving with Noisettes of Lamb

½ pint brown stock (from lamb bones)
1 medium-sized onion
1 tablespoon oil
½ lb salted peanuts
¼ pint sour double cream
2 dessertspoons curry powder
1 clove garlic
1 cooking apple
2 dessertspoons mango chutney

Chop the onion and fry it gently in the oil. Wash and dry the peanuts, chop them coarsely and add them to the onions with the curry powder. Stir for a minute before adding the crushed garlic and the peeled and chopped apple. Cook for a few minutes. Add the chutney and the stock and simmer the sauce for half an hour. Add the sour cream to the sauce and simmer it very gently for a few minutes.

Mrs Dimbleby's Juniper Berry Sauce for Roasted Pigeon Breasts

2 oz butter
1 small onion
1 stick celery
1 oz flour
½ pint red wine
1 dessertspoon redcurrant jelly
15 juniper berries
1 chicken stock cube
6 peppercorns
¼ pint port

Sweat the finely chopped vegetables in the butter until they are soft. Add the flour and cook gently until it is golden brown. Stir in the wine, the redcurrant jelly, the crushed juniper berries, the stock cube and the peppercorns. Bring the sauce to the boil and simmer it very slowly for 20 minutes. Add the port and cook it for 5 more minutes. Strain the sauce, pour some of it over the game and hand round the rest separately.

Mrs Dimbleby's Curried Mushroom Sauce for Roast Pheasant

½ lb mushrooms
butter, oil
1 heaped tablespoon plain flour
2 large tomatoes, skinned and chopped
2–3 teaspoons curry powder, to taste
2 teaspoons powdered cardamon
2 teaspoons ground ginger
1 teaspoon turmeric
1 tablespoon tomato purée
juice of ½ large or 1 small lemon
2 heaped tablespoons creamed coconut
2 teaspoons powdered cumin
2 teaspoons powdered coriander

Melt 1 tablespoon of olive oil and 1 oz butter in a fairly large saucepan. Remove from heat and stir in the sliced mushrooms and chopped tomatoes. Stir in the flour. Add a mixture of 1 tablespoon tomato purée mixed with 1 pint water. Add all the spices and the salt and stir in the lemon juice and the creamed coconut. This melts very quickly into the hot sauce. Bring to the boil, stirring often, then simmer for 10 minutes. Taste and add more curry or spices if necessary. If the sauce looks a bit thick add a little milk. Transfer to a serving bowl, cover and keep warm until ready to serve.

Mrs Dimbleby's Tarragon and Caper Sauce for Mackerel

1 tablespoon finely chopped tarragon
2–3 teaspoons capers, roughly chopped
1 teaspoon French mustard
1 oz butter
¾ pint milk
1 egg yolk, lightly beaten
cream or top of the milk
salt, black pepper
1 oz cornflour

Melt butter in a saucepan. Take off the heat and blend in the cornflour. Stir in the milk. Bring to the boil and simmer for 3 minutes, stirring. Add salt, pepper, tarragon, capers and mustard and simmer another minute. Take off the heat, stir in a little cream and lightly beaten egg yolk and pour into a sauce jug.

These five original and imaginative recipes come from Josceline Dimbleby's *A Taste of Dreams*.

Mrs Stanley's Sauce Landaise

1 small onion
12 g/½ oz butter
3 tomatoes
1 red pepper
½ clove garlic
bay leaf
pinch of mixed herbs
100 g/4 oz mushrooms
8 tablespoons stock
1 gherkin

Cook the chopped onion in a little butter, add the chopped, seeded and skinned tomatoes, red pepper or pimento, the hotness of which depends on your taste, garlic, bay leaf, herbs and mushrooms. Continue cooking for a few minutes, add the stock, chopped gherkin and seasoning, and simmer until slightly reduced. Remove the bay leaf. A little vinegar and sugar can be added to taste. Serve, without straining, with chicken or veal.

Mrs Stanley's Sauce Nenette

250 ml/½ pint double cream
½ tablespoon dry English mustard
2 tablespoons Italian tomato paste
2 tablespoons chopped parsley

This is a sauce for pork chops, preferably grilled.
Simmer the cream, with a little salt and pepper, until reduced by about one third (8–10 minutes). Mix the dry mustard with the tomato paste, stir into the hot cream, and let thicken for a few minutes (or even longer, if need be). If the chops have been grilled add some of the juices, otherwise a little stock. Finally simmer for 3–4 minutes, stir in the parsley, and pour into a sauceboat.

Mrs Stanley's Parsley Sauce

125 g/5 oz unsalted butter
250 ml/½ pint double cream
2 tablespoons chopped parsley
1 tablespoon chopped chives
blanched rind and juice of ½ lemon
½ crushed clove garlic

For lamb cutlets.
Melt unsalted butter in a heavy saucepan; when it bubbles pour in the double cream, and stir over a gentle heat until amalgamated. Add the mixture of parsley, chives, lemon rind and garlic. Season to taste with salt and lemon juice.

Mrs Stanley's Tarragon Sauce

25 g/1 oz flour
50 g/2 oz butter
1 teaspoon French mustard
1 egg yolk
250 ml/½ pint single cream
2 tablespoons chopped fresh tarragon
½ small onion or 1 spring onion
salt and pepper
½ lemon

For fish or chicken.
Put the flour, butter, mustard and egg yolk into a double boiler and gradually work in the cream. Add the finely chopped tarragon and raw onion, season with salt and pepper, and stir over simmering water until the sauce thickens. Finish with lemon juice.

Truffle Sauce from Dorset

125 ml/¼ pint Espagnole Sauce
125 ml/¼ pint Tomato Sauce
1 glass white wine
12 g/½ oz butter

Put chopped truffles with the wine into a small covered pan and reduce to one half. Add the Espagnole and Tomato Sauces. Boil, then remove from the fire and add the butter carefully in swirls away from the heat.

FRANCE

Alsatian Brandy and Cream Sauce

250 ml/½ pint Alsatian Riesling
125 ml/¼ pint chicken or game stock
125 ml/¼ pint cream
1 glass Fine Champagne
black pepper and salt
lemon juice
250 g/8 oz white grapes
250 g/8 oz black grapes
2–3 tablespoons unsalted butter

For Pheasant à la Vigneronne. From the Hostellerie du Cerf, Marlenheim.

Cook a young pheasant wrapped in bacon in a casserole with a carrot, an onion and 2 generous tablespoons of butter. When it is ready, lift it out and keep hot. De-glaze the casserole with the wine and the stock. Bring it to the boil and then reduce liquid over a fierce heat. When reduced by half, add the cream and boil up again for a few minutes. Heat the Fine Champagne in a soup ladle, flambé it, and pour it blazing into the sauce. Correct the seasoning and add a few drops of lemon juice, then strain into a clean saucepan. Stew the peeled and seeded grapes in butter for 3 minutes and add to the sauce with their buttery juices. Serve the pheasant cut up with sauce poured over and croûtons of bread fried in butter on which you have spread the mashed up sautéed liver of the pheasant (this too can be flambéed in brandy) combined with a little pâté de foie gras.

Mademoiselle de Rothschild's Sauce Aurore or Rothschild Sauce

2 shallots, finely chopped
1 carrot, finely chopped
1 onion, finely chopped
2 tablespoons unsalted butter
2 tablespoons oil
100 ml/4 fl oz dry white wine
1 teaspoon tomato purée
100 ml/4 fl oz water
1 very small bouquet garni
1 tablespoon cognac, flambéed
1 tablespoon double cream
1 tablespoon butter, cut into small pieces
potato starch

This is really a classic sauce (see also p. 34) but as this authentic version comes directly from a member of the family it is called after, it seems to fit in here. It is a delicious wine and cream sauce with a delicate tomato flavour.

Soften the shallots, carrot and onion in the butter and oil. Heat the white wine and tomato purée in another pan and reduce slightly. Strain the reduced liquid over the softened vegetables, add the water and the bouquet garni, bring to the boil and boil lightly for 20 minutes. Strain the liquid through a conical sieve into another saucepan, reduce slightly, then add the flambéed cognac, the cream and the pieces of butter. Whisk until all is absorbed and adjust the seasoning. Heat through and thicken the sauce with a small pinch of potato starch, diluted in 1 teaspoon of cold water.

Mrs David Bruce's Cream Sauce

3 large egg yolks
6 tablespoons cream
3 level tablespoons butter
salt
cayenne pepper
1 teaspoon lemon juice

Beat up the egg yolks; put them in a saucepan with the cream, butter, a very little salt, a few grains of cayenne pepper and a small teaspoon of lemon juice.

Stand the saucepan in a bain-marie and stir the mixture with a wooden spoon until it becomes quite thick and creamy, but do not let it boil. Then put it through a fine sieve and use. Excellent with Eggs Benedict, sweetbreads and fine quality plain boiled fish.

Sauce Moutarde Dijonnaise

325 ml/⅓ pint double cream
2 tablespoons strong Dijon or other favourite mustard
3–4 gherkins, thinly sliced
1 tablespoon shallots, finely minced
½ tablespoon wine vinegar
1 tablespoon dry sherry

For Roast Carré de Porc or Sautéed Pork Fillets.
Combine the cream, mustard, gherkins, minced shallots (previously sweated in butter), and vinegar in a bowl.

Pour off all the fat in your roasting pan. De-glaze pan with the sherry and add to the cream. Bring to the boil and boil for 2 minutes only, stirring with a wooden spoon. Correct seasoning.

Jamie's Sauce Poivre Vert au Naturel

Green Pepper Sauce for a Steak au Poivre.
Fry or grill your steak according to taste. Remove from pan and keep warm. De-glaze the buttery juices of the pan with a good tablespoon of brandy (or whisky, if preferred). Scrape the juices together and flambé briefly. Crush 1 tablespoon green peppercorns* in a bowl with 50 g/2 oz thick cream and a pinch of salt, and add to the juices in the pan. Bring to the boil, stirring vigorously. Simmer for 2–3 minutes, then pour over the steak and serve. Impressive and easy.
* Green peppercorns (*poivre vert au naturel*) can be bought in small 75 g/3 oz tins at any good grocers. They come from Madagascar and are less hot than the dried black kind we use in pepper mills. You must wash them by rinsing in a small sieve before you use them to remove preservative.

La Rouille

2–4 cloves garlic
2 small red chilli peppers
1 tablespoon crumb or bread dipped in a little fish bouillon or bouillabaisse, then pressed to extract liquid
2 tablespoons oil
200 ml/scant ½ pint fish bouillon or bouillabaisse

Put 2–4 cloves garlic, according to taste, into a mortar (preferably of marble or earthenware) with 2 small hot red peppers. Crush together finely with a wooden pestle until completely broken down and amalgamated.

Add a small piece of bread soaked in a little fish bouillon and squeezed dry of all liquid. Continue to mash with the pestle until a paste is formed. Then add in a fine thread the equivalent of 2 tablespoons of oil, working with a wooden spatula and dilute this paste with about 200 ml/scant ½ pint of fish bouillon or bouillabaisse. If the sauce is not a strong colour one may add 1 teaspoon of tomato paste diluted with 1 teaspoon olive oil.

GERMANY

Cream Sauce for Hare or Roe Deer

Boil 250 ml/½ pint good cream, add 50 g/2 oz meat glaze, salt, pepper and the juice of a lemon. Pass through a sieve or muslin and serve hot.

Hot Potato Salad Sauce

2 tablespoons oil
4 tablespoons wine vinegar
1 onion, finely chopped
salt and freshly milled black pepper
2 oz bacon, cubed and sautéed in butter

Put the oil and vinegar in a saucepan with the onion, salt, pepper and a pinch of sugar (optional). Add the bacon previously sautéed till crisp. Pour hot over thickly sliced boiled hot potatoes.

This sauce is also good with sliced green beans or whole snapper beans.

HUNGARY

Paprika Sauce

Put some bacon cut into small pieces into a saucepan; put it on the fire and fry it crisp. Chop an onion finely and fry it golden brown, add some paprika, to taste. Take 500 ml/1 pint of sour cream and let it boil until it becomes thick. Mix with the bacon and onion and a little potato flour mixed to a paste with water, if it is not thick enough. Correct seasoning. Strain and serve hot.

ITALY

La Bagna Cauda

6 cloves garlic, crushed
6 anchovy fillets, mashed
4 tablespoons olive oil
50 g/2 oz butter

A strong, garlicky hot dip from the Piedmont – only for those with very robust digestions!

Pound the garlic and anchovy fillets together and gradually stir in the oil. Put into a small pan with the butter and simmer for about 10 minutes. Keep hot in a chafing dish over a spirit stove. With the *Bagna Cauda* serve small pieces of raw vegetable: celery, sweet pepper, carrot, cabbage, for dunking. Each person takes a piece of vegetable on a fork and dips it into the sauce before eating.

POLAND

Sos Koperkowy

40 g/1½ oz flour
40 g/1½ oz butter
125–155 g/5–6 oz meat glaze
½ onion, chopped
2 tablespoons fresh cream
a handful of dill, chopped
salt and pepper
2 egg yolks

This is a dill sauce.

Brown the flour in the hot butter, add the meat glaze gradually, the onion, the cream, the dill and season with salt and pepper. Simmer for 10 minutes, stirring constantly. Cool, then add the egg yolks, previously mixed in a basin with a few tablespoons of the sauce, and heat up for a few minutes without boiling.

Shura's Sauce Polonaise

About 1 tablespoon melted butter
per person
hard-boiled egg, chopped
fresh fennel tops, and a very little
of the bulb, chopped
lemon rind, finely chopped
or grated (zest only)
capers, to taste

For pork or veal chops in breadcrumbs.
Gently heat all ingredients together till just warm and pour over crisply fried pork or veal. Garnish with lemon slices.

RUSSIA

Julian Amery's Sauce for Shashlik of Salmon or Sturgeon

1 glass white wine
2 anchovies, chopped
piece of onion
lemon peel
1 cup good broth
2–3 tablespoons cream

Put the wine into a pan with the anchovies, onion and lemon peel, and the broth. Stir in the cream and either pour the sauce over the fish or serve it in a sauceboat.

Smitane Sauce

1 tablespoon butter
75 g/3 oz onion, finely chopped
½ wine glass dry white wine
250 ml/½ pint Velouté or brown sauce
250 ml/½ pint thick or cultured sour cream or *smetana*
salt and pepper
lemon juice

Melt the butter in a saucepan and cook the onion in it until transparent. Add wine and cook until mixture is reduced by half. Add the Velouté or brown sauce, blend and simmer for 5 minutes, then add sour cream. Season to taste. Add a little lemon juice for a sharper effect.

NOTE: Velouté is used for white meats, a brown sauce for game and other meats.

Hot Sour Cream Sauce

3 tablespoons butter
2 tablespoons flour
1 teaspoon salt
¼ teaspoon pepper
500 ml/1 pint cultured or thick sour cream or *smetana*
1½ tablespoons lemon juice

Melt butter, add flour, salt and pepper. Blend well and simmer till flour is cooked, stirring briskly. Remove from heat. Gradually stir in cream and return to heat. When sauce is thick stir in lemon juice.

SCOTLAND

Mrs James Young's Barbecue Sauce for Roast Chicken

1 onion
2 oz butter
1 clove garlic, minced
1 tablespoon Worcestershire Sauce
1 tablespoon H.P. sauce
4 tablespoons tomato sauce
1 tablespoon tomato paste

Chop the onion finely and sauté in the butter, then add the garlic and all the liquids; cook for half an hour and then strain.

Rub the chicken that is to be roasted with a teaspoon each of dry mustard, powdered ginger and salt, then grind some black pepper over it. Roast in the ordinary way in a hot oven for 20 minutes, then pour over it the sauce and baste it with this every quarter of an hour until it is cooked. Carve the chicken, skim the fat from the sauce in the roasting pan. Reduce it a little by fast boiling, then pour it over the carved chicken.

VM's Hazelnut Sauce for Sauté of Chicken

2–3 tablespoons Madeira
1 pint cream
2 tablespoons meat glaze
7 tablespoons hazelnuts, ground

Remove the cooked chicken (wings and breasts of 2 chickens) from the sauté pan and keep it warm. De-glaze the pan by swirling the Madeira round it and scraping together all the juices. Add the cream and the meat glaze and simmer all together. Put the nuts into a very hot oven for a few minutes to loosen their skins, but do not let them burn. Rub off the skins and put the nuts through the finest part of your mincer. Do it twice, then rub them through a very fine sieve. Blend the nut purée into the sauce and keep it hot, but do not allow it to boil.

For garnish, you can fry up some little apple balls in butter and put them at one end of the serving dish. Pour the sauce over the sautéed chicken and serve.

Lady Victoria Wemyss's Tomato Sauce

6 large tomatoes
1 leek (white part)
small stick of celery
1 small carrot
12 g/½ oz bacon, chopped
325 ml/⅓ pint milk
1 tablespoon double cream

Peel the tomatoes, slice them and put them in a pan with the sliced leek, celery and carrot, the chopped bacon and milk. Season with pepper, bring to the boil and simmer for 30 minutes. Strain, add the cream and adjust seasoning.

This is a thin sauce and suitable for fish or chicken. If a thicker sauce is preferred, moisten a teaspoon of arrowroot with a teaspoon or two of milk, add to the strained sauce, bring just to the boil, and then add the cream.

SPAIN

Salsa Verde Española

Put a little oil in a saucepan and when hot add 2 or 3 cloves of chopped garlic. When the garlic begins to brown stir in a little flour and add gradually 1 litre/2 pints of hot stock and 1 heaped tablespoon of chopped parsley. Season with salt and pepper and let it simmer till reduced by half. Add a handful of cooked peas and a handful of asparagus tips and simmer for 10 minutes longer.

This sauce is often poured over hard-boiled eggs in Spain and the dish garnished with boiled new potatoes.

SWEDEN

Dill Sauce

Mix 1 tablespoon hot butter with 2 tablespoons flour, without browning, and gradually add 500 ml/1 pint hot stock. Season with 2 tablespoons fresh dill when available or half that quantity dried, 1½ tablespoons vinegar, 2 teaspoons sugar, and a little salt. Stir all well and finally add 1 egg yolk previously mixed with a little of the sauce.

UNITED STATES OF AMERICA

Chicken Barbecue Sauce I

3 tablespoons dripping
1 medium onion, chopped
1 clove garlic, minced
3 tablespoons soy or
Worcestershire Sauce
1 cup water
1 red pepper, chopped
2 tablespoons vinegar
2–4 tablespoons brown sugar
1 cup tomato ketchup
1 teaspoon prepared mustard
½ cup diced celery
½ teaspoon salt
¼ cup lemon juice

Melt the dripping and cook the onion and garlic in it slowly until golden. Add the other ingredients and simmer for 30 minutes. Finally add the lemon juice.

Chicken Barbecue Sauce II

1 bunch parsley, chopped
4 green peppers, seeded and sliced
2 large onions, sliced
olive oil
1 lb canned tomatoes, chopped
1 teaspoon mace
2 teaspoons curry powder
salt and pepper to taste
1 clove garlic, minced
flour
salt and pepper
paprika
handful of currants

Fry parsley, green peppers and onions in oil slowly for 15 minutes. Put into a large saucepan and add tomatoes, spices, salt and pepper. Simmer 15 minutes then add garlic. Dredge chicken with mixture of flour, salt, pepper and paprika. Fry till brown. Lay chicken in sauce and simmer in a covered pan for 1½–2 hours. Add currants 30 minutes before serving. Arrange cooked rice on a large platter, pour sauce over this and place pieces of chicken on top. Sprinkle toasted almonds on chicken.

Ferocious Barbecue Sauce

From Joy of Cooking, my favourite American cookbook.

Simmer for 15 minutes, stirring frequently:

12–14 oz tomato catsup
½ cup white distilled vinegar
1 teaspoon sugar
a liberal seasoning of red and black pepper
⅛ teaspoon salt

Add to this sauce:

¼ seeded lemon, diced fine
½ teaspoon ground cumin
1 teaspoon ground coriander
⅛ teaspoon Spanish paprika
⅛ teaspoon saffron
¼ teaspoon ground ginger

Combine and heat together for a few minutes, but only baste grilled meats with this sauce during the last 15 minutes of cooking. Too long cooking will make the spices in the sauce bitter.

Richmond Barbecue Sauce for Pork or Spare Ribs

1 tablespoon dry mustard
2–3 tablespoons maple sugar, grated (or other sugar)
1 teaspoon celery seeds
1 teaspoon salt
$\frac{1}{2}$–$\frac{3}{4}$ teaspoon red pepper flakes
1 teaspoon ground black pepper
1 cup tarragon vinegar

Combine all dry ingredients. Stir into vinegar and boil for about 5 minutes.

Texan Barbecue Sauce

1 cup onion, finely chopped
1 clove garlic
$\frac{1}{4}$ cup butter, melted
1 cup ketchup
$\frac{1}{2}$ cup dry sherry
1 tablespoon light brown sugar
1 teaspoon dry mustard
1 tablespoon lemon juice
$\frac{1}{2}$ cup vinegar
2 teaspoons Worcestershire Sauce
$\frac{1}{2}$ teaspoon salt
dash of chili sauce

Sauté onions and garlic in butter for 3–4 minutes. Add remaining ingredients and $1\frac{1}{2}$ cups water and bring to boil. Lower heat and simmer uncovered for 1 hour stirring frequently to prevent scorching.

Admiral Ralph Stevens' Sauces for Submariners: Barbecue Sauce

2 tablespoons chopped onion
1 tablespoon fat (butter or oil)
2 tablespoons vinegar
2 tablespoons brown sugar
3 tablespoons Worcestershire Sauce
1 cup tomato sauce or tomato ketchup
$\frac{1}{3}$ cup lemon juice
$\frac{1}{2}$ teaspoon salt
dash of chili sauce

Sauté onion in fat, add the other ingredients and simmer for 5 minutes over a low heat.

Three Sauces for Barbecued Spare Ribs of Pork

1) Marinade

4 tablespoons soy sauce
2 tablespoons dry sherry
1 teaspoon ground ginger
2 cloves garlic, crushed
fresh ground black pepper
4 star anise seeds

2) Roasting Sauce

3 tablespoons molasses
3 tablespoons orange marmalade
2 tablespoons sea salt
pepper
1 teaspoon arrowroot or cornflower
2 cloves garlic, crushed

Combine all the ingredients for the Marinade except the last and brush on to both sides of the racks of spare ribs. Break the star anise seeds into pieces and sprinkle them on top. Leave for 1 hour. Cover tightly with foil and steam for 1 hour at 325°F 170°C Gas 3. Take ribs from tin and cool. Pour the juices from the pan into a saucepan and add the ingredients for the Roasting Sauce. Heat mixture to boiling and allow to cook a few minutes. Liquidize and allow to cool. Remove any fat. Baste ribs with sauce and roast for 30 minutes in a very hot oven.

3) Chinese Mustard

To serve with the Barbecued
Spare Ribs:

2 tablespoons dry mustard
1 tablespoon turmeric
2 tablespoons wine vinegar
cold water to mix

Mix mustard powder and turmeric very thoroughly. Add the vinegar and enough water to make a very thin paste. It is very hot.
Serve with the spare ribs but separately.

Oriental Marinade

½ cup soy sauce
½ cup frozen orange juice
concentrate
½ cup salad oil
⅓ cup honey
2 tablespoons lemon juice
2 tablespoons white vinegar
1 tablespoon grated orange rind
¼ teaspoon ground ginger

Mix all ingredients together. Serve hot or cold. Good with pork or seafood.

Jamaican Sweet-sour Pineapple Sauce

¼ cup green pepper in strips
½ cup onion, chopped
3 tablespoons butter
1 tablespoon soy sauce
1 tablespoon cornstarch
1 cup crushed or chunk pineapple
2 tablespoons vinegar

Cook green pepper and onion in butter until soft. Add the remaining ingredients and cook until thick, stirring constantly.
Serve with small pork roast or pork cutlets, or left-over pork, or shrimp.

Teriyaki Sauce

¼ cup dry sherry
½ cup soy sauce
½ cup chicken stock
½ cup pineapple juice
1 teaspoon fresh ginger, grated

Heat sherry to boiling point. Add soy sauce, chicken stock, pineapple juice and ginger. Bring to a boil, remove from heat and allow to cool to room temperature before marinating the pork or chicken in it.

Mustard Butter Sauce

4 tablespoons butter
1 tablespoon lemon juice
½ teaspoon prepared English mustard
¼ teaspoon salt

Melt the butter in a saucepan and stir into it lemon juice, mustard and salt.
Serve hot with cooked broccoli or courgettes.

SAUCES FROM ALL OVER

2 COLD SAUCES

AUSTRALIA
Marmalade Mayonnaise

AUSTRIA
Princess Weikersheim's Chive Sauce

ENGLAND
Sir Phillip Joubert's Bagnarotte Sauce
Mrs Dimbleby's Smoked Cod's Roe Sauce

ITALY
Agre-dolce Sauce for Cold Meats
Maionese Tonnata
Peperata
Salsa Piccante alle Asciughe
Salsa di Capperi al'Olio
Salsa Genovese per Pesce Lesso
Salsa Livornese
Rutilio's Salsa Verde
Walnut Sauce

MEDITERRANEAN
Skordelia

NORWAY
Lady Dudley's Sauce Norwégienne

POLAND
Warsaw Sour Cream Sauce

RUSSIA
Caucasian Walnut Sauce
Walnut Sauce

SINGAPORE
Lady Head's Carcosa Sauce

SWEDEN
Sauce Suédoise

TURKEY
Beyendi Sauce for Kebabs
Harem Sauce
Lemon and Mustard Sauce
Pine Nut Sauce
Yoghurt Sauce I
Yoghurt Sauce II

UNITED STATES OF AMERICA
Sour Cream Sauce for Tuna Fish Mousse or Salad
Dill and Sour Cream Sauce
Rémoulade Sauce for Créole Shrimp
Elizabeth Arden's Special Dressing
Maria Blake's Mustard Sauce for Spinach Salad
Loret Hayden's Salad Dressing
Cold Creamy Mustard Sauce

YUGOSLAVIA
Ivar or Poor Man's Caviar

AUSTRALIA

Marmalade Mayonnaise
from Melbourne

This sounds peculiar but tastes good with a cold chicken or cold duck salad. Simply fold about 75 g/3 oz sieved marmalade into the mayonnaise.

AUSTRIA

Princess Weikersheim's Chive Sauce

3 thick slices of bread
125 ml/¼ pint milk
3 hard-boiled egg yolks
salt
½ tablespoon sugar
125 ml/¼ pint oil
1 tablespoon lemon or vinegar
1 teaspoon French mustard
Worcestershire Sauce
2 tablespoons chives

Remove crust from bread and soak it in milk. Then squeeze dry and pass it through a sieve with the hard-boiled egg yolks. Add salt and sugar and drip in oil as with mayonnaise. Add lemon juice, mustard and Worcestershire Sauce to taste. It should taste sweet-sour. At the last moment before serving stir in finely chopped chives.

ENGLAND

Sir Phillip Joubert's Bagnarotte Sauce

250 ml/½ pint Mayonnaise Sauce
1 tablespoon tomato ketchup
2 teaspoons fresh cream
1 teaspoon Worcestershire Sauce
1 teaspoon brandy
dash of Tabasco
few drops lemon juice
salt and pepper

Mix all ingredients and serve chilled.

Mrs Dimbleby's Smoked Cod's Roe Sauce

4 oz smoked cod's roe
8 oz cream cheese
single cream or top of the milk
black pepper, salt
juice of ½ lemon
parsley or fennel leaves to decorate

For smoked mackerel fillets.
In a bowl put the cod's roe, cream cheese and lemon juice and mash it up very thoroughly with a fork (or liquidize). Add a lot of black pepper and a small pinch of salt. If it is very thick add some cream or top of the milk. Pour over smoked fish and decorate with parsley or fennel leaves.

ITALY

Agre-dolce Sauce for Cold Meats

1 wineglass dry white wine
1 wineglass ketchup or tomato sauce
1 tablespoon prepared mustard
1 tablespoon Worcestershire Sauce
1 clove of garlic, minced
½ teaspoon whole rosemary
2 tablespoons vinegar
2 tablespoons brown sugar

Combine all ingredients in a jar and shake to blend thoroughly.

Maionese Tonnata

Make a stiff Mayonnaise with 2 yolks of eggs, no salt, 100 g/4 oz olive oil, and a very little lemon juice. Pound or put through a sieve about 50 g/2 oz tinned tunny fish in oil, incorporate the purée gradually into the Mayonnaise. Check seasoning, add a pinch of English mustard and salt if necessary. Excellent for all kinds of cold dishes, particularly chicken or hard-boiled eggs, for sandwiches, or for filling raw tomatoes for an hors d'oeuvre.

Peperata

40 g/1½ oz each beef marrow and butter (or 75 g/3 oz butter)
about 75 g/3 oz of fresh white breadcrumbs
40 g/1½ oz grated Parmesan
salt
ground black pepper
enough stock to moisten the mixture

A Veronese sauce to be served with *Bollito* or any plainly cooked meat or poultry, hot or cold.

Melt the butter and the beef marrow together in a double saucepan; the butter should not cook. Stir in the breadcrumbs and the cheese, add a little stock, enough to make a smooth paste. Season with salt and a generous amount of ground black pepper. To be served cold.

Salsa Piccante al' Asciughe

1 onion, finely chopped
1 carrot, finely chopped
1 stick celery, finely chopped
2 tablespoons olive oil
1 slice bread
10 anchovy fillets
2 tablespoons capers
1 clove garlic
1 teaspoon parsley
1½ tablespoons wine vinegar
2 tablespoons lemon juice
¼ teaspoon salt
black pepper
¼ pint olive oil and salad oil, mixed

Cook the onion, carrot and celery in the olive oil until tender. Put in liquidizer with all the other ingredients except the oils. Blend until smooth and then gradually add the oils. Keep in the refrigerator but serve at room temperature.

Salsi di Capperi al' Olio

5 tablespoons olive oil
2 tablespoons fresh lemon juice
2 tablespoons drained capers
1 tablespoon fresh parsley, chopped

Mix together the oil and lemon juice. Stir in the capers and parsley. Serve with cold or hot poached fish, cold chicken or meat. This is particularly good with cold lamb; it has a much fresher taste than ordinary Vinaigrette – it is also excellent for dressing salads.

Salsa Genovese per Pesce Lesso

a clove of garlic, very finely chopped
3 or 4 sprigs of parsley, very finely chopped
12 g/½ oz capers
3 stoned olives
1 salt anchovy
the yolk of 1 hard-boiled egg
1 heaped tablespoon of bread, previously soaked in vinegar
10 tablespoons of oil
1 tablespoon of vinegar
salt and pepper

Chop the garlic and parsley very finely and pound the caper and olives in a mortar with the anchovy, the yolk of egg and the bread. When pounded into a smooth paste, add the oil gradually, as in mayonnaise, and finally the vinegar. Season with a little salt and pepper.

A delicious sauce for boiled fish.

Salsa Livornese Sieve 6 hard-boiled egg yolks, add a pinch of grated nutmeg and pepper, 4 or 5 pounded and sieved anchovy fillets (or 1 large teaspoon of essence). Now add 500 ml/1 pint olive oil gradually in the same manner as for mayonnaise, using tarragon vinegar to taste. Finish with 1 teaspoon chopped parsley. Serve with cold meat.

Rutilio's Salsa Verde

1 tablespoon capers
2 cloves garlic
1 shallot or 12 g/½ oz onion
50 g/2 oz fresh parsley
salt and pepper
5 tablespoons olive oil
2 tablespoons lemon juice
1 sprig sweet basil

Drain the capers and peel the garlic and shallot or onion. Pass the capers, garlic cloves, shallot or onion and parsley through a mouli grater or electric blender, or chop the ingredients very finely and sieve. Put into a basin, add salt and pepper to taste and mix in the olive oil and lemon juice as for French dressing. Lastly add the finely chopped basil. The sauce should be fairly thick. Serve with cold boiled meat, chicken or with poached fish.

Walnut Sauce Pour boiling water over 50 g/2 oz shelled walnuts, leave a minute or two and then rub off the skins. Soak a thick slice of white bread, without the crust, in water, and squeeze dry. Pound the walnuts in a mortar with a clove or garlic, pepper, salt, and a little water. Add the bread, a little vinegar, and enough olive oil to form a thick sauce. Press through a sieve, add some chopped parsley. The sauce should be of the consistency of a thick mayonnaise.

Very good with a poached fish, either hot or cold.

MEDITER-RANEAN
Skordelia To 500 ml/1 pint basic Aïoli Sauce (see p. 60) add 100 g/4 oz ground almonds, 50 g/2 oz fresh breadcrumbs (or 1 small potato, boiled and sieved), 3 teaspoons lemon juice and 2 tablespoons chopped parsley.

NORWAY
Lady Dudley's Sauce Norwégienne Take three tablespoonfuls of Mayonnaise Sauce, one gill of whipped cream, a tablespoonful of grated horseradish, a little pepper and salt. Mix all together lightly – set on the ice and serve.

POLAND
Warsaw Sour Cream Sauce

4 egg yolks
250–300 ml/generous ½ pint sour cream
1½–2 tablespoons lemon juice
¼ teaspoon salt
1–2 tablespoons mild paprika powder
3 tablespoons fresh parsley, finely chopped

Beat egg yolks in top part of double boiler. Stir in sour cream and lemon juice and beat continuously over gently simmering water until the sauce thickens. Add salt and enough paprika to turn sauce a pretty pink, then stir in parsley just before serving. This is nice for boiled fish, pike or salmon.

RUSSIA
Caucasian Walnut Sauce

3 large slices of crustless white bread
250 ml/½ pint chicken stock
375 g/12 oz shelled and skinned walnuts
salt to taste
2–3 tablespoons double cream can be added, but this would make the recipe less authentic

This sauce is spread over a cold chicken, cooked in its own juices and with its own aspic.

Crumble white bread into blender and add the stock. Slowly blend in the walnut meats and blend to a paste, adding more stock if necessary. Refrigerate for several hours. When cold the sauce should be quite thick and should spread like soft butter.

Walnut Sauce

Shell and skin and pound in a mortar about 20 walnuts. Add 1 teaspoon of French mustard, the yolks of 2 hard-boiled eggs, 1 tablespoon fine brown breadcrumbs*, 1 tablespoon oil and 10 tablespoons vinegar. Mix well and serve with boiled or fried fish. (Add a little water to the walnuts as you pound them to make them cream.)
* In Russia rye bread would be used.

SINGAPORE
Lady Head's Carcosa Sauce

To 250 ml/½ pint of Mayonnaise made with a light salad oil (arrachide or very refined olive oil) add 1 chopped shallot and 1 finely chopped chili pepper. Then add the juice of half a lemon.

SWEDEN
Sauce Suédoise

Cook 2 medium-sized sliced apples in a little white wine. Reduce and pass through a fine sieve. When cold mix with the mayonnaise. Finish with a little grated horseradish.

TURKEY
Beyendi Sauce for Kebabs

This creamed aubergine and butter sauce is a pale green sauce or mousse which tastes and looks delicious. It can be as thick or thin as you wish according to how much butter or oil you add. For kebabs it should be fairly thick. It comes from Eskisehir or Kaisaria in Anatolia. Oil 4–5 fine young aubergines well with a spoonful or two of olive oil and sprinkle them with salt then bake over charcoal or in the oven. They will take about 30–40 minutes to cook in a hot oven. Cool and skin as best you can, spooning out the whole of the pulp into a blender bowl with a silver spoon.

Set blender at its lowest speed and feed into the aubergines 375 g/12 oz unsalted butter or up to 250 ml/½ pint olive oil. Add finely minced garlic, black pepper, salt and lemon juice to taste and then put it in a cool place until you want it. It has the advantage of keeping up to a week in a fridge and is good enough to eat as an hors d'oeuvre or side-dish on its own.

Harem Sauce

100 g/4 oz pistachio nuts
or walnuts (skinned)
4 cloves garlic
50 g/2 oz white bread (use the
crumb only)
olive oil
lemon juice or wine vinegar

This is a pistachio nut sauce from Istanbul.

Pound the nuts and garlic in a mortar. Soak the bread in water, squeeze it dry and work with the nuts into a smooth paste. Pour in a little olive oil very gradually until you have a thick sauce, and finally stir in lemon juice or wine vinegar to taste. The pistachio sauce is a pretty green colour and has a delicate flavour. To improve colour add a little spinach juice.

Lemon and Mustard Sauce

Squeeze the juice of 2 lemons into a bowl. Pour in slowly, beating while you pour, double the quantity of olive oil to lemon juice; then add salt, pepper, 1 teaspoon dried mustard and two cloves of chopped garlic. Stir thoroughly with a wooden spoon. Strain through a sieve and sprinkle in a little chopped parsley. An excellent sauce with grilled fish or game.

Pine Nut Sauce

Pound together in a mortar 100 g/4 oz pine nuts, two cloves of garlic and one teaspoon of salt. Drop in very slowly enough olive oil to make a thick smooth sauce. Thin a little with either vinegar or lemon juice.

Yoghurt Sauce I

Beat the yoghurt well with a wooden spoon and season it with salt and pepper. Mix in vegetable or meat stock or meat glaze and serve as a sauce over hot vegetable dishes, ragouts and stews. It can be luke-warm or cold, but never hot, and should only be added to a dish just before serving.

Tomato purée is often added, but this is a matter of individual preference and, in any case, it should only be enough to colour the yoghurt. Personally I think it spoils the fresh clean taste of the plainest sauce.

Yoghurt Sauce II

A cold yoghurt sauce or dressing for cucumber or apple-and-celery salad is made by simply beating a fairly creamy yoghurt with a spoon and adding a squeeze or two of lemon juice, then a very little salt, and lots of freshly ground black pepper.

UNITED STATES OF AMERICA

Sour Cream Sauce for Tuna Fish Mousse or Salad

1 cup sour cream
1 cup shallots, chopped
$\frac{1}{4}$ cup radishes, chopped
$\frac{1}{4}$ cup cucumber, grated
2 teaspoons lemon juice
1 teaspoon horseradish
salt and pepper to taste

Mix all ingredients thoroughly and chill for 2–3 hours before serving. Makes 2 cups.

Dill and Sour Cream Sauce

500 ml/1 pint sour cream
¼ cup onion, minced
¼ teaspoon celery seed
¼ teaspoon garlic powder
2 tablespoons fresh dill, chopped
or ½ teaspoon dried dill

Mix all ingredients together in a bowl and chill. Let stand no longer than 2 hours. Makes 2 cups.

Rémoulade Sauce for Créole Shrimp

4 tablespoons olive oil
2 tablespoons tarragon vinegar
1 cup celery, chopped
½ cup green onions, chopped
2 tablespoons Dijon mustard
2 tablespoons prepared horseradish
1 teaspoon salt
⅛ teaspoon pepper
¼ cup parsley, chopped

Combine first 4 ingredients in an electric blender for 1 minute. Stir in mustard, horseradish, salt and pepper. Pour this sauce over shrimp in a large bowl, sprinkle with parsley and chill before serving.

Elizabeth Arden's Special Dressing

1 tablespoon Worcestershire Sauce
¼ cup tarragon vinegar
1 white onion finely chopped
2 cups vegetable oil
4 egg yolks
1 teaspoon monosodium glutamate (optional)
1 teaspoon horseradish
1 bunch parsley leaves
1 bunch watercress leaves
1¼ tablespoons Veg-e-sal

Mix together in electric blender. Veg-e-sal may be purchased in a health store. It is vital to the recipe. This delicious dressing is good on any green salad. Make at room temperature. Makes 3 cups.

Maria Blake's Mustard Sauce for Spinach Salad

1 pint sour cream
1 tablespoon tarragon vinegar
1 tablespoon mustard
1 teaspoon salt
2 eggs

Put all above ingredients in top of double boiler over hot water, stirring constantly for 10 minutes or until thickened. Cool and refrigerate. Makes 2 cups.

Loret Hayden's Salad Dressing

1 8 oz packet cream cheese
¼ lb Roquefort cheese
1 cup basic Vinaigrette
1 tablespoon Worcestershire Sauce
salt and freshly ground pepper

Soften cheese and mash together with French dressing and Worcestershire Sauce. Season.

These last three recipes come from Mary Clifford's excellent *Washington Cookbook*.

Cold Creamy Mustard Sauce

2 tablespoons light cream
2 tablespoons tarragon vinegar
⅛ teaspoon salt
4 tablespoons mustard
2 tablespoons sugar
2 teaspoons green onion or shallot, finely minced

Mix all together and chill in refrigerator.

NOTE: You should use your favourite mustard, French or English. The quantities given are only a rough guide as the strengths of mustards vary considerably.

YUGOSLAVIA

Ivar or Poor Man's Caviar

4 aubergines
8 tablespoons olive oil
salt
4 cloves of garlic
1 small onion
2 sweet green peppers, blanched
½–1 hot capsicum pepper, according to taste, blanched
lemon juice
freshly ground pepper

This is a fierier version of the Turkish Beyendi Sauce on p. 148. It is much esteemed in Montenegro and Bosnia as an accompaniment to fish or meat grills. It also gives a fillip to a dull dish of cold meats. Sprinkle the aubergines with one third of the oil and some salt. Bake for 30–40 minutes in a moderate oven. Cool, split and scrape out the pulp with a silver spoon. Chop slightly and turn into an electric mixer with the rest of the ingredients except the lemon juice. Feed the rest of the oil into the aubergine pulp spoonful by spoonful. Sharpen with lemon juice and correct seasoning.

6

SAUCES
FOR PUDDINGS

Sauces for Puddings

1 Hot and Cold Sauces

Hot Brandy Cream Sauce
Sauce Sabayon
Quick Zabaglione Sauce
German Weinschaum Sauce
Sherry Sauce
Good Custard
Vanilla Custard Sauce and Brandy Custard Sauce
Mrs Stanley's Chocolate Sauce
Almond Sauce I
Almond Sauce II
Almond Dressing from Tennessee
Frozen Macaroon Topping
Pistachio Cream Sauce
Lèche Cream
Whipped Cream Sauce
18th Century Solid Syllabub
Lemon and Wine Sauce
Hot Lemon Sauce
Lemon Curd Sauce
Prune Sauce I
Prune Sauce II
Apple Sauce
Apricot Sauce with White Wine
Apricot Sauce with Honey
Honey Sauce
Honey Mint Sauce
Maple Syrup Sauce
Maple Honey Sauce
Chestnut Syrup Sauce or Crème de Marrons
Theodora's Muscat Syrup
Pineapple Syrup
Senior Wrangler Sauce
Calvados Butter Sauce
Hard Sauce
Rum Butter Sauce
Cumberland Rum Butter
Foamy Orange Sauce

Hot Brandy Cream Sauce

75 g/3 oz butter
125 g/5 oz icing sugar
3 tablespoons brandy
2 egg yolks
125 ml/¼ pint cream

Place the butter in the top of a double boiler over hot water. Gradually add the sugar and beat until creamy. Slowly beat in the brandy and egg yolks (one at a time). Add the cream and continue to cook until slightly thickened. Delicious over the plainest sponge cake or gingerbread. (Shake toasted almond flakes over the top, and call it a pudding!)

Sauce Sabayon

To be served with sweet, light puddings or compôtes.

Put into a saucepan a wineglass full of good Madeira or Marsala, two heaped tablespoonsful of pounded white sugar, the juice of one lemon, the yolks of four very fresh eggs. Whip all this well together. Put the saucepan into a bain-marie for five minutes whipping it well all the time and then serve. If you fail to get enough volume, whip one egg white separately and fold it in.

Quick Zabaglione Sauce

4 egg yolks
1 wineglass white wine
75–100 g/3–4 oz caster sugar

Beat egg yolks in a pan with a wire whisk, add wine and sugar. Place over medium heat and beat constantly, raising pan when a little steam appears. Continue beating and return to heat. Repeat until sauce thickens.

German Weinschaum Sauce
Wine-froth Sauce

Put two whole eggs and the yolks of three eggs in a basin with one teaspoon sugar, the juice of one lemon, thin strips of lemon peel and ¼ bottle of Moselle. Stand the basin above a saucepan of boiling water, and beat till very light and frothy.

NOTE: Great care must be taken with the last three sauces to ensure that the egg does not become overheated and scramble.

Sherry Sauce

125 ml/¼ pint milk
50 g/2 oz caster sugar
4 tablespoons butter
2 tablespoons sherry

Boil milk, sugar and butter together for 5 minutes. Add sherry.

Good Custard

500 ml/1 pint milk, as fresh and creamy as possible
1 bay leaf
a little nutmeg and/or a saltspoon of powdered cinnamon
2–3 eggs, large and fresh
2 tablespoons vanilla sugar

And it can be good; also called *Crème à l'Anglaise* in France, and *Zuppa Inglese*, in Italy.

Heat the milk to well below boiling point with a small bay leaf and cinnamon if wished. Stir the well beaten yolks of the eggs into the hot milk (or gradually pour it over them in a bowl, stirring vigorously). Return to the saucepan or double boiler and stir over hot water till sauce thickens and coats the back of your spoon, but do not boil. When thick enough remove immediately. Cool, and when cold, fold in stiffly beaten white of 1 egg. Keep in the refrigerator until wanted. It is infinitely nicer served chilled.

Vanilla Custard Sauce

1 tablespoon caster sugar
2 eggs
500 ml/1 pint hot milk
vanilla stick or ½ teaspoon vanilla essence

Place the sugar and eggs in a basin, beat till they are well blended. Gradually stir in the hot milk, then put it all into a double boiler. Add the stick of vanilla. Stir over hot water until it is thick, but do not boil. Remove vanilla stick before serving. If you wish a **Brandy Custard Sauce** add a tablespoon of cognac off the heat. Serve hot in a sauce boat but if wanted cold cover and stir from time to time to prevent a skin forming.

NOTE: Cream can be added to any of these custards if a richer sauce is wanted, but it takes away from the essential egginess of a good custard and I think is better served separately.

Mrs Stanley's Chocolate Sauce

150 g/6 oz chocolate (preferably bitter)
8 tablespoons milk
2–3 tablespoons sherry

Dissolve the broken-up chocolate in the milk over a low heat in a double saucepan, to ensure that the chocolate remains shiny. Finish with sherry to taste. For steamed chocolate soufflé.

Almond Sauce I

250 ml/½ pint creamy milk (or half and half)
25 g/1 oz sugar
25 g/1 oz sweet almonds, blanched and pounded*
3 bitter almonds, pounded
3 egg yolks
cognac

Boil the milk with the sugar, add the almonds and boil together for 10 minutes. Cool and when the sauce is still hot, but nowhere near boiling, strain it, and pour it over the strained yolks of eggs. Mix well and re-heat, but do not boil again. Just before serving add a very small glass of cognac. This sauce can also be chilled and served cold.

* Remember to add a few drops of water to the almonds when you pound them or they will oil.

Almond Sauce II

Blanch and skin 25 g/1 oz of sweet Jordan almonds and only 3 bitter almonds. Pound them in a mortar with a little orange flower water. Pound thoroughly, so that there are no lumps, and put into a stewpan with 10 tablespoons cream and 2 egg yolks. Whisk over a very low heat until cooked.

NOTE: Bitter Almonds are quite a different animal from ordinary sweet almonds. You must ask for them by name from a good grocer.

Almond Dressing from Tennessee

Beat one egg until light. Add one tablespoon of sugar and one of corn starch and blend with two tablespoons each of lemon and pineapple juice in a double boiler. Cook until thick, beating steadily with an egg beater. When cold, add two cups of whipped double cream and a quarter of a pound of finely pulverized almonds.

Frozen Macaroon Topping

8 almond macaroons
125 ml/¼ pint milk
65 g/2½ oz icing sugar
1 teaspoon vanilla
500 ml/1 pint double cream, whipped stiffly

Soften macaroons in milk. Flavour the cream with sugar and vanilla. Fold in the softened macaroons and milk. It's good with hot apple or steam puddings, or frozen in little paper cups or dariole moulds. To serve these peel off paper and place on peach halves, strawberries, raspberry sherbert, etc. The topping will gradually melt over the fruit.

Pistachio Cream Sauce

First skin 100 g/4 oz pistachios by putting them in the oven for a minute or two, and then rubbing them between a folded cloth. When they are skinned blanch them. Beat them up finely with a little rose-water (or whirl in liquidizer). Add the paste to 375 ml/¾ pint whipped double cream, sweeten to taste and deepen the pale green colour if you wish with a little vegetable colouring, or spinach juice.

Lèche Cream

This is a very simple sauce or pudding, whichever you wish. Simply heat an unopened tin of condensed milk in a saucepan of boiling water until it caramelizes. It will take about 3 hours in quietly simmering water, but less if you increase heat. It is *very* sweet but some people (children, campers, toffee chewers) love the golden sticky result.

Whipped Cream Sauce

75 g/3 oz icing sugar
3 egg yolks, beaten until thick
pinch of salt
2 tablespoons Cointreau
or other liqueur, or Bourbon,
or sherry
250 ml/½ pint double cream,
whipped

Beat sugar into eggs, add salt and gradually pour on Cointreau or other flavouring. Fold in whipped cream.

18th Century Solid Syllabub

Put 100 g/4 oz orange and lemon juice and 75 g/3 oz caster sugar in a basin. Add 250 ml/½ pint fresh cream and whip together till very thick.

Lemon and Wine Sauce

100 g/4 oz sugar
1½ tablespoons cornflour
375 ml/¾ pint white wine
3 large lemons
4 tablespoons butter

Place the sugar and cornflour in the top of a double boiler. Add the wine and bring to a boil over a low flame, stirring constantly until the mixture thickens. Place over boiling water and cook for 15 minutes. Grate the lemon rind and add ⅓ cup of the strained juice. Remove from the heat and add the lemon rind, juice and butter. Stir until butter has melted. Reheat over boiling water before serving.

Hot Lemon Sauce

100 g/4 oz sugar
1 tablespoon cornflour or arrowroot
¼ teaspoon salt
250 ml/½ pint boiling water
1 teaspoon lemon rind, grated
3 tablespoons lemon juice
2 tablespoons butter
1 heaped tablespoon sultanas
(optional)

Mix together the sugar, cornflour, salt and water. Bring to the boil and cook for about 5 minutes, stirring all the time. When smooth, thick and clear, take off the heat and stir in lemon juice, rind and butter. For some puddings and ice cream a spoonful of sultanas that you have plumped up in water can be added to make this sauce more interesting.

Lemon Curd Sauce
a quick method

Thin a small jar of lemon curd down in 125 ml/¼ pint of medium sweet wine. Add a walnut of butter, stir and simmer till smooth and shiny. Serve hot.

Prune Sauce I

½ kilo/1 lb prunes
250 ml/½ pint water
1 tablespoon soft brown sugar
1 tablespoon rum or brandy

Boil the prunes in water till soft. Add the sugar, rum or brandy. Rub through a sieve.

Prune Sauce II

Reduce the syrup in which prunes have been cooked to half the quantity, add a glass of sweet sherry and strain.

Apple Sauce

500 g/1 lb cooking apples
rind of ½ lemon
2–3 tablespoons water
1 clove
½ tablespoon caster sugar
or 1 tablespoon golden syrup
12 g/½ oz butter

Peel and core the apples, pare the lemon rind very thinly. Put them both in a saucepan with 2–3 tablespoons of water and the clove. Cover saucepan and cook gently until mushy. Remove clove – beat smooth with a wooden spoon, or sieve – stir in sugar or syrup – beat in butter. Serve hot in a sauceboat.

Apricot Sauce with White Wine

2–3 tablespoons apricot jam
1 wineglass white wine
sugar to taste (about 2 tablespoons)
lemon rind peeled thinly
1 teaspoon lemon juice

Mix everything together over gentle heat and remove lemon rind before serving.

Apricot Sauce with Honey

Take one cup of apricot jam and add to it one cup of hot water, half cup of strained honey and two tablespoons lemon juice. Boil together and reduce to a syrup. Strain. Then add Maraschino or apricot brandy.

Honey Sauce

4 tablespoons hot water
8 tablespoons honey
50 g/2 oz nutmeats, chopped
50 g/2 oz candied orange or lemon
peel or crystallized ginger

Combine all ingredients and stir well. Chill.

Honey Mint Sauce

125 ml/¼ pint orange juice
2 tablespoons lemon juice
2 tablespoons honey
1–2 tablespoons fresh mint,
finely chopped

This sauce is delicious with fruit compôtes.
Combine ingredients.

Maple Syrup Sauce

125 ml/¼ pint maple syrup
½ teaspoon grated lemon peel
a squeeze of lemon juice
¼ teaspoon freshly grated nutmeg
or ⅛ teaspoon ginger or cloves
2–3 tablespoons chopped nuts

Heat the syrup but do not boil. Add the other ingredients. If you wish to serve it hot, swirl in 1–2 tablespoons butter. If you wish it cold, chill.

Maple Honey Sauce

8 tablespoons strained pure honey
12 tablespoons maple syrup
2 teaspoons ground cinnamon
½ teaspoon caraway seeds

Combine honey and maple syrup and heat slowly. Add cinnamon and caraway and bring to a fast boil. Serve hot.

Chestnut Syrup Sauce or Crème de Marrons

You can either use tinned marrons purée or tinned marrons debris for this sauce. Cook a few spoonfuls of either with 1 wineglass white wine and a squeeze of lemon juice for about 5 minutes. Cool and use luke-warm or cold. Good with meringue puddings or plain ice cream.

Theodora's Muscat Syrup

¾ kilo/1½ lb sugar
1 kilo/2 lb gooseberries
12 sprigs of elderflower heads
250 ml/½ pint water

Dissolve the sugar slowly in the water, add the gooseberries and cook them very gently so the fruit does not burst. When they are cooked bring suddenly to a quick boil and plunge in the elderflowers still on their stalks. Leave them in the hot syrup for about 15 minutes until the elderflower flavour has come out. Then strain and put into jars. This is good as a sauce for ice creams, or as a glaze for fruit tarts.

Pineapple Syrup

Put 375 g/12 oz sliced fresh pineapple into a saucepan with 500 ml/1 pint water. Bring to boil and simmer till the fruit is quite tender. Strain it through muslin, twice, until the juice is quite clear. Put back in a clean pan, add 300 g/10 oz of sugar and melt slowly. Then bring to boil and boil rapidly for 10 minutes. It ought to be quite bright in colour and if put into jars with airtight lids it will keep for weeks.

Senior Wrangler Sauce

This is a superior Brandy Butter, as you would expect.
Take 100 g/4 oz unsalted butter and 100 g/4 oz icing sugar. Beat them together until quite light and white. Then add 2 tablespoons brandy and 1 tablespoon sherry; the brandy and wine to be put in slowly by degrees, and beaten until thoroughly mixed.

Calvados Butter Sauce

Made exactly the same way as Senior Wrangler except that you use Calvados instead of brandy and sherry. To be served with apple fritters (dust these with icing sugar and set for a minute under a hot grill before serving). The Calvados Butter turns a simple dish into a feast.

Hard Sauce

100 g/4 oz butter (unsalted)
150 g/6 oz caster sugar
1 egg white, beaten
2 tablespoons rum or bourbon
grated nutmeg

This is the American version of Brandy Butter Sauce.
Cream butter and sugar until very light, add egg white, continue beating and add flavouring a little at a time until sauce is very fluffy. Sprinkle grated nutmeg on top of sauce.
Here are some variations:
orange, lemon or ginger flavoured; beat in a little orange or lemon rind or finely chopped ginger.

Rum Butter Sauce

150 g/6 oz caster sugar
2 tablespoons cornflour
about 250 ml/½ pint boiling water
125 ml/¼ pint lemon juice
rind of 1 lemon
2 tablespoons brandy
¼ teaspoon grated nutmeg
125 ml/¼ pint light rum
2 tablespoons dark rum

Blend sugar and cornflour in 1 cup boiling water. Cook, stirring constantly, over medium heat, until mixture begins to thicken. Add remaining ingredients and cook 2 minutes, stirring constantly. Serve hot over mince pies or puddings.

Cumberland Rum Butter

Excellent Cumberland Rum Butter can be bought ready made in the Lake District, if you are selective. This can be frozen in dariole moulds and allowed to melt when served over iced puddings or whipped up with a little softened (unsalted) butter when served with hot ones.

Foamy Orange Sauce

60 g/2½ oz butter
112 g/4½ oz icing sugar
1 egg, separated
130 ml/6 fl oz orange juice
1 teaspoon grated orange zest
1 tablespoon brandy or Drambuie

Cream the butter until soft. Gradually beat in sugar, then egg yolk, orange juice and zest and liqueur. Just before serving fold in stiffly beaten egg white.

SAUCES FOR PUDDINGS
2 ICE CREAM SAUCES

Black Cherry Sauce
Hot Cherry Sauce
Cerises Monte Carlo
South Sea Island or Rum and Apricot Sauce
Admiral Ralph Stevens Sauce Superbe
Dark Rum and Raisin Sauce
Virginian Spiced Peach Sauce
Strawberry Sauce
Sauce Melba I or Raspberry Sauce
Raspberry Sauce or Sauce Melba II
Fresh Raspberry Sauce
Framboise and Cassis Sauce
Queen Sauce or Marie Malade
Theodora's Red Currant Sauce
VM's Good Plain Chocolate Sauce
Hot Chocolate Sauce
Black Barbados Sauce
Fudge or Chocolate Toffee Sauce
Butterscotch Sauce I
Butterscotch Sauce II
Caramel Sauce I
Caramel Sauce II
Lady Jekyll's Caramel Sauce
Toasted Almond and Butterscotch Sauce
Burnt Almond Sauce
Home Made Cream
Stand-up Cream

Black Cherry Sauce
pitted black cherries
thin shavings of 1 lemon
or orange peel
4 tablespoons Bourbon

Drain cherries and boil the juice and orange peel until liquid is reduced by half. Strain, add Bourbon and soak cherries in this for several hours. Serve steaming hot or cold.

Hot Cherry Sauce

½ kilo/1 lb cherries (Morellos are best)
½ kilo/1 lb sugar (depending on sweetness of cherries)
a little water
75–100 g/3–4 oz red currant jelly
Kirsch

Stone the cherries. Put the sugar in a saucepan with 1–2 tablespoons water. Heat till sugar dissolves, then bring to boiling point and boil for 5 minutes, skimming carefully. Add the cherries and their juice and cook quickly, as you would when making jam. When the evaporation from the cherries is less dense and they have been boiling steadily for about 10 minutes, take off the heat and drain off the cherries. Reduce the syrup a little more by fast boiling and return the cherries to the pan with the red currant jelly. Stir well and flavour with a very small glass of Kirsch. Serve in a separate heated bowl or sauceboat to the one used for the vanilla and/or raspberry ice cream.

Cerises Monte Carlo

This is more a compôte than a sauce but it enlivens plain vanilla or raspberry ice cream. Take 1 kilo/2 lb of fresh cherries and stone them. Put into a saucepan 225 g/½ lb lump sugar and 1 wineglass water. Set on heat and when the sugar has melted add the cherries and let them boil gently for a few minutes. Whilst they are boiling, mix ½ tablespoon arrowroot in a little cold water until it is quite smooth. Add this to the cherries, shaking the saucepan well and taking care that the sugar and arrowroot blend completely. Pour the mixture into a fireproof bowl or silver sauceboat and at the last moment before serving heat a large glassful of Kirchwasser in a saucepan, set it alight and pour it over the cherries. Send it flaming to the table with ice cream in a separate dish or glass; a silver punch bowl is ideal. Optional: a small jar of red currant jelly can be added to the sauce.

South Sea Island or Rum and Apricot Sauce

1 cup sugar
1½ cup apricot nectar
½ cup dark rum

Bring the sugar and apricot nectar to a boil and simmer for 5 minutes. Remove from the heat and add to the rum.

Serve warm or cold.

Admiral Ralph Stevens' Sauce Superbe

½ cup blanched almonds
½ cup firmly packed brown sugar
¼ cup apricot brandy
½ cup Bourbon
½ cup toasted, flaked coconut or almonds if preferred

Place the almonds in the blender and blend until well ground. Add the sugar, brandy and Bourbon and blend until smooth. Remove and mix in the coconut flakes.

Serve as a sauce over ice cream.

Dark Rum and Raisin Sauce

2 egg yolks
112 g/4½ oz sifted icing sugar
75 g/3 oz seedless raisins or sultanas
6 tablespoons rum
250 ml/½ pint double cream, stiffly whipped
1 teaspoon vanilla

Beat the egg yolks and then add the sugar and beat until it has dissolved. Mix in the raisins, then add the rum slowly and when well blended add the cream. Fold in the vanilla. Can be used hot or cold with ice cream or with creamy rice puddings.

Virginian Spiced Peach Sauce

6 firm fresh peaches
1 tablespoon lemon juice
⅓ cup sugar
½ teaspoon ground cloves
½ teaspoon nutmeg
½ cup brandy

Peel peaches, slice thinly or dice. Sprinkle with lemon juice and mix immediately to prevent discolouring. Mix spices with sugar, add brandy and warm just enough to dissolve sugar. Pour over peaches, mix and chill for 2 hours. Serve over vanilla or peach ice cream.

Strawberry Sauce

150 g/6 oz caster sugar
125 ml/¼ pint water
1¼ kilo/2½ lb sliced strawberries

Boil the sugar and water for 5 minutes. Pour over the sliced strawberries and allow to cool. Sliced peaches may be used instead of strawberries.

Sauce Melba I or Raspberry Sauce

Pass some fresh raspberry jam (about 500 g/1 lb) through a fine sieve to free it from all seeds. To this purée add a generous squeeze of lemon juice and 1 large tablespoon Kirsch and 1 large tablespoon Maraschino. Serve in a sauceboat or pour over ice cream and peaches.

Raspberry Sauce or Sauce Melba II

1½ kilo/16 oz packet frozen raspberries
1 teaspoon cornflour
1 tablespoon water
50 g/2 oz caster sugar
100 g/4 oz red currant jelly
4 tablespoons Cointreau

Thaw berries, heat and strain through sieve. Mix the cornflour with the water. Add to strained berries and simmer 5 minutes. Add sugar and red currant jelly. Dissolve thoroughly and add the Cointreau. Serve over freshly sliced peaches, cantaloupe melon balls or ice cream.

Fresh Raspberry Sauce

500 ml/1 pint fresh raspberries
1 oz icing sugar

Rub raspberries through a fine sieve or purée them in a food mill and then sieve. Add sugar and mix well. Let the berries stand in the sugar for 2 hours or more before cooking. Bring purée to the boil over a medium heat, stirring carefully. Simmer until it forms a heavy syrup. Cool.

Framboise and Cassis Sauce

Combine cooked raspberry syrup as above with 50 g/2 oz (¼ cup) Crème de Cassis and chill before serving. A beautifully coloured sauce that it is difficult to identify, but that tastes delicious.

Queen Sauce or Marie Malade

2 tablespoons marmalade
2 small glasses sherry

Boil together, stirring all the time. Do not sieve and serve hot and syrupy. Excellent with steamed sponge pudding or orange ice cream.

Theodora's Red Currant Sauce

100 g/4 oz lump sugar
1 eggshell
water
2 tablespoons red currant jelly
rind of ½ lemon, grated
rind of ½ orange, grated
1 tablespoon Maraschino liqueur

Put the lump sugar in a saucepan with the eggshell and water to cover. Boil gently for 15 minutes and then strain the syrup. Put the red currant jelly in a saucepan with the grated peels and the syrup. Bring to the boil and simmer gently until the jelly has melted, stirring all the time. Strain, add the Maraschino and serve either hot or cold.

VM's Good Plain Chocolate Sauce

100 g/4 oz good black cooking
chocolate (unsweetened)
375 ml/¾ pint water
100 g/4 oz Bournville Red Label
Cocoa
50–75 g/2–3 oz icing sugar
25 g/1 oz fresh butter

Boil the chocolate in the water for 10 minutes, mixing it in well with a wooden spoon. Put in the cocoa, and simmer and stir for 15 minutes more. When smooth, beat in the icing sugar and butter. Mix well, but do not boil. (Chopped and blanched almonds may be added.) The quality of this sauce depends on the quality of the chocolate – so if you want a rich sauce buy a good, black, unsweetened or semi-sweet bitter chocolate. If a plainer sauce is needed use a plainer chocolate.

Hot Chocolate Sauce

100 g/4 oz unsweetened black
chocolate
175 g/7 oz sugar (granulated)
150–175 g/6–7 oz evaporated milk
or single cream
1 tablespoon very strong coffee
a very little salt
½ teaspoon vanilla (or 1 teaspoon
Rum)

Melt chocolate in top of double boiler over boiling water. Add sugar and stir. Cover and cook for 30 minutes. Add evaporated milk (or cream), coffee, salt and flavouring.

Take off heat and stir occasionally until thick and smooth and cool. (It will thicken as it cools.) Serve cool or cold with ice cream or puddings. This sauce can be refrigerated and reheated over boiling water. The quantities can be doubled.

Black Barbados Sauce

2–3 tablespoons black treacle
50 g/2 oz butter
75 g/3 oz black chocolate
about 1 tablespoon dark rum
juice of 1 orange

Put all ingredients in a saucepan. Gently heat and stir, until the chocolate has melted, and serve hot with ice cream.

Fudge or Chocolate Toffee Sauce

50 g/2 oz unsweetened chocolate
1 tablespoon butter
5–6 tablespoons boiling water
175 g/7 oz granulated sugar
2 tablespoons corn syrup
1 teaspoon vanilla or 2 teaspoons
rum

Melt the chocolate and butter over hot water in a double boiler. Stir and blend well then add the boiling water. Stir well then add sugar and corn syrup. Let the sauce boil readily over direct heat. Do not stir. If you wish an ordinary sauce, boil it for 3 minutes, covered. If you wish a hot sauce that hardens over ice cream, boil it, UNCOVERED, about 3 minutes more. Add the vanilla or rum just before serving. When cold this sauce is very thick. It can be reheated in a double boiler over hot water.

Butterscotch Sauce I

½ kilo/1 lb dark brown Barbados
or sand sugar
8 tablespoons butter
125 ml/¼ pint double cream
1 tablespoon lemon juice

Combine ingredients in top of double boiler and cook for 1 hour, stirring occasionally.

Butterscotch Sauce II

100 g/4 oz brown sugar
50 g/2 oz granulated sugar
125 ml/¼ pint double cream
1 tablespoon corn syrup
1 tablespoon butter
1 small teaspoon vanilla

Bring all ingredients, except vanilla, to boil and continue cooking very gently for about 5 minutes. Remove from heat and add vanilla. Cool slightly before serving.

Caramel Sauce I

75 g/3 oz sugar, lump or caster
a little water
vanilla essence
250 ml/½ pint cream
2 egg yolks

Put sugar in an old, heavy pan on a slow fire and let it cook until it is light brown, stirring all the time with an iron spoon, and then add 1 tablespoon water and boil for a few moments. Cool a little and then off the heat add the cream and egg yolks, return to heat and stir and beat until it comes to boil. Then immediately remove from heat, continue beating and when nearly cool season with 1–2 drops vanilla. Serve at once.

NOTE: If you have caramelized a pudding like Crème Caramel, this sauce can be made in the bottom of the mould you have just turned out. Some caramel will be left in it and you simply melt this with a spoonful or two of water over heat and continue as above.

This sauce is a useful one for all sorts of puddings.

Caramel Sauce II

225 g/9 oz caster sugar
generous 125 ml/¼ pint cream
1 tablespoon butter

Use this sauce with Vanilla Ice Cream.

Put two thirds of the sugar and all the cream into the top of a double boiler. Brown the other third of the sugar to a liquid caramel in an old saucepan. When the cream is thoroughly hot add the caramel. Stir until it is completely dissolved and then until it is thick. Beat in the butter.

Lady Jekyll's Caramel Sauce

100 g/4 oz butter
300 g/10 oz soft brown sugar
225 g/8 oz golden syrup
a scant 250 ml/½ pint evaporated milk

Put the butter, sugar and syrup in the top part of a double boiler. Stir well over heat until smooth-looking – about 10 minutes. Remove from heat, beat well and add the evaporated milk, beating it in. The sauce can be used at once, or it is even better if you make it and allow it to stand for 1 hour and then reheat it in the double boiler.

Toasted Almond Butterscotch Sauce

75 g/3 oz caster sugar
75 g/3 oz light brown sugar
pinch of salt
2 tablespoons golden, or corn, syrup
8 tablespoons cold water
1½ teaspoons butter
4 tablespoons hot water
½ teaspoon vanilla essence

Cook white and brown sugar, salt, syrup and cold water until brittle when dropped into the cold water. Remove from heat and beat in the butter, hot water and vanilla. Serve immediately with vanilla ice cream.

NOTE: You can add toasted, flaked or slivered almonds to this sauce if you like.

Burnt Almond Sauce

100 g/4 oz brown sugar
3 tablespoons water
2 tablespoons butter
pinch of salt
1 tablespoon instant coffee powder
8 tablespoons hot water
1 teaspoon vanilla
50 g/2 oz slivered almonds
1 teaspoon butter

Cook sugar, water, 2 tablespoons butter and salt, covered, over moderately high heat for 3 minutes. Uncover and cook, without stirring, until the syrup forms a soft ball when tested in cold water. Cool slightly and add coffee dissolved in water and the vanilla. Toast almonds in oven at 350°F 180°C Gas 4 for about 8 minutes. Dot 1 teaspoon butter over them, mixing it in. Leave them in the closed oven with the heat turned off for at least 10 more minutes. Stir into sauce. Serve warm over ice cream.

Home Made Cream

125 ml/¼ pint milk
¼ teaspoon powdered gelatine
100 g/4 oz unsalted butter

Pour the milk into a small saucepan and sprinkle the gelatine on the milk. Warm the milk over a low heat, stirring to dissolve the gelatine, but do not let it get too hot. When it has dissolved add the butter and stir until this has melted. Pour the mixture into the liquidizer and turn to maximum speed for 1 minute. Pour into a bowl and chill. Beat before using.

Stand-up Cream

155 ml/6 fl oz single cream
3 tablespoons water
1 heaped teaspoon powdered gelatine

Put the cream into a bowl and whip till frothy. Measure 3 tablespoons water into a very small pan. Sprinkle on 1 heaped teaspoon powdered gelatine. Stir over low heat until absolutely clear. Then get someone to pour onto cream very slowly while you whip fast. As soon as it begins to thicken, stop. Put bowl into refrigerator and leave for 30 minutes. It will now be ready to spoon into an icing bag to be used to decorate the top of any pudding. It will hold a strong peak, even on a warm buffet table.

ICE FREEZER

APPENDIX

WHAT TO EAT
WITH WHAT

SAUCES FOR HORS D'OEUVRES, STARTERS, EGG DISHES

CLASSIC
Hot

Allemande
Américaine
Argenteuil
Aurore
Béarnaise
Béchamel
Bordelaise Blanche, à la
Bourguignonne
Cardinal
Champignons, aux
Chasseur, au
Châteaubriand
Chivry
Clamart
Continental
Créole
Crevettes, aux
Demi Glace
Diane
Diplomate or Riche
Espagnole
Estragon, à l'
Granville
Gratin, au
Hollandaise
Variations of Hollandaise,
    including
    Maître d'Hotel
    Mousseline or Chantilly
    Beurre Noisette
Hongroise
Hussarde
Indienne
Italienne
Joinville
Lapérouse
La Vallière

Lyonnaise
Madeira
Maintenon
Masséna
Matelote Brune
Mexican Tomato
Mornay
Moscovite
Normande
Parisienne
Périgourdine
Périgueux
Polignac
Polonaise
Portuguaise
Poulette
Printanière
Provençale
Ravigotte
Réforme
Richmont
Romaine
Rossini
Soubise
Suprême
Trianon
Velouté
Villeroy
York, d'
Zingara
Various Melted Butter Sauces,
    including
    Beurre Blanc
    Beurre Noir
    Beurre Noisette
    Beurre Polonaise
    Sauce Maître d'Hotel
    Sauce à la Meunière

CLASSIC Cold	Mayonnaise and Most Variations and Compounds, including	Rémoulade

CLASSIC
Cold

Mayonnaise and Most Variations
 and Compounds, including
 Aïoli
 Andalouse or *Niçoise*
 Bohémienne
 Bulgarienne
 Caboul or *East India*
  Mayonnaise
 Chaud-froid
 Génoise
 Gribiche
 Livournaise
 Maximilian
 Mayonnaise Chantilly
 Mayonnaise Escoffier
 Mayonnaise Mousseuse
 Mousquetaire

Rémoulade
Russian Mayonnaise
Suédoise
Tartare
Trianon
Verte or *Vert-pré*
Compound Butters,
 including
 Anchovy Butter
 Beurre Noisette or
  Hazelnut Butter
 Chivry or *Ravigotte Butter*
 Green Butter
 Lobster Butter
 Maître d'Hotel Butter
 Shrimp Butter
 Watercress Butter

NON-CLASSIC
Hot

Curry or *Indienne Sauce*
La Bagna Cauda
Melted Butter Sauce

Mornay
Salsa Verde Española
Sorrel

NON-CLASSIC
Cold

Aromatic Seafood Sauce
Cucumber Sauce
Cucumber Sauce with
 Sour Cream I and II
Virginian Sour Cream Sauce
Mrs Dimbleby's Smoked Cod's
 Roe Sauce
Lily MacLeod's Menarlo Sauce
A Delicate Sauce for
 Cold Curries
Cold Curry Risotto Sauce
Half and Half Dressing
1000 Island Dressing
Green Goddess Dressing
Mayonnaise Sauce à la Farquhar
Jubilee Mayonnaise
Green Pea Mayonnaise
Cucumber Mayonnaise
Quick Sauce Verte
'Hot' Sauce for Shrimp Cocktails
Shrimp or Prawn Cocktail Sauce
A good Sauce for Prawn Cocktails
Gloucester Sauce
Cambridge Sauce

Joan's Salad Dressing
Boiled Dressing for Salads
A Butler's Salad Dressing
Caldy Manor Salad Sauce
Elizabeth Arden's Special
 Dressing
Maria Blake's Mustard Sauce
 for Spinach Salad
Loret Hayden's Salad Dressing
Cold Creamy Mustard Sauce
Salsa di Capperi al'Olio
Salsa Piccante al'Asciughe
Dill and Sour Cream Sauce
Sour Cream Sauce for Tuna Fish
 Mousse or Salad
Maionese Tonnata
Lady Dudley's Sauce Norwégienne
Sir Phillip Joubert's
 Bagnarotte Sauce
Lady Head's Carcosa Sauce
Yoghurt Sauce I and II
Princess Weikersheim's
 Chive Sauce (Austrian)

SAUCES FOR FISH

FOR SOLE

CLASSIC
Hot and Cold

Most *Mayonnaise* and *Hollandaise*
  Variations, including
  Alphonse XIII
  Américaine
  Amiral, à l'
  Argenteuil
  Bercy
  Beurre Noisette or
    Hazelnut Butter
  Bordelaise Blanche, à la
  Bourguignonne
  Bretonne
  Cardinal
  Champignons, aux
  Chivry
  Crevettes, aux
  Diplomate or *Riche*
  Dugléré
  Foyot
  Giselle
  Granville
  Gratin, au
  Holstein
  Hongroise
  Hubert
  Huîtres, aux
  Indienne
  Italienne
  Joinville

  Lapérouse
  Maître d'Hotel
  Marchand de Vin, au
  Maréchale
  Marguéry
  Marinière
  Mathilde
  Mexican Tomato
  Mornay
  Nantua
  Niçoise
  Normande
  Orly
  Pauvre Homme
  Piccadilly
  Polignac
  Portuguaise
  Printanière
  Provençale
  Ravigotte
  Réjane
  Russe, à la
  Souchet
  Sully
  Tzarine
  Victoria
  Vin Blanc, au
  Walewska or *Valeska*

NON-CLASSIC

Dr Kitchener's Melted Butter
Fennel Sauce
Scallop and Mushroom Sauce

Victorian Hen Lobster Sauce
Old-fashioned Oyster Sauce
Mrs Crickmeer's Ritz Sauce

FOR TURBOT OR HALIBUT

CLASSIC
Américaine
Amiral, à l'
Champagne
Dugléré

Huîtres, aux
Saint-Malo
Régence

NON-CLASSIC
Rhoda's Cream Sauce for Halibut
Scallop and Mushroom Sauce

Cambridge Sauce
Gloucester Sauce

FOR SALMON

CLASSIC
Amiral, à l'
Béarnaise
Génevoise or *Génoise*
Huîtres, aux
Huîtres à Brun, aux

Nantua
Foyot
Most *Mayonnaises*
  and *Hollandaise* Sauces

NON-CLASSIC
Indian Sauce
Sorrel Sauce
Warsaw Sour Cream Sauce

Cucumber Mayonnaise
Green Pea Mayonnaise

FOR TROUT

CLASSIC
Most *Mayonnaise* and *Hollandaise*
  Variations, including
  Américaine
  Bretonne
  Champagne
  Doria

Génevoise
Hussarde
Nantua
Régence
Vin Blanc, au

NON-CLASSIC
Almond Butter for Grilled Trout
Mayonnaise Sauce à la Farquhar

Lily MacLeod's Menarlo Sauce

FOR SHELLFISH

CLASSIC
Most *Mayonnaise* and *Hollandaise*
  Variations, including
  Américaine
  Bercy
  Bretonne
  Bordelaise Blanche, à la
  Cardinal
  Champagne

Hongroise
Indienne
Marinière
Mornay
Nantua
Poulette
Russe, à la
Victoria

NON-CLASSIC	Quick Sauce Verte	Shrimp or Prawn Cocktail Sauce
	Mayonnaise Sauce à la Farquhar	A Good Sauce for Prawn Cocktails
	'Hot' Sauce for Shrimp Cocktails	

FOR MACKEREL

CLASSIC	Fenouil, au	Moutarde
	Indienne	

NON-CLASSIC	Fennel Sauce	Mrs Dimbleby's Tarragon and
	Green Gooseberry Sauce	Caper Sauce for Mackerel
	Lemon and Mustard Sauce (Turkey)	

FOR WHITING

CLASSIC	Duguesclin	Marchand de Vin, au

NON-CLASSIC	Victorian Cockle Sauce	Good Fish Sauce

FOR SMOKED FISH

NON-CLASSIC	Lady Dudley's Sauce Norwégienne	Caucasian Walnut Sauce (Russian)
	Suédoise	
	Mrs Dimbleby's Smoked Cod's Roe Sauce	Hot Horseradish Sauce (Austria)
		Dill and Sour Cream Sauce
	Lemon and Mustard Sauce (Turkey)	Cold Creamy Mustard Sauce

CHOICE OF VARIOUS OTHER SAUCES SUITABLE FOR FISH

CLASSIC	Anchois, aux	Livournaise
	Aurore	Maltaise
	Bâtarde	Matelote Blanche
	Choron	Morley
	Crème	Nantaise
	Créole	Vert-pré
	Fines-Herbes	Velouté
	Génoise	Tomato Demi Glace

NON-CLASSIC	Caper Sauce	Old-fashioned Parsley Sauce
	Mustard Sauce	Sour Cream Sauce for Tuna Fish
	Good Fish Sauce	Mousse or Salad
	Anchovy Cream Sauce	Virginian Sour Cream Sauce
	Old-fashioned English Egg Sauce	Victoria Sauce
	Victorian Cockle Sauce	Cambridge Sauce
	Watercress Sauce	Gloucester Sauce
	Rémoulade Sauce for Créole	Aromatic Seafood Sauce
	Shrimp	Hot Horseradish (Austrian)
	Walnut Sauce (Italian)	Rutilio's Salsa Verde
	Warsaw Sour Cream Sauce	Caucasian Walnut Sauce

MAYONNAISES SUITABLE FOR ALMOST ANY COLD POACHED FISH

NON-CLASSIC	Lady Head's Carcosa	Sir Phillip Joubert's
	Salsa Livornese	Bagnarotte Sauce
	Skordelia	Suédoise
	Maionese Tonnata	Salsa Genovese
		Lady Dudley's Sauce Norwégienne

SAUCES FOR MEAT

FOR BRAINS

CLASSIC

Beurre Noir
Bourguignonne
Duxelles
Financièrè, à la
Half Glaze (Demi Glace)
Italienne

Matelote Brune
Périgueux
Poulette
Ravigotte
Suprême
Villeroy

FOR KIDNEYS

CLASSIC

Béarnaise
Bercy
Bordelaise Rouge
Champignons, aux
Chasseur, au
Indienne
Madeira

Marchand de Vin, au
Portuguaise
Robert
Vert-pré
Villeroy

NON-CLASSIC

Juniper Sauce

Mrs Dimbleby's Brandy and Orange Sauce

FOR NOISETTES, TOURNEDOS AND FILLETS MIGNONS

CLASSIC

Albert
Béarnaise
Bercy
Bordelaise
Brögli
Champignons, aux
Chasseur, au
Châteaubriand
Choron

Grand Veneur
Half Glaze (Demi Glace)
Italienne
Lyonnaise
Madeira
Masséna
Moëlle, à la
Mornay
Nancy

Niçoise
Paloise
Parisienne
Périgourdine
Périgueux
Poivrade
Polonaise
Pompadour

Portuguaise
Provençale
Richmont
Régence
Rossini
Sicilienne
Vert-pré
Zingara

NON-CLASSIC Theodora's Anchovy, Egg and
    Herb Sauce
A Victorian Mushroom Sauce

Jamie's Sauce Poivre Vert
    au Naturel
Mrs Dimbleby's Cream Curry and
    Nut Sauce

FOR STEAKS

CLASSIC Béarnaise
Bercy
Bordelaise
Champignons, aux
Châteaubriand
Hussarde
Lyonnaise

Marchand de Vin, au
Mexican Tomato
Nancy
Parisienne
Polonaise
Sicilienne
Vert-pré

NON-CASSIC Victorian Grill Sauce for Meat
Mushroom and Madeira Sauce

Juniper Sauce

FOR LAMB

CLASSIC Bretonne
Châteaubriand
Duxelles
Financière, à la
Italienne
Madeira
Maintenon
Maréchale
Mornay

Mousquetaire
Orsay
Parisienne
Périgueux
Pompadour
Provençale
Réforme
Villeroy

NON-CLASSIC Tennessee Mint Sauce
Mint Sauce
Sauce for Hot or
    Cold Roast Lamb
Theodora's Prune and
    Blackcurrant Sauce

Dr Kitchener's 1822 Port
    Wine Sauce
Mrs Stanley's Parsley
    Butter Sauce
Marinade Sauce
Currant Orange Sauce

FOR BOILED MUTTON AND BOILED BEEF OR SILVERSIDE

CLASSIC
Paloise	Vert-pré
Bretonne	Albert
Soubise	Ravigotte
Villageoise	Orsay

NON-CLASSIC
Caper Sauce (Austrian)	Dill Sauce (Swedish)
Dill Sauce (Austrian)	Hot Horseradish (Austrian)
Sos Koperkowy	Peperata

FOR COLD MEAT

CLASSIC
Vinaigrette	Gribiche
Most Mayonnaises and Horseradish Sauces	

NON-CLASSIC
Piquante	Agre-dolce Sauce
Lemon and Mustard Sauce (Turkish)	Peperata
Salsa di Caperi al'Olio	Princess Weikersheim's Chive Sauce
Rutilio's Salsa Verde	

FOR VEAL CUTLETS AND VEAL ESCALOPES

CLASSIC
Chatham	Paprika
Crème	Périgourdine
Financière, à la	Printanière
Fines-Herbes	Provençale
Flamande	Suprême
Hongroise	Vert-pré
Maintenon	Viennoise
Maréchale	York, d'
Marigny	Zingara
Matelote Brune	

NON-CLASSIC
Creamed Mushroom Sauce	Smitane Sauce
Sour Cream Sauce	Hot Sour Cream Sauce
Cheese Sauce	Shura's Sauce Polonaise
Cucumber Sauce	Sorrel Sauce
Paprika Sauce (Hungarian)	

FOR LAMB AND VEAL SWEETBREADS

CLASSIC
Bordelaise Blanche, à la
Champignons, aux
Châteaubriand
Financière, à la
Maintenon
Marinière
Périgourdine
Poulette
Régence
Soubise
Suprême
Madeira
Villeroy

BARBECUE SAUCES FOR CHARCOAL GRILLS

Richmond Barbecue Sauce
Admiral Ralph Stevens' Sauce
  for Submariners
Texan Barbecue Sauce
Chicken Barbecue Sauce I and II
Ferocious Barbecue Sauce
Beyendi Sauce for Kebabs

FOR ROAST PORK OR PORK CUTLETS

CLASSIC
Flamande
Piquante
Tomato Demi Glace
Suédoise
Verjus, au

NON-CLASSIC
Jamaican Sweet-Sour
  Pineapple Sauce
Apple Sauce
Shura's Sauce
Orange Sauce
Sauce Moutarde Dijonnaise
Teriyaki

FOR BARQUETTES

CLASSIC
Joinville
Mornay
Nantua
Normande
Salmis
Victoria

FOR BOUCHEES

CLASSIC
Bohémienne
Crevettes, aux
Hollandaise
Joinville
Nantua
Périgourdine
Suprême

NON-CLASSIC
A Delicate Sauce for
  Cold Curries
Gloucester Sauce
Cold Curry Risotto Sauce
Jubilee Mayonnaise

FOR TONGUE

CLASSIC   *Champignons, aux*   *Piquante*
            Flamande   *Ravigotte*
            Italienne   *Romaine*
            Madeira   *Rémoulade*

NON-CLASSIC   *Cherry Sauce*

FOR HAM

CLASSIC   *Half Glaze (Demi Glace)*   *Madeira*
            Cerises, aux   *Périgueux*

NON-CLASSIC   *Virginian Raisin Sauce*   *Quick Cumberland Sauce*
                Mustard Sauce   *Orange Sauce for Ham*
                Raisin Sauce   *à la Wombwell*
                Cumberland Sauce   *Orange Sauce*

SAUCES FOR POULTRY AND GAME

FOR QUAIL

CLASSIC
Archiduc, à l'	Madeira
Cerises, aux	Régence
Duxelles	Villeroy
Half Glaze (Demi Glace)	

FOR PHEASANT AND GUINEA-FOWL

CLASSIC
Archiduc, à l'	Périgueux
Bohémienne	Pignole
Champignons, aux	Régence
Crème	Salmis
Half Glaze (Demi Glace)	Villeroy
Madeira	

NON-CLASSIC
Celery Sauce	Caucasian Walnut Sauce
Spatchcock Sauce	Mrs Dimbleby's Curried
Smitane Sauce	Mushroom Sauce
Alsatian Brandy and Cream Sauce	

FOR WILD DUCK

NON-CLASSIC Wild Duck Sauce – First Lifeguards' Recipe

FOR PIGEON BREASTS

NON-CLASSIC Mrs Dimbleby's Juniper Berry Sauce

FOR PARTRIDGE

CLASSIC

Bourguignonne	Madeira
Demi-Deuil	Salmis
Half Glaze (Demi Glace)	Suprême

NON-CLASSIC

Smitane Sauce	Alsatian Brandy and Cream Sauce

FOR CHICKEN SAUTE

CLASSIC

Alexandra	Half Glaze (Demi Glace)
Algérienne	Hongroise
Archiduc, à l'	Huîtres, aux
Aromates, aux	Indienne or Curry
Bercy	Italienne
Bohémienne	Lyonnaise
Bordelaise Blanche, à la	Marigny
Bourguignonne	Mathilde
Bretonne	Mironton
Catalane	Niçoise
Chasseur, au	Périgueux
Doria	Portuguaise
Doriac	Provençale
Estragon, à l'	Suprême
Fenouil, au	Tortue, à la
Fines Herbes	

NON-CLASSIC

Theodora's Chicken Liver and Lemon Sauce	Aubergine Sauce for a Gratin of Chicken
Salsa Fria	Kentucky Pan-broiled Gravy

FOR CHICKEN FILLETS OR SUPREMES

CLASSIC

Alexandra	Marinière
Ambassadrice, à l'	Mornay
Archiduc, à l'	Orly
Doria	Périgueux
Financière, à la	Polignac
Hongroise	Porto, au
Italienne	Régence
Indienne or Curry	Rossini
Maréchale	Villageoise I and II

NON-CLASSIC

Grape Sauce	Pine Nut Sauce (Turkish)
Caucasian Walnut Sauce	

FOR CHICKEN

CLASSIC

Alexandra
Ambassadrice, à l'
Argenteuil
Aurore
Champignons, aux
Chivry
Demi-Deuil
Estragon, à l'
Financière, à la
Half Glaze (Demi Glace)
Hollandaise
Hongroise
Huîtres, aux
Imperatrice, à l'
Indienne
Ivoire
Madeira
Maintenon

Maréchale
Matignon
Niçoise
Normande
Parisienne
Périgourdine
Polignac
Pompadour
Portuguaise
Printanière
Régence
Rossini
Russe, à la
Sicilienne
Souveraine
Trianon
Vert-pré

NON-CLASSIC

White Celery Sauce
Almond Sauce for Chicken
    Croquettes
Bread Sauce, The Right Way
Bread Sauce, A Victorian Recipe

18th Century Sauce for Fowls
Harem Sauce
Smitane Sauce
Teriyaki Sauce

FOR TURKEY

CLASSIC

Catalane
Champignons, aux
Estragon, à l'

Financière, à la
Half Glaze (Demi Glace)
Suprême

NON-CLASSIC

Jubilee Mayonnaise
Spatchcock Sauce

FOR DUCK, DUCKLING AND GOOSE

CLASSIC

Archiduc, à l'
Bigarade
Bordelaise
Half Glaze (Demi Glace)
Madeira
Nora

Olives, aux
Porto, au
Rouennaise
Salmis
Verjus, au

NON-CLASSIC	*Theodora's Green Sauce for*	*'Hanoverian' Sauce*
	Ducklings	*Marmalade Mayonnaise*
	Orange Sauce	*Cherry Sauce*

FOR VENISON AND ROE-DEER

CLASSIC	*Cerises, aux*	*Grand Veneur*
	Chevreuil, au	*Moscovite*
	Conti	*Nesselrode*
	Czarine, à la	*Viennoise*
	Diane	

NON-CLASSIC	*Red Wine Sauce*	*Hot Sauce*
	Spatchcock Sauce	*Damson Sauce*
	Sour Cream Sauce	*Cream Sauce (German)*
	Theodora's Chestnut Sauce	*Smitane Sauce*
	Mrs Rundell's Currant Sauce	*Hot Sour Cream Sauce*

FOR HARE

| NON-CLASSIC | *Theodora's Prune and* | *Cream Sauce (German)* |
| | *Spices Sauce* | |

SAUCES AND DRESSINGS FOR SALADS AND VEGETABLES

FOR SALADS

NON-CLASSIC

Half and Half Dressing
1000 Island Dressing
Green Goddess Dressing
Joan's Salad Dressing
Boiled Dressing for Salads
A Butler's Salad Dressing

Caldy Manor Salad Sauce
Elizabeth Arden's Special
  Dressing
Loret Hayden's Salad Dressing
Maria Blake's Mustard Sauce
  for Spinach Salad

FOR ARTICHOKES

CLASSIC

Crème
Hollandaise
Italienne
Melted or *Drawn Butter*
Mornay
Polonaise

Villeroy
Vinaigrette
Mousseline or *Chantilly*
Mayonnaise Mousseuse
Béarnaise

FOR POTATOES

CLASSIC

Mornay

NON-CLASSIC

Dill Sauce (Austrian)
Hot Potato Salad Sauce

Salsa Verde Española

FOR ASPARAGUS

CLASSIC

Hollandaise
Melted or *Drawn Butter*
Beurre à la Vièrge or
  Sauce Mousseuse
Maltaise

Mayonnaise Mousseuse
Mornay
Mousseline or *Chantilly*
Vinaigrette

FOR CRUDITES

Tartare I and II   *Yoghurt Sauces I and II*

FOR CAULIFLOWER

Crème   *Mornay*
Italienne

FOR BEANS (FRENCH)

Hollandaise   *Blender Hollandaise*

FOR MARROWS AND ZUCCHINI

Crème   *Provençale*
Hollandaise

FOR SPINACH

Béchamel   *Mornay*
Crème

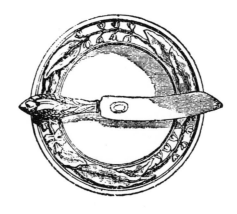

INDEX